CRUISING GUIDE
to the
NOVA SCOTIA COAST

Including Prince Edward Island, the Magdalens
&
Sable Island

Charles A Westropp, Editor

Alexander Weld, Publisher

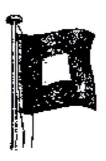

Pilot Press

Weston, Massachusetts

Direction *under power off the coast of Nova Scotia, approaching Little Hope Island with its fog gun booming. In 1946 it was one of the last guns to be used along the northeast coast. It was activated by acetylene gas and sparked by a timing mechanism. The light was sadly destroyed in a storm in December 2003 and not replaced*

from *Saga of Direction* by Charles H. Vilas, CCA
Sketch by Margaret Van Pelt Vilas

ISBN 0-9635668-3-0

PREFACE

Over the fifty-three years of its publication, *The Guide* has accumulated a loyal band of correspondents -- sailors, seamen and cruising folk who share a love of cruising and the Canadian Maritimes. These correspondents are the Guide and each entry, each piece of information was written by them. Their names are listed -- even after many of them have made their final voyage. You are standing on deck with some great seamen -- Rod Stephens, Peabo Gardiner, Charlie Bartlett, Mac Grant, Judge Bok, Dr. Starr, John and Nancy McKelvy... I could go on -- accomplished men and women in many fields and great sailors in the field we have in common.

So come aboard and leave the office, factory, schoolroom, scene of the crime, and let's go for a cruise. As Charlie Bartlett said, this book is for "the cruiser with limited time who appreciates a few tips from those who have been there before."

We don't presume to know every harbor in Nova Scotia, New Brunswick, P.E.I. or Quebec, but we know about some splendid places you may wish to visit, and some great snug harbors you may want to hole up in when a piece of weather comes by. But this area is relatively pristine and filled with cruising pearls waiting to be discovered by you. We urge you to share your discoveries with us as those who have come before are now sharing their finds with you.

The Cruising Guide to the Nova Scotia Coast is the work of Charles W. Bartlett (1905-1984), a former Rear Commodore of the Cruising Club of America and a recipient of the Club's prestigious Nye Trophy, "for long and various services to the Cruising Club of America, especially the inauguration of the Cruising Club Guide to Nova Scotia, Newfoundland and Labrador."

"Charlie" (as he was known to all) was a gunkholer at heart. During the war he was a Lieutenant Commander in the western Pacific, after which he returned to his law practice and cruising the Canadian Maritimes on his beloved *Gurnet Light*. In those early post-war years, Canadian pilot books were oriented toward the needs of large ships, and many Canadian charts were copies of nineteenth-century British Admiralty Charts, beautifully but finely engraved in black ink, all hard to read, especially in a seaway when one was tired.

Charlie suggested in 1950 that the Club co-sponsor a guide to the Nova Scotia coast with the Royal Nova Scotia Yacht Squadron in Halifax. The original contributors were: Judge Curtis Bok, Paul Sheldon, Don Gardiner (Charlie's classmate at Dartmouth), Peter Richmond, John Cooley, Peabody Gardiner, Carl Vilas, Joe Guild, George Killam of Yarmouth, N.S., and Dr. George MacIntosh and MacCallum Grant, both of Halifax.

The Guide continues to be endorsed by its original sponsors, the Cruising Club of America and the Royal Nova Scotia Yacht Squadron, whose members provide much of the information herein. For these endorsements the Editor is deeply grateful. As the new editor I hope that my efforts will be helpful to all who cruise the waters of the Canadian Maritimes.

SOME EDITORIAL CONSIDERATIONS

Since the Publisher and my spellchecker are creatures of the U.S., the American spelling customs prevail. When the abstract word "harbor" is used, it is spelled the American way, whereas if we are talking about Shelburne Harbour, the Canadian spelling is used because that is the proper name of a place on the chart.

This Editor seeks to avoid being too finite with entry directions because: (1) Buoy numbers change and buoys are removed from station, and (2) Compass courses are sometimes not very reliable where there are strong cross currents. Presumably the reader has the common sense to figure this out.

Not all people perceive a harbor in the same way, especially when that harbor is only visited once. There is an old adage: "One person's caviar is another's fish eggs." The Editor tries to combine a blend of reports on any particular harbor or place.

The Editor generally avoids comments on shore entertainment unless it appears to be permanent. Provincial Hotel restaurants (e.g. Liscomb Lodge) are listed because chances are they will be there in the next few years. We avoid using the names of "meeters and greeters" for the same reasons.

UPDATES AND CONTRIBUTIONS

The value of this book depends on how current its descriptions are (and this is the reason we try to date all material here). The Editor cannot overemphasize the necessity of users of this guide to send in new and/or updated material. We all profit from users who are considerate enough to share their information in *The Guide*, and to all those who have contributed to it, thank you. Those who wish to contribute, please send your contributions to:

Charles Westropp
6336 London Street
Halifax, Nova Scotia
Canada B3L 1X3
cmdre@ns.sympatico.ca
A web site: www.pilot-press.com
disseminates changes to this guide annually, usually in January.

NEWFOUNDLAND AND LABRADOR GUIDES

Two sister publications to this guide are *The Cruising Guide to Newfoundland* and *Cruising Guide to the Labrador*.

CAUTION

A final note: Cruising the Nova Scotia coast is not for everyone and can be very dangerous due to extreme tides and sudden fogs. There are few marinas (in the U.S. East Coast sense of the word) and boatyards and repair facilities are few and far between. (You should check your insurance policy before entering Canadian waters because of this!)

For obvious reasons the Cruising Club of America and the Royal Nova Scotia Yacht Squadron and the editors and authors of this Guide cannot assume responsibility for the accuracy of the material contained herein. As every cruising man knows, if you don't bounce once a while, you haven't been anywhere.

TABLE OF CONTENTS

CHARTS, PUBLICATIONS AND NAVIGATIONAL AIDS

Since the first edition of this publication in 1952, the Canadian Government has made enormous strides updating the old copper-plate British Admiralty Charts which were issued in the 1950's. The new Canadian Charts have color keys, most depths are in meters, and the beautiful profile drawings of landfalls and headlands have been dropped.

Over the past half-century, ever-new electronic navigation systems have been introduced. Suffice it to say, if you have used one of these systems elsewhere, you will be familiar with it in Canada.

In the period between the two World Wars, a very fine Radio Direction Finder system was developed. On the southeast Coast of Nova Scotia there were RDF stations every 20-30 miles apart, providing reasonably accurate fixes or beacons to home in on (as most transmitters were in lighthouses at harbor entrances). This made an excellent "poor man's navigation system." All you needed was a good radio receiver attached to a polaris to catch the null.

Today there are only three RDF stations working in the area covered by the Guide, all the rest having been scrapped as being too costly. Don't throw your RDF receiver away though. You never know when it might be helpful (perhaps when you lose the main ship's power source and you may be near one of the remaining RDF signals or even a radio station with a transmitter marked on your chart). Also, RDF is viable in many other parts of the world.

In the 1960's many Canadians adopted the "Decca" system, a private system one subscribed to, and the charts of the period were marked with "Decca lines." This system was phased out in the 1970's and need not detain us.

Now we come to Loran C, which is a system controlled by an international governmental consortium with transmitters in the U.S. and Canada to provide information for navigational fixes (if you have the proper receiver).

Loran: Although Loran can be inaccurate when working close inshore – errors of up to a quarter of a mile – coverage is good in the area covered by this guide. It was the intention to discontinue Loran but it now appears here to stay for the foreseeable future. It is a good back up to GPS and very repeatable. Local fishermen still rely on Loran to find their gear in fog.

The General Positioning System (GPS):
WAAS enabled GPS is the obvious choice as the primary navigation "aid". Sole dependence on this or any other single system would be foolish and I still recommend a traditional approach to coastal navigation using our senses, common sense as well as all the electronic gadgetry available today.

Electronic Charts: The Canadian Hydrographic Service until recently had contracted a company in Newfoundland "NDI" to be the sole provider of its charts in electronic format. C-Map, Navionics and other electronic chart providers paid NDI royalty fees for the product. The fees charged by NDI are being disputed by the industry. CHS is at the present (February 2005) attempting to terminate NDI's sole source contract, which has been challenged in court by NDI. The bottom line is that electronic charts of Canadian waters will still be available from the electronic chart providers, but who pays royalties to whom, and how much, is currently before the courts.

Buoys: The Canadian government in the past decade has been changing the buoyage in this area, particularly around the smaller harbors and inside passages. If you buy charts directly from the Hydrographic Service in Ottawa, the chart will be updated to the time stamped on the chart. With so much recent change in buoyage, older charts can become outdated quickly.

The buoyage system is well explained in the Sailing Directions publications of the Hydrographic Service. Some remarks, however, are in order. Most Canadian buoys are red or green or a combination thereof. Generally, red is to starboard and green to port when proceeding from a larger to a smaller body of water (as in the U.S.). A new (European-inspired) system has been introduced in the last decade, however, where buoys are distinguished by combinations of black and yellow colors with distinctive pairs of cones on top of the buoy. (The positions of the cones and combinations of colors all mean different things as explained in Sailing Directions.) We dwell on this because many hundreds of buoys have been moved or discontinued recently. If you come across a yellow and black buoy, it probably has been placed there since 1995. If you have an old chart, make sure the black and yellow buoy you come across is not misidentified as another buoy, which has been removed. BEWARE; all buoys look alike on radar.

Chart Distribution: Charts should be purchased well ahead of your cruise because charts for more remote regions are not readily available (even when you are in the area you need the chart for!) and chart sales offices are hard to find. Publications and chart prices fluctuate along with U.S.-Canadian exchange rates. Sometimes it is better to deal directly with Canadian Hydrographic Service in Ottawa and sometimes better with a nearby dealer after considering U.S.-Canadian

exchange rates.

All Canadian marine publications may be purchased at:

Hydrographic Chart Distribution Office
Department of the Environment
1675 Russell Road
P.O. Box 8080
Ottawa, Ontario
CANADA K1G 3H6

There are a number of Canadian Hydrographic Service chart dealers in Canada, but their inventories are often limited. Two good dealers are:

The Binnacle
15 Purcells Cove Road
Halifax, Nova Scotia
CANADA B3N 1R2
www.binnacle.com

The Nautical Mind
249 Queen's Quay W.
Toronto, Ontario M5J 2N5
Canada
www.nauticalmind.com

There are numerous Canadian chart dealers in the U.S., three dependable dealers are:

Armchair Sailor
543 Thames St.
Newport, RI 02840
www.armchairsailor.com

Bluewater Books and Charts
1481 S.E. 17th Street
Ft. Lauderdale, FL 33316
www.bluewaterweb.com

Landfall Navigation
151 Harvard Ave.
Stamford, CT 06902
www.landfallnavigation.com

Publications: Important Canadian Government publications you should have on board are:

Sailing Directions, Nova Scotia (Atlantic Coast) and Bay of Fundy, First Edition 1990.

Canadian Tide and Current Tables, Bay of Fundy and Gulf of Maine, Volume 1, Atlantic Coast and Bay of Fundy, published annually.

Atlas of Tidal Currents, Bay of Fundy and Gulf of Maine.

List of Lights, Buoys and Fog Signals, Atlantic Coast, published annually.

Radio Aids to Marine Navigation (Atlantic and Great Lakes), published annually.

If you cruise in the Gulf of St. Lawrence, you should carry on board as well:

Sailing Directions, Gulf of St. Lawrence, First Edition, 1992.

Canadian Tide and Current Tables, Volume 2, Gulf of St. Lawrence, published annually.

In addition, the following cruising guides are recommended:

Cruising Nova Scotia, published by Diversity Special Interest Publishing P.O. Box 2705 Halifax NS B3J 3P7. This has replaced Cruise Cape Breton and has good sailing directions for the harbors of the Bras d'Or Lakes as well as the rest of the Province. As this is a government-industry sponsored book it is revised from time to time

Cruising the Eastern Shore by Mike Cox, published in 1997 by Nimbus Publishing 3731 Mackintosh Street P.O. Box 9301, Station A, Halifax NS B3K 5N5. This is a splendid little guide for the routes and anchorages from Halifax to Canso with lots of chartlets and photos.

Dr. Peter Loveridge's A *cruising guide to Nova Scotia: Digby to Cape Breton Island. Published by McGraw-Hill* is very useful for those intending to spend any time cruising in his home waters from Digby to Shelburne.

TIMES AND DISTANCES

For those coming from New England, or further to the west, there is much to be said for "getting there" (i.e. making your way east quickly). Whether you depart from Race Point (the outer tip of Cape Cod) or Nantucket one would probably set a course for Brazil Rock. These distances are roughly 220 and 230 nautical miles respectively on a course of about 85° magnetic. This is an "Ocean Passage" that crosses the entrance to the Gulf of Maine. If you have the time and inclination cruise along the Maine coast and take off from Mt. Desert Island and head for Yarmouth, about 100 miles, or Shelburne at about 165 miles. Or one can cruise further east along the Maine coast, to Eastport, then it's about 20 miles to Grand Manan (North Head), 35 miles to Westport (on Digby Neck) and another 30 miles to Yarmouth. One can stop at the intervening ports and await weather or tide for the next leg. Whatever route you take, pay particular attention to the currents around Seal Island and Blonde Rocks. Currents in this area can reach 1.5 knots and can be particularly dangerous – overfalls and swirls.

When crossing, from say Mt. Desert Island in Maine, the "normal" crossing time is about 12 hours so the tidal flood and ebb tend to cancel each other so there isn't the need to adjust ones course for the current. It's obviously vital to adjust your course when approaching the coast. The same is pretty much true when sailing east from Cape Cod.

Once you have reached Brazil Rock or rounded Cape Sable you have it made. It's about another 100 miles to Halifax . But as the guide describes, there are hundreds of delightful harbors to explore between Cape Sable and Halifax. If you're heading further east, it's about 150 miles from Sambro Light (off Halifax) to the St. Peters Canal at the southern entrance to the Bras d'Or Lakes.

And again there are innumerable wonderful anchorages to stop in along this section of the coast.

One can hurry along the coast, or cruise leisurely from harbor to harbor. But remember, **it usually takes twice as long going to the westward as it does going to the eastward**.

In settle summer weather the wind generally goes flat at night and very often is quite light off the coast during the morning, but by midday a moderate southwesterly usually develops.

An efficient and sometimes pleasant way to get to Nova Scotia is by going on the Marblehead-Halifax Race. The Boston Yacht Club and the Royal Nova Scotia Yacht Squadron sponsor this race jointly. It is held biennially in odd-numbered years and starts on the first Sunday after July 4th. With a racing crew and incentive to do reasonably well, you can be in Halifax three days after leaving Marblehead. In Halifax there are excellent air connections and you can exchange your racing crew for your family. After some R. and R. in Halifax (a very interesting and friendly city) you can be off to the Bras d'Or (150 miles to the east) or return at a more leisurely pace to the U.S.

As everyone knows, coming back is something else again. Your friendly southwesterly will have turned enemy. Now there is a tremendous temptation to sag off into the coast of Maine, which will add greatly to your distance if bound for Cape Cod or further west.

The Royal Nova Scotia Yacht Squadron after the Marblehead to Halifax Race in 2003

FUEL

In Nova Scotia, fuel for pleasure craft is taxed at a higher rate than fuel for commercial enterprises. Although many small harbors have fuel docks, such fuel is generally unavailable to yachts. Fuel for yachts must be "marked" (i.e. dyed a different color) to prove the higher tax has been paid. This fuel is only available in yachting centers such as Chester, Halifax or Baddeck, although in the past decade more U.S.-style marinas have been built which offer fuel for pleasure craft.

Every effort has been made in this guide to indicate harbors where fuel is available, but it is impossible to be absolutely accurate. Except for yachting centers, fuel is hard to find. Always top-off when the opportunity avails.

In extremis, you can resort to the taxi-and-jerry-can routine. It is best to carry a jerry can aboard for such an occasion.

Propane: This is available at several Ultramar service stations in Halifax. However, be aware that there is a provincial law requiring your tank valves to have been "officially" inspected in the last two years. ("Officially" means that they have been inspected by a qualified propane gas dealer and certified by him to be safe.) Lacking proof of inspection, a dealer may refuse to fill your tanks (as happened to one Guide correspondent). This is an admirable law but it can cause delay and problems. If cruising extensively in the province, have the propane dealer in your homeport prepare some sort of document attesting to the safety of your tanks.

Propane is now generally available at most Service stations as well as at general and hardware stores.

WEATHER REPORTS AND TELEPHONE SERVICE

All areas covered by this guide are served by VHF marine weather forecasts on WX1 and WX2 channels operated by Environment Canada (an agency somewhat like NOAA in the U.S.). The maritime areas surrounding Nova Scotia are broken into subdivisions which are named and located on the map below. These forecasts are generally reliable and accurate.

In addition to the normal VHF marine weather reporting, Environment Canada has put the weather reports on the Internet. These can be accessed at:

HTTP://WWW.NS.EC.CA/WEATHER/N S_MAR.HTML

Most commercial AM radio weather reports are very land-oriented, local, and of not much use.

If you have a single-sideband receiver, you may get high seas weather by following the instructions in *Radio Aids*. Unfortunately, the times and frequencies of these broadcasts seem to fluctuate, and at this time we cannot be more informative about this.

Public telephone service is provided in most areas by contacting the nearest Canadian Coast Guard Station on VHF Channel 16. Once you have explained that you wish to have telephone service, they will advise you which channel to shift to. Then you can make your call.

For easier telephone access, we suggest using a cellular telephone. Cellular service is available west of Halifax, in parts of the Bras d'Or Lakes, and Prince Edward Island. There is a "dead spot" on the Eastern Shore. There is no cellular service around the Magdalens. Gary Schneider recommends that if cellular is important to you a thorough check of cellular companies offering Canadian coverage be made. Promises of coverage are easier to find than service. As a general rule you can only expect cellular coverage near sizeable towns.

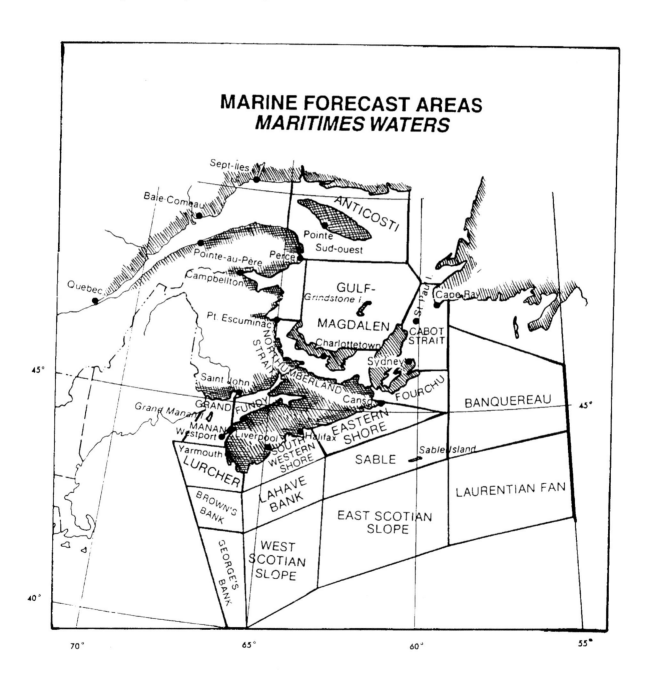

13

SAILING THE COAST OF NOVA SCOTIA

Comments by Harold E. Smith:

The difficulties and dangers of this coast have been greatly exaggerated, but they do exist. The greatest danger is the ever-present probability of fog. Whether there is more fog off the outer coast of Nova Scotia than in the Gulf of Maine is a question I leave to experts, but the Nova Scotia variety is thicker, wetter, and *colder*. Also it is apt to come in on much shorter warning --- in fact at times without any warning whatever.

Other than fog, navigation presents no extraordinary difficulties.

Comments by Curtis Bok

It is believed that both flood and ebb tides have an offshore set along the [southeast] coast, which the books onlyhint at. Corrections from 3 degrees to 6 degrees have been found necessary, modified by local inflow and outflow from the larger harbors and bays. Average current is about 3/4 knot,and constant tidal ranges average between four and seven feet.

Especially east of Halifax, the many fine harbors are guarded by a band of dangers from two to five miles wide, most of them unmarked. There are two general systems of buoys: the sea-buoys offshore, and a string of buoys marking the principal dangers inshore. The coast would be a wicked lee shore, and because the fog can close in almost without warning, it is wise to stick to the buoys and resist the temptation to cut corners even in clear weather.

This area is quite primitive, the harbors containing occasional small villages or hamlets. Most of them afford only simple provisions, and gasoline can also be obtained, though usually not through a hose. Rarely is water laid on in this region.

While solid fog can certainly occur, this coast rather specializes in "patches" in which one may spend from half an hour to five or six. Unless the fog is regional, it tends to thin out or burn off close to shore. The holding ground in the harbors is almost universally good.

Comments by Arnold B. Chace

Anyone cruising in these waters should surely have a radar reflector rigged at all times and should use the simple metal type, as the local fishermen say the plastic covered ones are very inefficient. Due to the persistent fog at sea, every man-made floating object is equipped with a radar reflector. This includes boats, navigational buoys and fish net or line marker buoys. This can be very confusing on a radar screen searching for a buoy with 100' visibility. Some inside buoys have reflectors. Some do not.

SAILING IN AND ACROSS THE BAY OF FUNDY

Comments by Harold Smith

The tidal current in the Bay of Fundy is 2 1/2 to 3 knots at most in the open parts of the Bay. However, in harbor entrances and passages between the islands it is really strong --- at least 5 to 6 knots in Grand Passage and Digby Gut, and 7 to 8 knots in Petit Passage. What it must be in Minas Basin and Petitcodiac River I dread to contemplate, but navigation in the open Bay represents few difficulties, with one exception. In the Bay of Fundy, a strong southwest wind blowing against an ebb tide kicks up a mean, vicious, short sea which can be very trying to a small ship. Rather than trying to make progress against it, it is far better to return to harbor and await a change of tide or wind. Between the Lurcher and Brazil Rock there is no more difficulty than cruising off any other coast.

Comments by John McKelvy

In the past ten years more traffic has appeared in the Bay of Fundy, especially at night. St. John, New Brunswick, has a lively trade with cargo ships of some size, and one can count on a fleet of fishing boats leaving Yarmouth at night to ply the Bay with nets. The newest shipping enterprise is a 300-foot catamaran ferry capable of 50 knots speed which daily makes two round trips from Bar Harbor, Maine, to Yarmouth, Nova Scotia. This also operates at night.

It is very difficult to tell (even with radar) the courses of fishing boats at night. They also tend to "flock." Given these conditions and an occasional freighter going to or from St. John, the crew on watch crossing the Bay can have their hands full. Most of these traffic problems occur during the early morning when bound east for Seal Island. The west-bound passage is less lively because a boat headed for Maine usually passes Cape Sable in the afternoon and is well out in the Bay before the Yarmouth and St. John traffic comes along. Sometimes a fishing boat will rake you with a searchlight, which doesn't necessarily mean you are too close, but that they are just curious.

Some defensive moves are:

Call **"Fundy Traffic"** the Vessel Traffic Management for the Bay on Channel 14 or 16, they will give you a good picture of all large shipping moving in the Bay.

Stay south of a line between Bar Harbor and Yarmouth --- this at least eliminates the catamaran.

Shine your spreader light or a searchlight on your sails (if you are a sailboat) so any other boat close by will at least know what you are and that you're not very fast.

Don't change your course too quickly or constantly unless it's obvious you don't have the right of way. Let the other vessel get some idea of what you intend to do.

Crossing the Bay at night isn't always tricky and I have had some of my most pleasant night sails on the Bay. Given time, you will become used to it.

CUSTOMS

2005

As a result of the dreadful events of 9/11 the procedures to enter Canada have been tightened up and Canada Customs is now part of an organization called The Canadian Border Services Agency. In the past a system called CANPASS made advanced clearances to Canada much easier. CANPASS is still available but is designed for boat owners who **frequently** cross the border. There is a considerable amount of paperwork to complete as well as a $40 Can. fee for a five year CANPASS.

The bottom line is that a CANPASS is not really worth the effort, but if you want one contact:

Customs Processing Center
400 Place d'Youville
Montréal, Quebec
CANADA H2Y 2C2

Telephone(514) 350-6137

When entering Canada on a recreational boat **you must report to a designated telephone reporting marine site**. It is important to note that failure to report at one of these designated telephone reporting marine sites may result in penalty action.

When you arrive at one of the reporting sites listed below call this number, which is manned 24 hours a day. Make sure you have your boat's and crew's documentation handy

(888) 226-7277

When you have called you will be given a report number, which you should display on the dockside of your boat. This does not mean that a Customs officer will come to inspect you, but they do on a random basis. With a long and convoluted coast line Nova Scotia is a favorite place for drug smugglers to land

their wares by yacht. You may be searched by a team of Border Service Agency people complete with sniffer dogs.

The following are the designated telephone reporting marine sites, which as you can see are really quite convenient for any vessel entering from the States.

NOVA SCOTIA:

Yarmouth: Killam Brothers Wharf, Yarmouth Marginal Wharf, Lobster Rock Wharf

Shelburne: Shelburne Harbour Yacht Club

Liverpool: Brooklyn Marina

Lunenburg: Lunenburg Yacht Club, Lunenburg Public Wharf

Halifax: Royal Nova Scotia Yacht Squadron, Armdale Yacht Club, Maritime Museum of the Atlantic, Dartmouth Yacht Club, Shearwater Yacht Club, Bedford Basin Yacht Club

Port Hawksbury: Port Hawksbury Wharf at Canso Canal

St. Peters: St. Peters Lion's Club Marina

Sydney: Royal Cape Breton Yacht Club

NEW BRUNSWICK:

Campobello: Head Harbour Wharf, Welshpool Wharf, North Road Island Wharf,Curry Corner Wharf, Leonardville Wharf, Wilson's Beach Wharf

Deer Island: Richardson Wharf, Fairhaven Wharf, Lord's Cove Wharf, Stuart Town Wharf, Leonardville Wharf

Grand Manan: Seal Cove Wharf, North Head Wharf

St. Andrews: St. Andrews Town Wharf, Bayside Marine Terminal

Saint John Harbour: Market Slip

Saint John River: Saint John Powerboat Club, Royal Kennebecasis Yacht Club

PRINCE EDWARD ISLAND:

Charlottetown: Charlottetown Yacht Club

Summerside: Summerside Yacht Club

CONTRABAND:

Anything over 40 oz. of liquor per crew member, plus 200 cigarettes or 50 cigars is over the limit. Meat or meat products are not allowed unless tinned, nor are fruit or vegetables.* Years ago there were many complaints about boarding and searching for drugs. Today there are more complaints concerning searches and seizure of liquor being brought into the province over quota amounts.

The U.S. yachtsman often reasons that Nova Scotia Provincial Liquor Commission Stores are difficult to find and they don't carry preferred wines and spirits. It is therefore best to stock up for the cruise before leaving the U.S. (They are motivated by convenience and not by trying to cheat the Canadian Government out of tax revenue.) Nonetheless, the law is the law. Illegal liquor can be and is confiscated.

Our suggested solution (though partial) is to fill your spirits quota with the products you can't get in Nova Scotia (Chateau Lafitte, Glen Morangie malt, or what have you), and head for Halifax (where the greatest variety of spirits may be found) to stock up for the rest of the cruise. (the Provincial Liquor Stores are much improved of late, although smaller places do have much less variety – ed)

U.S. yachtsmen are well-regarded in Canada and we would like to keep it that way. DO NOT MAKE LIFE HARD ON CANADIAN CUSTOMS OFFICIALS. Almost without exception they are pleasant and forbearing.

*I have never been questioned about meat, fruit or vegetables and feel sure there is no problem about these if carried as ship's stores..

.

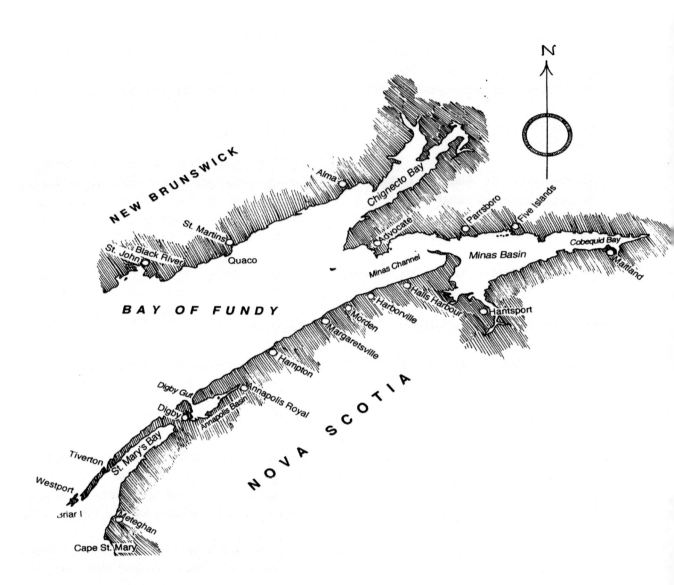

N

NEW BRUNSWICK

Alma

Chignecto Bay

St. Martins

St. John   Black River

Quaco

Advocate

Parrsboro

Five Islands

Cobequid Bay

Maitland

Minas Basin

BAY OF FUNDY

Minas Channel

Halls Harbour

Harborville

Hantsport

Morden

Margaretsville

Hampton

Digby Gut   Annapolis Royal

Digby   Annapolis Basin

Tiverton   St. Mary's Bay

NOVA SCOTIA

Westport

Briar I

Meteghan

Cape St. Mary

18

GRAND MANAN, NEW BRUNSWICK
NORTH HEAD

44° 45.7 N, 66° 44.94W

Charts: #434201, #434001

Gary Schneider   *2003*

DIRECTIONS: Entrance to North Head is straightforward, and the harbor provides an easy stopover for passages to Nova Scotia or the St. John River. (An easy day sail from Maine/N.B.to Grand Manan and then another day sail to Westport -ed)   From Roque or Cutler it is an easy one-tide-run with boosts of up to two and one half knots up the Grand Manan Channel. If approaching from the north and west, one should be aware that there are now salmon pens in Whale Cove and fish weirs at the head of Fish Head as well as along the shore south of the head.   However, they are close to shore.   The entrance to North Head is well marked with Swallow Tail light and Red bell buoy XV6.   There is regular ferry service between North Head and Black Harbor, NB and there are several tour boats, which offer sailing, fishing and whale watching from North Head.

ANCHORAGES AND BERTHS: In bad weather it is probably possible to tie up to the public dock, but given the number of fishing boats, one might consider alternatives if the protection of the breakwater is not required. It is possible to anchor in Long Island Bay, and there is plenty of room, despite the concern to avoid fish weirs. In addition there are several town moorings, large yellow floats with poly pennants, in Flagg Cove. This area is a bit open but we sat out a two-day rainy SE blow of thirty knots in relative comfort. One of the day sailing vessels uses a mooring here, distinguished by the oversized pair of poly pennants.

When they threw us off, they politely advised that any of the other yellow moorings could be utilized. The next one we picked up had a single well spliced 1-inch poly pennant.

REMARKS: As is the case elsewhere in Canada, customs offices have been closed; the office in Grand Manan no longer is functional. The town does have a post office, liquor store and food supplies. As it is served by a substantial ferry, there is considerable emphasis on the summer tourist trade in the immediate area of the town.

FACILITIES: None

UPPER BAY OF FUNDY*

(Including Margaretsville, Halls Harbour, Advocate, Parrsboro, Five Islands,
Hantsport, Black River, N.B., St. Martins, N.B., and Alma, N.B.)

Charts: 4010, #4399, #4140, #4337

Rewritten and condensed from material by A. P. Loring, R. L. Ireland, R. S. West, and R. S. Carter. The bulk of this information is based on a comprehensive cruise made in this area in 1984 by R .S. Carter. 1988

That part of the Bay of Fundy east of a line drawn between St. John, New Brunswick, and Digby, Nova Scotia, is seldom, if ever, visited by yachtsmen because of fog and extreme tidal ranges. As one would expect when surrounded closely by land, the fog occurs less often in Minas Basin than the lower part of the Bay. Burntcoat Head in Minas Basin holds the world's record for tidal range at 53 feet. Obviously the tides are crucial to progress up and down the coast, and one must be guided by when the tide will allow you to enter and leave the different harbors. Cargo ship traffic is here to serve the gypsum and lumber industries, and these freighters will also use the tides just as you will. Boats drawing up to 6 feet can enter the harbors mentioned here.

Some of the harbors have little indication on the chart what a harbor will be like, but *Sailing Directions* tells which ones have wharves and the depth of water at high tide at each wharf. THERE ARE NO "LOW WATER" HARBORS IN THIS AREA, but if one is willing to ground out each night, leaning against a wharf or jetty, and one is willing to explore on his own and not be too apprehensive about fog and currents, the visiting yachtsman will find the scenery (when it is clear) spectacular, the people friendly, and the harbors at high tide snug and often beautiful.

For grounding out, choose harbors with piers and a suitable bottom at low tide. A fender board should be rigged outside your conventional fenders to bear on the pilings. On securing to the pier, lead the main halyard from the masthead to a securing line made fast to whatever is available across the pier. Set up a modest tension, which must be adjusted as the tide drops, or alternately, tie a weight (a jerry-can of water will do) to the midpoint of this line to retain tension. Bow and stern lines must be adjusted and should have all the length possible. The lines and fender board must be tended until the boat takes the ground. After this, with the halyard set up taught, she shouldn't go anywhere. Those with powerboats may follow the custom of the area and have "turtles" built to fit under the outboard quarter to make sure she leans against the dock. Remember to have a bucket of seawater aboard before you are high and dry so you can flush the head!

The coast between Minas Basin and Digby is very bold and at times spectacular. The harbors are usually very well protected, but small. According to local residents, Hampton**, Margaretsville, Morden**, Harborville at Gibbons Brook** and Halls Harbour are satisfactory. Often these harbors are accessible to a 6' draft boat for only an hour or so before and after high water. Generally, when viewed from seaward, these harbors appear as a stubby bit of breakwater projecting perhaps halfway from the edge of the grass to the water, usually with a dilapidated flat face on its eastern side, against which a boat can lie when the wind is not easterly.

Margaretsville is better than most and Halls Harbour is the most recommended.

Caution should be used on entering these harbours as they have not been reported on in the last ten years.

**These harbors appear as "fly specks" on Canadian Chart #4010 and the Guide has no further direct information on them based on personal experience.

MARGARETSVILLE

45°02.9'N, 65°03.6'W

Chart #4010

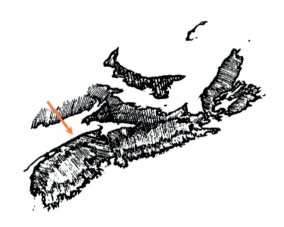

DIRECTIONS: Margaretsville Harbor is formed by two wharves or breakwaters which are only open to the northeast and can be entered within three hours of high water. A square lighthouse is on the point just to the west of the outer breakwater. When coming from the west, leave the light about 1/4 mile to starboard and then head toward the land. The entrance will open when you have passed the outer wharf.

BERTHS: The best place to lie is against the eastern side of the outer wharf. Here the bottom is level and soft.

REMARKS: One correspondent writes that Margaretsville, "could still be murder in a northeast storm."

HALLS HARBOUR

45°12'N, 64°37'W

Chart # 4010

1988

DIRECTIONS: Halls Harbour can be entered within two hours of high water. A breakwater extends out on the westerly side of the entrance, and a small, square lighthouse on iron stilts is on the easterly side. Keep as close to the breakwater as possible when entering, as the channel is narrow. At the head of the breakwater the channel turns left and opensinto a completely landlocked basin surrounded by woods.

BERTHS: The wharf on the easterly side is next to a small store. The bottom is soft and slants gently away from the wharf.

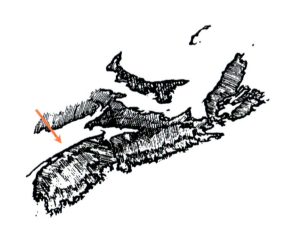

REMARKS: One of the smallest and prettiest harbors on this coast.

FACILITIES: Very limited.

ADVOCATE

45°19.4'N, 64°47.2'W

Chart #4010

1988

DIRECTIONS: Advocate, lying between Cape d'Or and Cape Chignecto, both of which have impressive cliffs, can be entered within about two hours of high water. From the lighted bell at the entrance, head easterly toward a light on a red tripod with a small red building next to it. The channel is well buoyed. After passing the light, go in a northerly direction until you see two beacons. Turn toward the east end of the harbor, thence follow the channel along the shore to the government wharf next to the steel bridge.

REMARKS: The town stretches for about two miles along the waterfront.

BERTHS: At the government wharf.

FACILITIES: Very limited.

THE HARBORS OF MINAS BASIN

When entering Minas Basin, keep well toward the northerly shore and give Cape Split (a dramatic sharp point of 200' sheer basalt cliffs, ending in a series of broken needles of rock) a wide berth. The tide runs hard off most of the headlands and in many places forms rips.

As previously mentioned, be aware of the large steamers (30,000 tons) that transit the Avon River to Hantsport to load gypsum.

Local residents do not recommend going beyond Economy Point.

PARRSBORO

45°23.5'N, 64°19.2'W

Charts: #4010, #4399

DIRECTIONS: Parrsboro is the first good harbor inside Minas Basin and can be entered two hours before and after high water.

BERTHS: Large steamers use the westerly side of the government wharf where they can lie on a bed of timbers at LW and load lumber. The northerly end is more sheltered and has a soft and fairly level bottom.

REMARKS: None.

FACILITIES: Basic supplies and liquor may be had in the town; no fuel or water.

FIVE ISLANDS

45°24'N, 64°04.2'N

DIRECTIONS: This is a lovely harbor inside five very bold islands about a mile offshore. When entering, leave Moose Island and the small island next to it to starboard and head for the small lighthouse at the entrance to East River. There is a long sandbar that makes out from the eastern side of the light which should be left to port.

BERTHS: Once in East River, go up beyond the light and you will find a deserted wharf that is completely protected.

REMARKS: None.

FACILITIES: None.

HANTSPORT

45°04'N, 64°10'W

Charts #4010, #4140

DIRECTIONS: Entrance here is greatly simplified by having Chart #4140 aboard. The approach up the Avon River is clearly marked by buoys.

ANCHORAGE AND BERTHS: Tie to the government wharf (the southerly of the two wharves indicated on #4140) and ground out on the gravel vessel bed.

It is possible to anchor in the midchannel shoal area approximately two miles downstream from Hantsport.

In a northwesterly blow, Bob Carter recommends anchoring in the bight just southwest of Cape Blomidon in the approximate area 45°15'N, 64°20.5'W in 12

feet at LW and 60 feet at HW. This is obviously no place to be in any wind from the east and the current runs across the wind, creating the danger of dragging the anchor.

It is unwise to set two anchors here as the contrary wind and current directions will cause the lines to foul.

REMARKS: Hantsport is a busy gypsum port which is so highly-automated that a 30,000-ton freighter can be loaded and leave on a single tide. It can be a dirty place.

FACILITIES: Most supplies are available except fuel and water. Simple repairs can be made by hiring repairmen from Halifax, approximately an hour away by road.

THE NEW BRUNSWICK SHORE

The New Brunswick Shore east of St. John is very bold and wild. According to local residents, Black River, St. Martins, and Alma are the best harbors between St. John and the Petitcodiac River. Except for St Martins and Alma, the coast is without towns.

BLACK RIVER, N.B.

45°15.2'N, 65°48.2'W

Chart: #4010

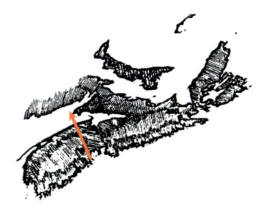

DIRECTIONS: The entrance light erected on a steel tower can only be seen when you are south of it. Coming in, head directly for the end of the pier. There is a sand spit opposite and about 100 feet off the end of the wharf.

BERTHS: The south side of the pier has five feet of water at low tide, but it is exposed and a roll is apt to make in. On the west side of the pier you are protected from this roll. About 200 yards upstream there is a series of poles where the local lobstermen lie and ground out during the winter months.

FACILITIES: None.

ST. MARTINS, N.B.

45°21.2'N, 65°32.

Chart #4010

DIRECTIONS: St. Martins Harbour is easy to make from the west and is formed by two breakwaters at the entrance of a small stream. It may be entered between 2 1/2 to 3 hours of high water.

BERTHS: At the head of the harbor is a wharf used by the local fishermen with approximately 8 feet at high water and a soft mud bottom. The westerly breakwater is not suitable for lying against. The breakwater on the south side of the harbor affords a hard bottom free of rocks, but care should be taken to lie near the center of this breakwater and not too close to either end as both ends are rocky.

REMARKS: This harbor is well protected with a number of dwellings around it.

FACILITIES: None.

ALMA, N.B.

45°36'N, 64°56.7'W

Charts: #4010, #4337

DIRECTIONS: This is an easy place to get into if you have Chart #4337 aboard. Alma is in the Upper Salmon River which is the northern boundary of Fundy Park. The entrance to this harbor is practically invisible until you are almost at the breakwater which is on the western side of the harbor. One can carry five to six feet into the harbor 2 hours either side of high water.

BERTHS: There is a pier coming out from the eastern shore with a soft mud bottom.

REMARKS: At the head of the harbor is a fixed bridge which is the entrance to Fundy Park. This is an active town with stores, gas stations and motels.

FACILITIES: Liquor and limited supplies are available, but not fuel and water.

DIGBY AND ANNAPOLIS BASIN

Charts: #4010, #4396

DIRECTIONS: Annapolis Basin is a triangular-shaped, landlocked inlet, running approximately northeast and southwest. It is about five miles long, and at its southern end about three miles wide. It is advisable to have Chart #4396 for peace of mind, though it may be possible to get into Digby Gut on Chart #4010 in good visibility.

DIGBY

44°37.5'N, 65°45.2'W

Gary Schneider and previous material.   2003

ANCHORAGE AND BERTHS: It is possible to anchor north of Digby to the west of the red channel markers. The bottom appeared to be sandy gravel. However, one can expect some fishing boat traffic in the early morning hours. Even though we had swung out into the channel a bit, the twenty or so boats which came by us between four and seven AM all held their distance and a lot of them even throttled back before they went by us.   See below concerning water depths shown on the charts.   The town landing shown on the chart is predominately used by scallop draggers, and herring seiners. The float shown on the chart off of one of the large piers is no longer present. There are two floating docks with finger piers inside which do not show on the chart. Water depths at low low might be a problem for some vessels, however, the tide range is normally adequate to accommodate a 6 ft. vessel. Nightly charge for space on the float was $28 Canadian for boats over thirty feet;

Digby Gut is not easy to identify when approaching from east or west because the pine-clad shoreline has no prominent marks, including Prim Point Light, which is small and hard to find. When in doubt, find the whistle buoy a mile north of the Gut, from which position the Gut opens up. The tide in the Gut runs about six knots at full strength. However, the Gut is deep, its bottom is clear, and there are few eddies to contend with.

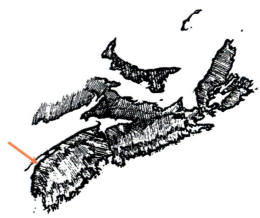

$25 US.   There appeared to be water available at the floats and some had power. There is also a gas and a diesel pump at the top of the steps; the Annapolis Basin charter office is in charge of docking fees and fuel. Fuel access is obtained only at high water by tying inside the floats next to the stairs/ramp. Looking at the location at low one can see the rocks on the shore side and the remains of old piers on the northern side of the marina. These rocks will be under you while you are fueling so timing is everything. We would recommend checking with the office prior to maneuvering a vessel into position. Many of the Western Nova Scotian Yacht Club appear to be berthed here. The Yacht club itself is further in and only operational on weekends, tho there are reportedly Friday night gatherings and Wed. night and Sunday races.

It is also possible to anchor off the town pier. There are at least two large moorings east. We spent a couple of evenings on one, accessed through the Digby Marine Store where, the store owner, charged us the princely sum of ten bucks a night, Canadian. This is a large yellow plastic ball, bigger than a 55 gallon drum with two nicely spliced ¾" Poly pro pennants that were pretty new and free of slime. Do not be too concerned that the charted depth in the area of the mooring is only four or five feet. The chart datum appears to be set for low, low water. Even though we were there for a number of low tides, we never saw less than fifteen feet on the depth machine. Should you be there at a Spring low, then the chart depth might be of more concern. This mooring is used by the committee boat during racing, and may not be available.

REMARKS: Digby (pop. 2,300) was settled by Loyalists from the United States. One of these, a certain John Edison from New Jersey, became Town Assessor in 1808 and his great grandson was Thomas A. Edison, the great inventor.

A prominent landmark on the west shore just before Digby is the Pines Hotel, run by the Province of Nova Scotia. Several correspondents have recommended renting a room there for the purpose of providing a bath for all hands. The dining room at last report was very good and if you are lucky you will find the famous Digby scallops on the menu. Digby is the Nova Scotia terminus of the ferry from St. John and suffers somewhat from tourist trap commercialism, although there are some pleasant craft shops in the area.

John McKelvy recalls having sailed all the way to Digby from Massachusetts in his 39' yawl for the first time in 1963 (a voyage of some note at the time). We were given a berth on the only float on the ferry dock. In the evening a little kid (probably from the Pines), dressed in a blue blazer, shorts, and a tie came down the dock and read our transom out loud:

AEOLUS
HYANNIS PORT

"Where is Hyannis Port," he queried. "Somewhere in New Brunswick?" ... We knew we had "gone foreign."

ANNAPOLIS ROYAL

44°44.6'N, 65°31.4'W

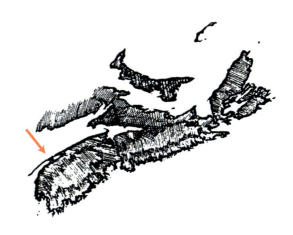

DIRECTIONS: This is a pleasant sail of about 15 miles ENE of Digby, rounding Goat Island. It is well marked, and at low tide mud banks make out from the shore.

ANCHORAGE AND BERTHS: Anchor close to the dock near restored Fort Ann. The dock dries out an hour before and after low tide, but it also has a vessel bed and you are welcome to tie up if you are willing to ground out at low water. One correspondent complained that the holding ground was poor here, but others express no such complaint. The once-swift local current has been tamed by a dam and hydroelectric turbine. (It is not an easy place to land. The Pilot recommends anchoring near the hydro plant at the head of the basin. This is now not an option as there are fishing boats moored bow to stern in the area. My recommendation is to borrow a car and motor from Digby – ed)

REMARKS: The buildings and grounds of Fort Ann have been restored and are worth seeing. This site was originally a French stronghold named Port Royal which became a thorn in the side of the fledgling British North

American Empire until 1710 when an expedition of New Englanders expelled the French for good. The fort was maintained as a garrison until 1854.

Horticulturists should visit the Annapolis Royal Historic Gardens.

On the way up the Annapolis River to Annapolis, there is a reconstruction of Samuel de Champlain's "Habitat," where he and a few others settled after their failure at St. Croix Island, and prior to their journey to (and foundation of) Quebec in 1608. This building is located on the channel opposite Goat Island.

FACILITIES: One correspondent writes of Annapolis Royal: "The entire community has been 'revised' and is now a place of boutiques, restaurants [and a] theatre." There is no fuel or water available here; however, at last check there was a liquor store.

PASSAGE NOTES
(Digby to Cape Sable Including Schooner Passage)

Charts: #4118, #4244, #4243, #4242

From Digby to Petit Passage there are no low water harbors. The shoreline can be followed safely at a distance of 200 yards all the way from Digby to the north end of Brier Island, except the west point of Sandy Cove, where a berth of 600 yards should be given.

George Killam provided the following directions through Petit Passage and Grand Passage, against the tide, in 1952. They are still as valid today as when they were written. Prudence however, might dictate planning any trip through this area with a fair tide.

PETIT PASSAGE

Chart # 4118

Petit Passage affords a short cut into St, Mary's Bay and has a breakwater on the Tiverton side where yachts can safely tie up afloat at all tides. **If entering this passage from the north against the tide**, run across under Boar's Head Light and follow the eddy down the western shore to the breakwater. The only obstruction on the western shore is a rock with 1 1/4 fathoms over it located 400 yards, 12 degrees from Boar's Head. (See Tiverton below.)

In **leaving Tiverton going south on the flood tide**, run down the eddy to the long point of rocks below the breakwater, then cross the passage to the eastern shore and follow down into St. Mary's Bay. In this way a five-knot boat can get through a seven-knot current.

If your boat will stem the current around Eddy Point, do so and follow the eddy all the way through. Give the western shoreline a wider berth below Eddy Point, as a small shoal makes out at this point at low water.

A heavy tide rip runs at the lower end of the passage on ebb tide, but this can be avoided by following down the western side on the edge of the eddy.

In **going north through the passage against the tide**, follow up the western shore to Eddy Point, then if you cannot stem the tide around the point, cross over to the eastern shore and run up to well above Tiverton breakwater before crossing to the Tiverton side again.

There are no low water harbors in St. Mary's Bay except Little River Cove (44°26.7'N, 66°07.6'W, see below) in which small yachts can safely lie at low water. From Tiverton to Westport the shorelines of Long Island can be followed safely at a distance of 150 yards.

Give the whole coast of Brier Island from North Point around through the west to the extreme southern tip a wide berth of six miles or more and thus avoid dangerous shoals and heavy tide rips.

GRAND PASSAGE

Chart #4118

In entering Grand Passage from the north, run to a red bell buoy (HA4), then follow the western shore down to the government wharf. There are mixed reports concerning the holding ground for yachts in the cove below the dock (see Westport, below).

In **going south from Westport**, use the small passage west of Peter Island. *If ebb tide*, keep in the middle of the passage until below the point opposite Peter Island, then haul over to the westward to the edge of the eddy and thus avoid a tide rip. Bold water runs practically to the rock line through this passage. *If flood tide*, keep in the eddy to the point, then after rounding the point against the tide, haul over to westward and follow the eddy through.

From Westport or Tiverton there is a clear run across Cape St. Mary's (see Cape St. Mary's below)... but I would not suggest a stop there unless in smooth water.

YARMOUTH TO SCHOONER PASSAGE

Charts: #4243, #4244

In leaving Yarmouth, after clearing Sunday Point on the east side of the harbor mouth, yachts drawing under 9' can steer for a lighted Mo A buoy just south of Chebogue Point, keeping about 300 yards off the land at Chebogue Pt. From this bell buoy, steer 162° mag. about 4 1/2 miles to another bell buoy off the entrances to both Schooner and Ellenwood Passages. From this bell buoy steer 144° mag. keeping midway between Candlebox Light and a green buoy off Owl's Head Island. If going through Ellenwood Passage, steer south from the Mo A buoy to a spindle off the end of Ellenwood Island, keeping just a berth off the spindle; then steer for a wharf about halfway down the island.

From Candlebox Light through Schooner Passage, the course is 172° mag., passing Johns Island on the west with Harris Island on your east side. The lower wharf at Johns Island is a good place to tie up, but note should be taken of a possible strong tide when docking.

In passing down by Peases Island, keep close to the island and pass out between the island and a red automatic buoy southeast of the island.

SCHOONER PASSAGE AREA HARBORS

(Including Turpentine Cove and Johns Island Wharf)

TURPENTINE COVE

43°39.1'N, 66°02.0'W

Chart #4244

Rewritten from material written by Judge Bailey Aldrich, William Sayres Dr. Bayard Clarkson. Charles Westropp and Charles Gibson.   *2003*

Running southward through Schooner Passage, be sure to proceed well south of GRG buoy located south of Candlebox before turning northeast; the water south of Turpentine is quite shoal. Green and red spars north of Harris Island now clearly mark the southern entrance to Turpentine Channel and if you proceed south from GRG buoy until these are seen, you will have no difficulty entering the channel. You will find a small-protected

anchorage of adequate depth and out of the current. There are reported to be some abandoned wharves in fairly good condition here as well. This is reportedly the best stop on the straight run from Cape Sable to Yarmouth. Charles Gibson rode out a 30kt blow but reported a lively night with wind against a strong tide. Probably not the place to be in anything but light conditions.

JOHNS ISLAND WHARF*

43°38.7'N, 66°02.3'W

Chart #4244

Vernon C. Gray

Earlier mention of the wharves on the east side of Johns Island has been made. There are two suitable for lying alongside and both are in good repair. We tied up to the centermost wharf (outer face). The tide rises to 15 feet but averages 12 feet. You are out of the main stream of current and can have a reasonably

comfortable night. We found a truly lovely spot.

*Caution should be used entering this harbor as it has not been reported on in the last ten years.

SCHOONER PASSAGE TO CAPE SABLE ISLAND

(Including Westport, Cape St. Mary, Little River Cove, Meteghan, Yarmouth, Wedgeport, Lobster Bay (Upper Reaches), Pubnico, Stoddart Cove, Clark's Harbour, and Cape Sable.)

George Killam   *1952*

From Pease Island to Pubnico Harbour, the course is 125° mag., a distance of 10 miles. There is a wharf with only 3 to 4 feet of water at low tide at Lower East Pubnico about one mile inside the lighthouse. A good anchorage can be found about 200 feet southeast off the end of the wharf.

In going direct from Pease Island to Cape Sable or Clark Harbour, give the Old Man Shoal a wide berth on a flood tide, as the tide sets strongly to the northwest at this point.

Then steer for Pubnico Mo A whistle buoy, west of Johns Island Ledge, and from there to the bell buoy off the harbor entrance.

[From here one has the choice of stopping at Clark Harbour (see below) or rounding Cape Sable Island. Please note, however, that the tide runs up to 4 knots in this area, and the course from Pubnico Mo A whistle to the bell (ND2) off Outer Island comes dangerously close to Duck Island Ledges. Furthermore there are ledges and rips extending 3 miles south of the sand dunes off Cape Sable Island.]

WESTPORT

44°16.0'N, 66°21.1'W

Chart #4118

From earlier material by H. Smith, V. Gray, W. Brewer, and Charles Westropp   *2000*

DIRECTIONS: Westport is situated on Brier Island, the outermost of the islands which extend southwesterly from Digby Neck. It is separated from adjacent Long Island by a strait known as Grand Passage. The tide runs at not less than five knots, sometimes more, through this passage. The entrance to Grand Passage from either north or south presents no particular difficulty in clear weather, but is no place for a stranger to attempt during fog. North Point is prominent and is easily identified, and the only danger is Cow Ledge, which is marked. Once past this buoy, the channel is clear all the way to Westport. Just east of Westport lies Passage Shoal right in mid-channel, with only 5 feet of water on it marked by a red and green can. The entrance

from the south may be made on either side of

Peter Island, which is readily distinguishable from offshore. The westerly channel, which most of the natives seem to prefer, is entirely safe, provided you keep strictly in the middle. If the easterly channel is used, be sure to leave the beacon north of Peter Island on the port hand.

Leaving Grand Passage and bound west, be sure to give Southwest Ledge a wide birth, as it extends a good five miles southwest of the island, a wide berth. In the calmest weather a vicious sea makes up over the shoalier spots.

ANCHORAGE AND BERTHS: Anchoring is possible, but not recommended. The tide is hard and full of eddies; the bottom is hard sand and very irregular. However, in 1991 a Guide correspondent reported the holding ground in the fishermen's mooring area to be satisfactory. He used a Bruce anchor and the bottom was sand. There was a timber dinghy landing on shore used by the locals.

There is now a fully protected harbor where the Government wharf used to be. In the harbor there is a floating dock on The East side that is used by local fishing boats. We nested on one in what must be one of the most secure "cocoons" around. There is very little water in the Western half of harbor (it dries!) on the shore side.

REMARKS: Westport is attractive. Brier Island is an unspoiled little place, far removed from the "summer resort" crowd and notable as having been the boyhood home of Captain Joshua Slocum. The south and east sides are well worth visiting, the rock formation on the extreme southwesterly end being mostly short pinnacle rocks, strongly reminiscent of Fingal's Cave or the Giant's Causeway. The easterly side of the island is well wooded with deep, narrow coves running into the land.

Westport is the headquarters for the Brier Island Ocean Study, engaged in collecting data on the local cetacean population. There is no better place to observe birds, marine mammals, and other ocean species than the area just west of Brier Island and extending to Boar's Head, the north tip of Long Island. To support their efforts, they run a whale watch vessel from Westport twice daily in summer.

Bill Brewer describes an experience he had there in the summer of 1987 as follows:

"Sailing slowly along the 40 fathom curve, we saw a dozen humpbacks feeding on herring and euphasid shrimp, letting us approach very close as they concentrated on the abundant feed. A large finback rose majestically a few boat-lengths away, equally unconcerned with our presence. Schools of white-sided dolphin were all around us, dividing their attention between the yacht and the small bluefin tuna which were leaping into the air ahead of them. Shearwaters, phalaropes, and petrels were sharing the abundance with herring gulls and both common and arctic terns. On shore great blue herons sat in bunches patiently digesting their last meal. With a little luck on weather, one can begin to understand the extraordinary productivity of these northern seas."

FACILITIES: In 1991 the Westport Inn sold good plain meals and had a dry goods store in the basement. No fuel or water is available.

CAPE ST. MARY*

44°05.0'N, 66°12.4'W

Chart #4118

Rewritten from earlier material by G. C. Kirstein.

DIRECTIONS: The entrance is marked by the customary buoys (a red and white Mo A bell buoy, one mile south southwest of Cape St. Mary's Lighthouse and a green can close to the wharf).

ANCHORAGE AND BERTHS: There is the usual government wharf with fishing boats alongside. This dock is dredged to 7' along its entire length. [There is no place to anchor. - ed.]

REMARKS: The harbor has no merit except as a refuge. I do not recommend it, but I can state we were awfully glad to see it after being in rough seas for 2 days and 2 nights.

FACILITIES: There are no stores and no fuel or water is available.

Caution should be used entering this harbor as it has not been reported on in the last ten years.

LITTLE RIVER COVE*

44°26.6'N, 66°07.6W

Chart #4118

Rewritten from earlier material by B. Aldrich.

DIRECTIONS: This is an easy harbor to make and there are no entrance buoys. The harbor is formed by a breakwater-wharf with a small red flasher on the end.

ANCHORAGE AND BERTHS: This cove has been dredged to 7 - 8 feet. There is a small but usually crowded anchorage, as well as space either alongside the wharf or one of the fishing boats tied to the wharf.

REMARKS: This is a small but attractive harbor with some wharves up the narrow mouth of the river, safe from all winds except heavy easterlies.

FACILITIES: Only basic supplies are available at the general store about 1/2 mile from the wharf.

Caution should be used entering this harbor as it has not been reported on in the last ten years.

METEGHAN

44°11.8'N, 66°10.1'W

Chart: #4118

Jurgen Kok   *2000*

DIRECTIONS: Run from the bell buoy HC2 through the marked fairway to the flashing light at the end of the breakwater, and take a sharp right to enter the protected basin. The government wharf has been rebuilt and enlarged and now is accessible to most yachts on all tides.

ANCHORAGE AND BERTHS: Inside the breakwater there are several floating docks, including a "marina" float under construction, as well as berths alongside the wharves both within and outside the protected basin. All are at least eight feet deep.

REMARKS: Meteghan is one of the few deep harbors on St. Mary's Bay and is conveniently situated for a passage to or from Petit Passage. This is a good place to enter Nova Scotia from Saint John, or to launch a return trip to Maine. During both a quick stopover and stranded during bad weather, we found Meteghan to be a friendly and interesting harbor, with a long beach and a thriving fishing and shipbuilding infrastructure. The town and Harbormaster are making an effort to attract fishing boats and visiting yachts to the renovated harbor.

FACILITIES: A well-stocked supermarket with fresh meat, fish, and produce is a short walk up the road from the wharf. Truck deliveries of water and fuel can be arranged by the harbormaster. Other amenities include a pay phone, an ATM, a well-stocked hardware store, gas station, and a post office. Several commercial fisheries operations are near the wharf, but the fish market was closed during our visit. A 300-ton marine railway is located next to the government wharf. Four miles north, on Meteghan River, the A. F. Theriault & Sons Shipyard does building and repairs on yachts and workboats in fiberglass, aluminum, steel and wood, and can also fix propellers and just about any problem a boat may have.

YARMOUTH

43°50.0'N, 66°07.3'W

Charts: #4243, #4245

Condensed from material by J. McKelvy, by W. Feldman, with new information from R. Michener.   *2002*

DIRECTIONS: Chart #4245, the large scale harbor chart, should be used on entering the harbor itself, though in an emergency and with reasonable visibility, Yarmouth can be entered without this chart by using logic and common sense (red to port, green to starboard, etc.).

From the west coming across the Bay of Fundy, find the Lurcher Mo A buoy (YA). From Mo A YA, proceed east northeast to the flashing bell (Y3). Exact compass courses in this area will vary, as at most times there is a strong tidal current across your course. From green Y3 steer approximately 60° (again taking into account a strong cross-current) to red bell Y4 (just west of Hen and Chickens Shoal). From here you can follow the buoys east-northeast past Bunker Island and into the harbor. In thick weather, the buoys are easy to follow as they are no more than 1/2 mile apart and the fog signal on Cape Forchu (2 blasts every 48 seconds) and the fog signal on Bunker Island (one blast every 14 seconds) give you some relative bearing.

From the east, it is possible to skirt the shoreline coming from Pubnico and through Schooner Passage (as outlined in SCHOONER PASSAGE TO CAPE SABLE and YARMOUTH TO SCHOONER PASSAGE). However, in thick weather it is more advisable to follow the sea buoys (whistles for the most part) around the northwest to Yarmouth Fairway bell. From here a course of 40° mag. will bring you to green bell Y3 from which you can lay courses into the harbor as suggested above.

ANCHORAGE AND BERTHS: The best anchorage is northeast of Doctors Island. The holding ground is good. Yachts are urged to report to Fundy Traffic on VHF Channel 14 at the reporting points 1L, 1Y, and 2Y (as indicated on CHS charts 4011, 4243, and 4245) and when docked or leaving the docks or moorings in Yarmouth harbour. This is particularly important (even when the visibility is good) with the advent of the new high-speed catamaran ferry service between Bar Harbor and Yarmouth, as it is potentially dangerous for any vessel to be in the harbor's narrow channel at the same time as a large vessel is entering or leaving the harbour. Fundy Traffic needs to know who is out there and will inform yachts of potential conflicts.

Several free moorings have substantial pennants attached. The rental moorings are marked by red floats and are managed by the wharfmaster whose office is located on the Killam Wharf (902-742-5210). Restrooms, showers and laundry facilities are near the wharfmaster's office. A floating dock with water on it lies just north of the Coast Guard Dock which visitors are welcome to use.

REMARKS: Yarmouth, a city of 9,000 souls, is so no-nonsense, hard working seaport without frills or urban renewal. It is the terminus for two ferries, the Scotia Prince (daily from Portland, Maine) and the Cat, a 300-foot motorized catamaran (twice daily from Bar Harbor Maine). It has fair sized fishing fleet and oil tanker traffic to Bunker Island at the beginning of the channel leading into the harbor. Add to this an occasional freighter and you have traffic problems. Because of this traffic, if a thick o'fog comes in (or other visibility problem), you would be well advised to anchor temporarily in one of the bays before Bunker Island and wait until the visibility improves, even if you have radar.

If you must enter the harbor in poor visibility, call Fundy Traffic Control and be advised of traffic in the harbor.

To illustrate the danger of navigating here in poor visibility; in the night of September 4, 1998, the outbound *Cat* collided with a Canadian in-bound dragger, the 65-foot *Lady Megan II*. Both had radar and both were communicating with each other on VHF. The *Lady Megan* became stuck under the bridge between *Cat's* twin hulls and her captain was crushed to death in the wheelhouse.

Yarmouth is near a major airport for crew changes; it is a good jumping off point for crossing the Bay of Fundy, and although uncomfortable in a westerly blow, it is a safe harbor.

FACILITIES: Food and supplies are readily available. Water is to be had on the float north of the Coast Guard Dock as previously mentioned. Fuel would have to come by an arrangement with a tanker truck.

WEDGEPORT*

43°42.7'N, 65°59'W

Chart: #4244

Rewritten and condensed from earlier material by Dr. Isaac Starr and J.B. McLean. Dr. Starr wrote a comprehensive report on this harbor in the first edition of the Guide in 1952. J.B. McLean wrote an update in 1970 and since then there has been no further report. The directions are for the harbor marked "Lower Wedgeport" on the Goose Bay (west) side of "Tusket Wedge" and not for the harbor on the Tusket River (east) side of Tusket Wedge on chart #4244.

DIRECTIONS: There are heavy tidal currents running E-W in this area for which compensation must constantly be made. Due to the currents, when coming out of Schooner Passage from the west, Dr. Starr recommended in 1952 that you steer from the flashing red buoy (NS4) south of Peases Island to clear Old Woman Ledge. Thence, go north northeast toward Big Fish Island light until you have cleared Western Bar Island abeam, thence northwest, clearing Wedge Point to starboard, and on up the marked channel in Goose Bay. These directions have their merits in poor visibility without radar, but more buoys have been set since then, and there appears to be a safe, well-marked channel going inside Old Woman, then, just east of Big Tusket and Lobster Islands. The approach from the east is relatively clear.

Once inside Goose Bay, stay in the marked channel and <u>do</u> <u>not</u> <u>turn</u> <u>for</u> <u>the</u> <u>dock</u> <u>until</u> <u>it</u> <u>is</u> <u>approximately</u> <u>abeam</u> and you can distinguish the marks for the final channel in at approximately 90° to starboard of your course. This last channel into the dock is difficult to negotiate on an ebb tide because the boats moored in the area swing south across the channel.

ANCHORAGE AND BERTHS: It is possible to anchor out in the main channel (not the one dredged into the dock) and Dr. Starr states, "the dock can be reached in any tide." [If anchoring, beware of the 180° shift in the tide -ed.]

REMARKS: Forty years ago, Wedgeport (pop. 800) was the site of the international Tuna Cup matches and behemoth tuna of 800-900 lbs. were landed here. These fish are no longer in the area and Wedgeport has settled into a fishing-lobstering community. "There is nothing unusually attractive about this harbor," writes Dr. Starr.

FACILITIES: Basic supplies are available in the town.

*Caution should be used entering this harbor as it has not been reported on in the last ten years.

LOBSTER BAY* (UPPER REACHES)

43°40'N/43°46'N, 65°48'W/65°53'W

Chart: #4244

This section was originally written by Dr. Isaac Starr under the title "Argyle Bay" in 1952 with an update in 1975. Since 1975, Chart #4326 has been replaced with #4244 and some navigational marks have been added to the area. Dr. Starr's original directions are given here, corrected to conform to new Chart #4244 and with new material contributed by Mr. David Barker who visited the area in 1982.

Going out of Tusket River mouth, no northward passage is possible for several miles, and the next take-off point is Whitehead Island, its shape a beautiful example of a glacial drumlin. There are two excellent courses: The western passes close to Whitehead, Pumpkin and Lears Islands, leaving them all close to starboard when entering. This course leaves to port Jones Ledge, straight south of the south cape of Jones Island, and if approaching from the east, it is possible to shorten your course by using the good water between the cape and the reef as do those with local knowledge. An anchorage is marked on the charts east of Jones Island, but protection would only be fair and I have never seen anyone use it.

With Lears Island abeam to starboard, one must continue true north until one clears the shoal off the north cape of Lears, which is as long as the island itself. Rocks at its end are out of the water on most tides. Clearing this point one aims about true northeast at Channel Island (two small islets joined together at low water, one of them partly wooded) and Camp Island, both of which are essentially left to

port. The mainland is reached at Mortons Neck, and the course turns true north following the mainland shore where there is a wharf and a number of fishing boats anchored to the north of it. No water or fuel is available on this dock, but it is possible to have fresh well water trucked in for your tanks.

Proceeding north beyond Nanny Island are the ruins of a second wharf. With this second wharf abeam, one must leave the mainland shore and head for the southeast point of wooded Rankins Island, identified by a clearing near it visible from the south. Approaching this point, one follows close to the east shore of Rankin Island, leaving the dangerous reefs south of Globe Island to starboard and taking the narrow, but deep and clear passage between Rankin and Globe Islands into a beautiful bay sheltered by wooded islands. This anchorage provides a spectacular view of farms and fields.

On the southwest point of the mainland under Spinney Hill [identified by a 19-meter spot on Chart #4244] is the small marine railway of the Ardnamurchan Club, and the Club's boats are moored out of the current southeast of this point. Visitors entering the harbor should aim at this point and anchor out of the current southeast of it. The Ardnamurchan Club is a private organization.

Caution should be used entering this harbor as it has not been reported on in the last ten years.

PUBNICO*

43°37'N, 65°47.2'W

Chart: #4242

Rewritten and condensed from earlier material by Alexander Fowler.

DIRECTIONS: This harbor is easily entered under any weather conditions. From the bell off Pubnico Point, steer 62° mag. for the light on Beach Point. Observe the nun off Beach Point to starboard and continue north, observing the green flasher and can that mark the ledges making out to the west of Pubnico Point. Proceed from these buoys to the substantial government wharf on the western shore of the harbor (indicated on the chart as a square shape with openings).

ANCHORAGE AND BERTHS: There is a strong tidal current in Pubnico Harbour, and though anchoring is not recommended, it probably could be done out of the channel with a Bahamian mooring.

The marina-like government wharf provides most welcome shelter on a rugged night. There is plenty of water for 6' draft vessels to tie inside and 18' on the outside.

REMARKS: This is an attractive harbor, and the local people, like Nova Scotians elsewhere, are friendly and helpful.

FACILITIES: There are stores with basic supplies within a mile of the dock. There is no fuel or water on the dock.

*Caution should be used entering this harbor as it has not been reported on in the last ten years.

STODDART COVE*

43°28.2'N, 65°43'W

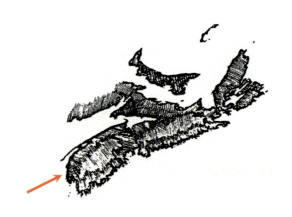

Chart: #4242

Rewritten and condensed from earlier material by Joseph Guild and Hugh McTeague.

DIRECTIONS: Stoddart Cove, located between Stoddart Island and Inner Island, is really part of a passage between these islands with only 1/2 fathom at the narrow eastern end. Entry is extremely simple; leave the two green marks to port and Stoddart Island light to starboard and don't go too far to the east.

ANCHORAGE AND BERTHS: The cove is out of the swift currents hereabouts and the holding ground is good, but it is open to the northeast. There are no wharves.

REMARKS: This harbor, once important before Barrington Passage was bridged by a causeway, is no longer on the "beaten path" and is a great anchorage if you want to be alone. The lighthouse is no longer manned and the only inhabitants are some sheep and cows on Stoddart Island.

FACILITIES: None.

*Caution should be used entering this harbor as it has not been reported on in the last ten years.

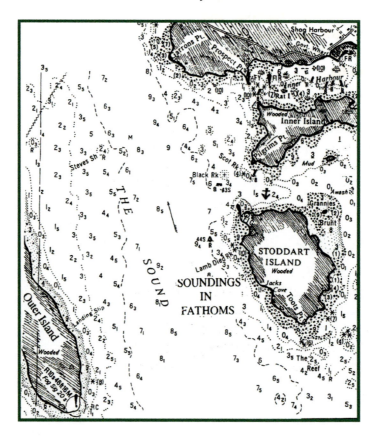

CLARK'S HARBOUR*

43°26.3'N, 65°38.7'W

Chart; #4242

Rewritten and condensed from earlier material by B. Aldrich, G. Kirstein and A. Zink.

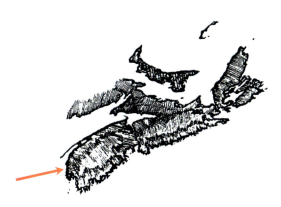

DIRECTIONS: From the west, find the red bell (ND2) south of Outer Island and shape a course for West Head (and remember there are strong cross currents here that you must compensate for). Round the red bell marking Hospital Reef and the flasher marking Hospital Ledge to starboard and swing southeast following the channel buoys into the harbor. All this is obvious when you look at chart #4242.

From the east, the safest course is to stay well clear of Cape Sable light (including Horse Race, Southwest Ledge, Pinnacle Rock, Cromwell Rock, and all that), then bear north to Hospital Reef and then in, leaving Green Island and all the ledges to the east of it to starboard.

There is a shorter passage from the east... *one that is not for the weak of heart.* As one correspondent states, "There is a mental problem in this passage, no question." It is used, however, by the Canadian Coast Guard 44' cutter at all tides and by 100' draggers at better than half tide.

This is it: Leave the green bell (JS53) northeast of Cape Sable light and Black Rock to starboard and stay well south of the lighthouse. When the light bears northeast, set a course for the red and white Mo A buoy (NA) due east of the lighthouse,

leaving it to starboard. from there, go to the red nun (NA2), leaving it to starboard and steer for the red and white Mo A (NAC), and leave it to starboard. Proceed to the flashing red light off Fish Island. On this leg you will pass Pork Ledge, which is steep-to on the channel side and should show if you get too close. Having passed Pork Ledge, stay a little offshore until Little Green Island bears east, then pass between it and the red nun south of it. Thereafter follow the channel buoys in.

ANCHORAGE AND BERTHS: Anchor where you can find the room out of the channel. As this is a well-used harbor, you may wish to set a trip line in case you snag something with the hook. The wharf in Clark's Harbour has a reported depth of 5' at low water. If you draw more and wish to be tied up at low water, use the (comparatively) new wharf at West Head where there is reported to be 10' at low water.

REMARKS: This is a busy harbor with a coast guard station.

FACILITIES: Basic supplies are available in the town.

*Caution should be used entering this harbor as it has not been reported on in the last ten years.

CAPE SABLE

Chart #4242

Rewritten, digested and condensed from earlier material by I. Starr, B. Aldrich, C. Bartlett, and J.B. McLean with additional insights by J. McKelvy.   1998

To date, this editor has rounded Cape Sable some twenty times and none of them have been relaxed. Because of the frigid water, in clear weather he has seen images of ships steaming upside down on the horizon and buildings popping up on land ten miles distant. In addition, fog can develop here instantaneously, the land is flat and presents a poor radar target (the racon on Cape Sable light notwithstanding*), and there is no good right-angle cross bearing for the R.D.F.

Chart #4242 has loran lines laid in, all well and good when your loran is working. Nonetheless, this is "an hairy place."

Two schools of thought exist about rounding Cape Sable: Either go well inshore or stay well offshore.

The inshore school, championed by Dr. Starr and Judge Aldrich, greatly depends on the state of the tide. A glance at the tidal streams information on chart #4242, or the ***Atlas of Tidal Currents in the Bay of Fundy and Gulf of Maine,*** will show that it is best to be at Cape Sable on the very last of the ebb, if eastbound, or the first of the flood, if westbound.

Bound east, the recommended inshore course is: From west of Green Island, run an easterly course for Black Point, leaving Green Island to port and Green Island Ledge and Hungarian Rock (both unmarked) to starboard. Having cleared Green Island Ledge and Hungarian Rock to starboard, bear down to a southeasterly course and leave the nun (NA2) marking Forfeit Rocks to port, thence to the red and white Mo A bell (NA), leaving it to port, and go from there to a point 1/4 mile south of Cape Sable lighthouse. By staying only 1/4 mile off the lighthouse you avoid the terrible tide rips at Horse Race. Continuing east, you leave Black Rock (which always shows) and the green bell (JS53) to port.

If bound to or from Maine east of Mt. Desert Island, some correspondents recommend going between Seal and Mud Islands, a course that should only be taken in good visibility as there are no navigational aids in this area.

Of this inshore route Charlie Bartlett said: "I just plain don't like this place. Given a good strong breeze the tide rips are something to behold. One minute your bow is scooping up green, the next your stern is trying to pour it down your back. Where the chart says 'Tide Rip', it means it."

Numerous Halifax Race navigators have expressed another negative vote for the inshore route. They feel that, although the inside route is appealing if you can time yourself to pick up a favorable tide, there is often a different weather pattern inshore (usually a flat calm) and this would more than offset any tidal advantage.

To be sure, the cruising man can always turn on the iron mainsail and go through the inshore course in reasonable safety.

A good, safe, and reasonably peaceful eastbound route recommended by this editor is to pick up Blonde Rock whistle (N4) 4 1/2 miles south of Seal Island, and proceed on course 105° mag., passing the red whistle 3 miles south of Cape Sable, to Brazil Rock buoy, a distance of 24.5 miles. At Brazil Rock, you enter the southeast coast of Nova Scotia, an area fraught with interesting harbors and without hard currents, rips, and enormous tide ranges.

The Cape Sable lighthouse racon had a range of less than three miles in July, 1987, not the 8 given in **Radio Aids to Navigation**.

PORT LA TOUR

43°30.1'N, 65°28.2'W

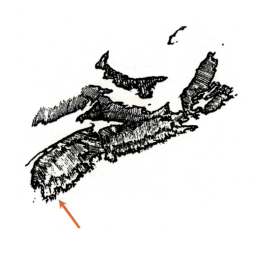

Chart: #4241

Rewritten and condensed from earlier material by W.K. Colby, S. Gerard, P. Richmond, C. Vilas, S. Campbell and L. Gray with additional information by Walter Wales 1997

DIRECTIONS: The buoys in this harbor have been changed in the last two years, so pay attention to your chart and move cautiously. (Beware, you may very well be carrying an obsolete chart.)

For entry either from the east or west, Find the La Tour Fairway buoy (Mo A JA) located 3 miles east southeast of Baccaro Point. In approaching from the east, care must be taken to differentiate between the fixed light with the fog horn on Cape Negro and the flashing light with the diaphone on the Salvages. The latter, about which there has been considerable confusion in the past, consists of a large, square, white house or barn-like structure with a cupola sticking out through the roof which is the lighthouse. This is extremely visible in clear weather and, as all the surrounding landscape is low, it can appear to be sitting on whatever land or rock pile that intervenes. In fact, from the vicinity of Green Point, it appears to be sitting on Blanche Island. Chart #4241 indicates that Blanche Island is 4 meters (13 feet) above high tide, but it gives the impression of a grassy sand bar and it is well to give it comfortable berth. It is probably not high enough to give much of a fog lift, so it would be highly advisable to locate thefairway whistle (Mo A JA) before entering under such conditions.

In approaching from the west, the Bantam Rocks flashing red whistle (JS 56) would be most useful to find in fog, but stay outside of it. If you have to, hunt for the La Tour Fairway buoy in open water. There is a strong rip around Bantam Rocks and between there and Baccaro Point, and the current runs strong through Outer and Inner Rocks. The most conspicuous objects on the flat landscape are a series of radomes and radio masts just north of Baccaro Point lighthouse; their red aircraft warning lights together with the Baccaro Point (3 flashes every 10 sec.) light should identify it. The Baccaro Point fog horn blast every 20 seconds should not be confused with the Salvages diaphone or with the Cape Negro (1 blast every 60 seconds) horn. The approach from Cuckold Rock flashing bell (JJ 51) inside Inner Rock and Taylor Rock is perfectly feasible with good visibility, but the buoys are small and can be less visible than the breakers. Watch out for nets.

The best approach is from La Tour Fairway (Mo A JA) straight through to Page Island flashing bell (Mo A JN). From Page Island flashing bell, proceed a little east of north mag. Leave Hogshead Ledge, Robinsons Ball, Mohawk Ledge and the jumble of buoys in that area to port, then arc back a little to the west to flashing green blinker JN 53 north of Mohawk Ledge. From there go straight into the harbor.

46

ANCHORAGE AND BERTHS: The best anchorage is found between the two wharves on the northern side of the harbor (labeled Upper Port La Tour on the chart), or one can tie up at either of the wharves.

There is also a concrete-walled, artificial basin at Seal Point, just east of the breakwater at Upper Port La Tour where several correspondents reported weathering a hurricane in comfort and safety.

REMARKS: This harbor is named after an early trader who built a fort here (the ruins of which can still be seen). It is popular because of its location as the first port after rounding Cape Sable from the west and the last before rounding Cape Sable bound west across the Bay of Fundy. Many informants have mentioned its convenience and its feasibility in most any kind of weather. It also should be perfectly feasible to enter at night provided you have half a mile or so of visibility to see the lights. Tides and fish nets may be problems.

FACILITIES: There is a small general store on the north (Upper Port La Tour) side of the harbor which can provide basic necessities.

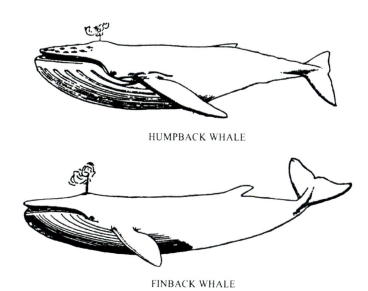

HUMPBACK WHALE

FINBACK WHALE

NEGRO HARBOUR

(with notes on Northeast Harbour and Ingomar)

43°33.6'N, 65°25.3'W

Chart #4241

Rewritten and condensed from earlier material by W. Brewer, Y. Morland, J. Robinson, E. Cabot, C. Bartlett, R. Lemmerman, W. Feldman, and A. Weld . 2001

DIRECTIONS: This is an easy place to enter in thick weather. From the east, enter through the narrow passage between the red buoy off East Point and the green bell off Budget Rock. (Budget Rock bell is hard to hear.) Proceed northwest toward Big Island (located well up the harbor), leaving the navigational marks in their usual order. There is also a less desirable, very narrow channel which passes close to the red buoy southwest of Budget Rock.

From the west, the "West Entrance" shown on the chart is more useful. Care must be taken here to center your course around the ledges north of the Salvages lighthouse and the area of the Triangle Rocks. Most of these hazards are visible.

ANCHORAGE AND BERTHS: There are four anchorages in the area, presented here going from the most to the least protected.

1. Proceed north, passing between Big and Round Islands, to the red buoy 1/2 mile north of Big Island. Turn 90° to the west, rounding the visible reef extending north of Davis Island, then turn south and anchor in 12 feet of water close to the northwest end of Big Island.

2. Anchor about one mile south of Big Island, get in as close to the western shore as possible.

3. Anchor in the north side of the bight formed

at the bar that connects the two ends of Cape Negro Island. However, beware of the electric cable that comes ashore here to supply the power to Cape Negro light. This anchorage is reported to have a surge in an east wind, and in 2001 was breached for about 75 yards.

4. In an easterly, go onto Northeast Harbour and anchor under the beach. One correspondent spent three days here waiting for an easterly to blow itself out and found the holding ground excellent.

There is a channel into the government wharf at Ingomar, marked by spars and tree limbs, with a controlling depth (in 1979) of five feet. It is best to seek local advice here before attempting to go in.

REMARKS: Negro Harbour offers convenient shelter and respite from the prevailing southwester. The anchorage behind Big Island is peaceful and out of the swells.

In 1979 Richard Lemmerman wrote, "Ingomar is primarily a herring fishing village and the sheds on the shore side of the government wharf contain great vats of herring and brine. The local people are most insistent that you sample them. Each vat is marked by the day it was put down and there is always one particular date when the herring is spectacular."

FACILITIES: None other than basic supplies at the general store in Ingomar.

SHELBURNE

43°45.2'N, 65°19.2'W

Charts: #4241, #4209

Rewritten and condensed from earlier material by D. Tunick, Dr. B. Clarkson, S. Campbell, H. McTeague, J. McKelvy, R. Carter, A. Emil, David Young, Brian Pollard, Walter Wales, Dr. Bernard Perry, Wallace; updates by Feldman and R. Michiner.
2002

DIRECTIONS: It is necessary to have Chart #4241 aboard and this chart will see you into Shelburne. Chart #4209 is a large scale harbor chart which refines the harbor details, but it is unnecessary (though comforting) to have aboard.

Shelburne was once the easiest harbor to enter west of Halifax, but no longer so due to the removal of the R.D.F. beacon and fog signal on McNutts Island. In thick weather, McNutts Island should be approached cautiously from a southeasterly direction until the lighthouse or shore is actually in sight, the southeasterly portion of this island being very bold. From this landfall, skirt the southeastern quarter of the island until at the northeast bluff area, from which one would lay off a course for the flashing buoy off Sandy Point (approximately 340° mag.), then run up the harbor for another 4 miles to the town. Very likely the fog will scale up and the visibility improve as you continue inshore.

ANCHORAGE AND BERTHS: There are a number of good anchorages available. The first is located on a line between the north end of McNutts Island and Carleton Village. (This looks open in a strong southerly -ed.) Also in this area, one-third mile north of the underwater cable crossing on the west side of **McNutts Island** is a small government wharf where one may tie up and then walk the three miles south to the lighthouse which has a fine

view. No depths are given next to the wharf on the chart, so use caution. Correspondent

David Young writes, "The south side of the wharf has the best water. There are a few stones off the north side that are not very far down, but can be avoided." Obviously you should tie up here only temporarily in good weather.

There is an anchorage off **Gunning Cove** just northwest of the green buoy. Here is a pleasant, quiet anchorage, off the fish wharves, where you can save yourself the extra four miles going up to the government wharf and town of Shelburne.

The Shelburne Harbour Yacht Club in 2002 built a new marina facility just south of the Town Wharf. Fuel, water and berths are available for visiting yachts. In 2004 there were 10 berths available for visiting yachts at $25 Can. per night.

The **Government Wharf** just south of the town is a massive structure where berths are usually available. Perfect protection from any southerly "fetch" up the harbor can be had on the northern side of the wharf which is not usually crowded. Like all government wharves, the dock is dirty with creosote piles and some fine gravel, so fenders and fenderboards should be used as well as a mat to wipe your feet. The tidal range in Shelburne is 8 feet, so add some scope to your dock lines.

Finally, there is a **town anchorage and dock** just northwest of the government wharf. The town dock is approximately 70 feet long and is just up a buoyed channel on the eastern (town) shore between McGowan's Restaurant (painted conspicuously red) and the Fishermen's Memorial. The dock has 10-14 feet on the south side and 6 feet on the north.

Up the buoyed channel to this dock lies an attractive anchorage where local yachts moor, and if you are lucky a mooring may be available here. (Check with someone who may be on the dock or at the Yacht Club about this.)

REMARKS: Shelburne is named for the Earl of Shelburne who was prime minister of England when the preliminary treaty ending the War for Independence was signed in 1782. His Lordship was accused at the time of "being soft" on the American rebels, but his view from Westminster was that England was locked in a global war with France over the control of the West Indies and India, and the American rebellion was a backwater operation from which he wished to release the army and navy in order to have them elsewhere in more important engagements.

So it was ironic that this town, settled by American Loyalists, was named after a prime minister who some felt betrayed the Loyalist cause. (This irony was pointed out in Kenneth Roberts' novel *Oliver Wiswell*, an excellent yarn about the Loyalist cause and the foundation of the Loyalist colonies in eastern Canada.)

Shelburne (pop. 2,400) enjoyed a reputation for shipbuilding in the nineteenth century and was the birthplace of Donald McKay, the great marine architect and proponent of the clipper ship.

The Canadian Coast Guard normally uses the government wharf as a base for one of its larger sea-going cutters. The officers and men of these vessels are normally very friendly and if you get invited aboard (as some Guide correspondents have been), don't be shy. The electronics on the bridge alone are worth seeing.

In 1983 many of the old colonial buildings were restored for the town's bicentennial. A further influx of old buildings and beautification came in 1993 when the movie *Scarlet Letter* (Hester Prynne and all that) was filmed here.

The result is a really delightful ersatz-colonial town with some nice restaurants, museums (try the Shelburne County Museum, the Dory Museum, or the barrel factory). There are nice craft stores as well with skillfully made items (comforters, carved birds, toy boat models, etc.).

North of the historic district by the waterfront is the modern town with a drugstore gas station, post office, food, liquor, laundromat, etc. This is a typical Nova Scotia town, oriented toward the land and not redolent of the town's seafaring past.

Little is known of Shelburne during the years of World War II when there was a naval base in the harbor, but one of the most dramatic incidents of the era occurred on May 13, 1945, when German submarine U-889 surrendered at the end of the war. Thomas Raddall (the C.S. Forester of Canada), on duty as a reporter at the time, describes the incident:

> "We ran outside and lay rolling twelve miles off McNutts Island, until the submarine was sighted coming slowlywith the shadowy forms of *H.M.C.S. Buckingham* and *Inch Arran* [frigates] in the mist astern. She was U-889, 750 tons, with twin anti-aircraft guns on a platform abaft the conning tower, and two more on the tower itself."

Questioned by newsmen through an interpreter, the young German captain now relaxed and talked freely, laughing at some of the questions. After trials in the Baltic, U-889 had departed Norway on April 4, making her way towards the North American Coast. She did not surface until May 8, having been more than four weeks underwater using the schnorkel.

"Asked what he intended to do after the war, the captain said his home city of Hamburg was in ruins and he would like to live in Canada --- 'After all, your government is very much like ours.' (A newsman chortled, 'Another vote for MacKenzie King.')"

From *In My Time*
by Thomas H. Raddall.

FACILITIES: Shelburne Marine is a well-equipped shipyard. They are capable of doing most of your repairs if their schedule permits.

If you have a special problem pertaining to your vessel, start your inquiries at the Shelburne Harbour Yacht Club.
www.shelburneharbouryachtclub.com
The members know everything and everybody in town and are very helpful. While not the policy of this guide to mention "meeters and greeters" Harry O'Connor is somewhat of an institution as the "Yacht Ambassador" of the Club. He is knowledgeable and very helpful. (I give him a heads up when I know a yacht is heading for Shelburne. – ed)

No facilities are available in Gunning Cove.

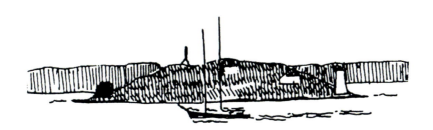

LOCKEPORT

43°42.1'N, 65°06.5'W

Charts: #4240, #4209

Rewritten and condensed from material by C. Bok, C. Bartlett, A. Weld, J. McKelvy, R. Carter; update by R. Michiner. 2002

DIRECTIONS: The charts for this area show strings of rocks, ledges and sunkers running north-south several miles offshore from Lockeport, and on a clear day some of these give a "smothered-in-foam" appearance. Coming from the east it is tempting to use Ram Island Passage (between Ram Island and Hemeon's Head), but this is an undesirable route in anything but the clearest weather. Much of the shoreline is low and presents a poor image for getting a proper position on a radar set in bad visibility.

Coming from seaward, Gull Rock is a good place to start from as it is conspicuous, rather resembling a castle with a lighthouse perched on an island. It has a strong horn pointing 130° (true), blasting every 30 seconds for three seconds. From Gull Rock north to the green bell (KK61), the buoyage is conventional, but beware of tidal currents up to 1/2 knot crossing your course. From green bell KK61, head north to the green bell (KK69) south of the flashing light on Carter Island.

Then head west into Lockeport Harbour between the breakwaters. These have red and green lights at their ends marking the entrance.

ANCHORAGE AND BERTHS: The White Gull Marina and Restaurant (902-656-2822) has two 180-foot floating docks on the SW side of the inner harbor.

There are two public wharves in the inner harbor to which one can tie up. The long wharf to the southeast has 12 feet of water at its end and nearly as much on each side.

There is no anchoring in the harbor.

REMARKS: Lockeport (pop. 1,000) was named after Jonathan Locke, a member of loyalist settlers who fled Plymouth, Massachusetts, during the American Revolution. To add insult to injury, Yankee privateers raided the town, causing hardship.

Today, Lockeport is a no nonsense, no frills, Nova Scotian fishing port somewhat down on its luck due to the closing of the offshore fisheries. Though lacking in beauty, it is nonetheless very snug, providing shelter from behind its breakwaters for any kind of blow. It looks very good indeed when you have beaten the fog in and a spell of weather is on its way.

FACILITIES: Fuel and water are available at the Marina. A grocery store is one road up from the fuel dock. A liquor store is across from the White Gull Restaurant at the head of the dock. Propane is available at Home Hardware just left of the restaurant.

LITTLE HARBOUR

43°42.9'N, 65°01.8'W

Charts: #4240, #4209

Rewritten and condensed from earlier material by D. Drinkwater and C. Bartlett with new material by David Young.   1993

DIRECTIONS: Boats <u>drawing</u> <u>six</u> <u>feet</u> <u>or</u> <u>more</u> <u>should</u> <u>only</u> <u>enter</u> <u>or</u> <u>leave</u> <u>at</u> <u>half tide or higher</u>, as there is a shoal spot south of the outer wharf. Also, <u>do</u> <u>not</u> <u>cross</u> <u>Middle Ground</u> <u>Shoal</u> <u>in</u> <u>a</u> <u>strong</u> <u>southeasterly</u>, as the sea breaks.

Leaving green quick flasher KC53 to port, head for a spot 150 feet south of the wharf which has a fixed white light on the end (approximate course 292° mag.). This course will cross a shoal known as "Middle Ground Shoal" which has 9 feet on it at low water.

ANCHORAGE AND BERTHS: From the spot 150' south of the wharf mentioned above, turn southwest and anchor slightly less than 1/4 mile away in the deeper part of the harbor with the fishing boats. Only three feet of water is reported next to the wharves at low water.

REMARKS: This harbor had extensive dredging in the fall of 1992, but a shoal spot remains just south of the outer end of the wharf. There is a small surge in here in all weather and a bad surge in a southeasterly. This harbor is untenable in an easterly.

FACILITIES: There is a small store about 1/4 mile up the road from the wharf. There is also a trash container and oil receptacle on the wharf.

PORT L'HEBERT

43°49.4'N, 64°55.3'W

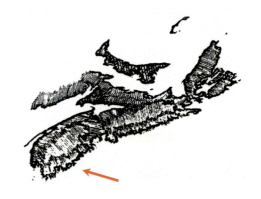

Chart #4240

John Cooley and John McKelvy   1993

DIRECTIONS: From the Port Hebert Mo A buoy (UX), you can approach the lighthouse on the tip of Shingle Point (Lighthouse Beach) on a course of 09° (mag.). Tillys Head, high and thickly-wooded, will be on the port bow making the west side of the harbor stand out against an otherwise undistinguished coastline. Thrumb Point, projecting seaward on the east side of the entrance, will be on the starboard bow and not easy to pick up in thick weather. Just beyond Tillys Head, the water shoals to 12 feet, and it is reported that the sea breaks in heavy weather. Continue on course 09° (mag.) to within a half mile of the light, then shift to the right to keep on the east side of the two green buoys (UX53 and UX55) below Shingle Point (Lighthouse Beach on the chart), the more northerly of these being within 200 yards of the lighthouse itself. These buoys are close alongside sunken ledges which narrow the entrance and form the one serious hazard in working into this harbor.

The maximum velocity of current at springs is reported to be 1 3/4 knots from Shingle Point to the government wharf, the time of slack corresponding quite closely to high and low water on shore. After passing the second green buoy, the channel widens and with a head wind it is possible to run past on the starboard tack, heading about NW into good water. Close above this point there is a small sand bar to the west and a government wharf to the east.

ANCHORAGE AND BERTHS: John Cooley indicates that the anchorage should be in the area to the NW of Shingle Point. It is the editor's experience that the tidal current "veritably whistles" through the harbor and any attempt to anchor should be made with a "Bahamian mooring" (i.e. with two anchors --- one set downstream to deal with the ebb tide and one set upstream to deal with the flood).

There is only one working government wharf here, at the site of the abandoned packing plant. It is used by a dozen fishermen and there is reported to be 10 feet off it. Many mariners prefer tying to this wharf rather than running the risk of dragging in the anchorage because of the velocity and change of the tidal stream.

REMARKS: Port Hebert (pop. very few) is (according to John Cooley's research in 1953) named after a certain Hebert who was Samuel de Champlain's apothecary. "Why was an apothecary such an important person? ...because he had charge of the liquor."

Cooley goes on to say, "Above the government wharf the channel is narrowed by an extensive sand flat on the west side which dries at low water. This flat, as well as the sandy beach on the east, provides clams of excellent quality, although the inroads of commercial diggers has reduced the supply sharply." [Could there be any left? -ed.]

FACILITIES: There is no fuel or water available, nor are there any stores or supplies.

LITTLE PORT L'HEBERT

43°45.4'N, 65°02.6W

(.5' SSW of Port Hebert)

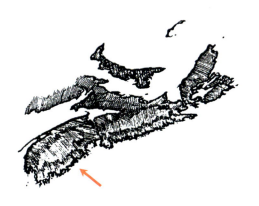

Dick and Ginny Walters   *1993*

"Heading northeast in a 15-20 knot southwest wind, we turned to port one mile short of the Port Hebert whistle. The fog scaled up on the lee side and we found our way between the reefs into a lovely, completely protected cove

inhabited by sheep and seals. There are berries and wildflowers as well."

Avoid either end of Green Rock by a considerable margin as well as the rock shown on the chart 1/4 mile southwest of Green Rock. (This usually breaks.)

PORT JOLI

43°51'N, 64°52'W

Chart: #4240

Shellman Brown   *1996*

DIRECTIONS: Enter from the south on a course roughly N by E. This inlet shoals gradually. When the government wharf and private marine railway (both no longer in use) are abeam, cross over to the west shore and anchor off the MacDonald fish house in 15 feet of water.

REMARKS: This is a quiet anchorage of relatively easy access. [It appears to be open to the south -ed.]

FACILITIES: None.

PORT MOUTON

43°55.3'N, 64°50.6'W

Chart: #4240

Rewritten and condensed from material by Curtis Bok, Dr. Bruce Tremblay, Alexander Weld, Wm. Brewer, J. McKelvy, Alvin Zink; update by L & M Bailey and W. Tobin. 2001

DIRECTIONS: From the east, a straight course can be held from the Liverpool whistler to the Spectacle Island lighthouse. From the south and west, pass through the Western Channel, leaving close to port the Cardinal buoy (BYB) marking Middle Rock between Bull Pt. and Port Mouton Island. This entrance could be dangerous in heavy weather, and in such should be passed up for Eastern Channel, avoiding Devastation Shoal and passing between Mouton Island and Brazil Rocks.

In spite of what is on chart #4240, coming from the south it is possible to pass west of Spectacle Island and through the narrow channel by the red flasher marking the half tide rock to Carters Beach. The course in leaves the green flashing buoy (US57) to port and the red flasher 50 feet to starboard on the way in from the south. This editor has noticed countless fishermen going through here hell bent for election. Nevertheless, the safer course would appear to be to round Spectacle Island and approach the beach from the north.

REMARKS: Port Mouton (pop. 250, and pronounced locally as Muh-tune) is so named because a sheep was lost overboard here from Champlain's ship in 1604.

ANCHORAGES AND BERTHS: The anchorage behind Spectacle Island in hard sand is surrounded by sugary soft beach sand and beach grass and reminds one of the great beaches that stretches from Sandwich to Provincetown on Cape Cod. It is worth a walk or picnic ashore.

In winds from NE-SW, the cove on the west side of Mouton Island provides good protection and good holding. It might be rolly.

FACILITIES: One-half mile from the government wharf is a small store where basic necessities may be purchased.

One could once purchase ice, water, and occasionally fuel in Willow Cove. This was before the fisheries collapsed. Perhaps someday there will be a revival in the fisheries, but for now the only supplies available nearby are at the store previously mentioned.

LIVERPOOL*

44°02.5'N, 64°42.9'W

Charts: #4240, #4379

Rewritten and condensed from material by C. Copelin, F. & M. Calderone, G Bryant, P. Richmond, R. Black, F. Slavic, G. Kirstein and A. Zink with new material by Walter Wales.

DIRECTIONS: Chart #4379 is best because of its large scale, but chart #4240 is adequate in reasonable visibility if you apply common sense to the channel marks in the inner harbor.

ANCHORAGE AND BERTHS: It is unadvisable to anchor off the town because the current in the Mersey River is swift and there can be much commercial traffic in the channel. Anchoring in the northwest part of the bay is chancy as well. The bottom is rocky with poor holding ground. It is best to tie up.

The government wharf on the north side of the harbor is reported to have fourteen feet of water on its end and little space to tie up. Various private wharves are located on the south side of the harbor.

REMARKS: In 1972 George Kirstein remarked, "Liverpool is a somewhat colorless town which there is little point in visiting unless it is necessary to take advantage of its excellent supply stores."

FACILITIES: Basic food and supplies are here. Water is available on some docks, but in spite of an obvious Irving fuel depot being here, fuel is not available.

*Caution should be used entering this harbor as it hasn't been reported on in the last ten years.

BROOKLYN (HERRING COVE)

44°03'N, 64°41.5'W

Walter Wales and C. Westropp   2004

DIRECTIONS: Brooklyn (across the Mersey from Liverpool) is easy to enter.

ANCHORAGE AND BERTHS: Anchoring in this harbor is not recommended because for many years this harbor was a holding place for log booms and an anchor could easily become stuck on the bottom.

There is a new marina here and a yacht club (founded in 1995). Minimum depth at the slips is 7.5 feet and 10ft at the moorings at low water.

REMARKS: This isn't a scenic place, but it has perfect protection and all the folks here "are the best."

FACILITIES: The marina has power and fresh water at the 10-15 slips available for guests. There are no fees for visitors using slips and moorings but a donation to help with upkeep is appreciated.. A public telephone and a small store (with ice) are within a half-mile walk.

For engine repairs, try Jason Bennett, 132 Shore Road. Telephone: 354-3607.

PORT MEDWAY

44°07.9'N, 64°34.7'W

Chart: #4211

R. Michiner   *1993*

DIRECTIONS: From the green Medway Bell (UA51), come to course 10° (mag.) leaving Medway Head to port and Frying Pan, Toby, Middle and Great Islands to starboard. Three miles in you should come to a red-green-red flasher (UAA) to starboard and a green spar to port. By the green spar, alter course to 325° (mag.) for the next green spar at Nautilus Rock. From the Nautilus Rock spar the channel in is obvious.

ANCHORAGES AND BERTHS: Anchor in close to the village. The holding ground is good. The government wharf has twenty feet of water on it at the outer end.

REMARKS: This is a typical harbor on the southwest coast. Once in by the town the anchorage is snug. The town itself is not very interesting.

FACILITIES: Limited supplies are available in the town's general store and water is available at the fish factory (when in operation). No fuel is available.

VOGLERS COVE

44°09.4'N, 64°32.1'W

Chart: #4211

David Buckman   *1991*

DIRECTIONS: This harbor is part of Medway Harbour as is Port Medway. Enter Medway Harbour as you would Port Medway from green Medway Bell (UA51) to the red-green-red flasher (UAA). Then swing north to UD53 and UD54. This channel is wide enough to tack a small boat in. There is 10 feet of water up to the government wharf just east of Calf Point.

ANCHORAGES AND BERTHS: Anchor off the government wharf. Sometimes there is a mooring available in Conrad Cove. [Depths unknown here --- ask for local guidance -ed.] There is eight feet at low water on the east side of the government wharf.

REMARKS: The small village is very attractive, but the harbor could get lumpy with a hard southerly or southwesterly blow. It is good in any wind from the north.

FACILITIES: There is a well-stocked Quik Mart in town. A pay phone is at Voglers Cove West, about 1/4 mile west on the road. There is no water or fuel.

LAHAVE RIVER

44°17.6'N, 64°21.4'W

Charts: #4384, #4394, #4395

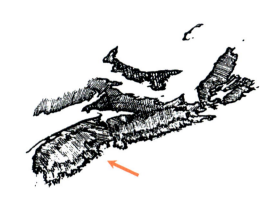

Rewritten and condensed from earlier material by W. Britton, G. Kirstein, H.B. French, H. Forrest, V.C. Gray with later material by S. Dumaresq.   *1997*

DIRECTIONS: "LaHave" refers to the geographic area composing the mouth of the LaHave River including the bays and anchorages located between Cape LaHave Island, West Ironbound Island and the upper reaches of the river as far as Bridgewater (a town which is navigable to medium-draft, ocean-going vessels).

Bound from the west, one must steer in a generally northeasterly direction from Indian Island whistle buoy. Keep Cape LaHave Island to port and slowly alter course to the north in order to enter the anchorage at False La Have, Mosher Island or Spectacle Island or points on the mainland or up the river.

Bound from the east, one may depart Pollock Shoal bell (TC52) on a course of 284° (mag.) for the Mosher Island lighthouse, passing between West Ironbound Island and Gaff Point. Once past this danger, one may set a course for the anchorages previously mentioned or turn to a more northerly course and locate the La Have fairway buoy (Mo A) from which one can run up the river. As with most areas on this coast in the lee of the prevailing west wind, visibility should improve further inshore.

ANCHORAGES AND BERTHS:

1. Mosher Harbour behind Mosher Island gives good protection from a southwest wind and swell, but in a southerly, move close in to the west end of Spectacle Island. Here the holding ground is good (solid mud) and this

area gives some protection from the northeast as well.

2. Snug Harbour (to the south of Dublin Shore, west of Bushen Island) is a well-protected spot and though the chart indicates a rocky bottom, good holding ground in mud has been reported. Soundings at low water (1979) suggest depths of 5-8 feet on the northeast side on entering and shoaler conditions on the southwest side and past the mid-point into the cove. Some difference of opinion exists as to how snug Snug Harbour can be, but one correspondent reports lying in this anchorage with a 29' Columbia, a 29' Northwind, a 32' North Sea Yacht and a 42' C&C all at the same time.

3. False LaHave offers a good anchorage just west of the two rocks off Bell Island in normal southerly wind conditions with no sea swell.

Halibut Bay on Cape La Have Island is <u>not</u> <u>recommended</u> as the bottom is reported to be "solid rock" and some rolls come in.

4. Bantam Bay (south side of Cape LaHave Island), while not suitable as an overnight anchorage, has one of the most impressive beaches in Nova Scotia. This is well worth a luncheon or afternoon stop before proceeding to a secure anchorage in the La Have Islands.

5. At **Crooked Channel*** (Between Turner Point on Cape La Have Island and George Island) it is possible to work your way up the buoyed channel past Turner Point and head for Cape Bay. Do not go past the shallow channel which runs to the west across the northernmost end of Cape LaHave Island, and

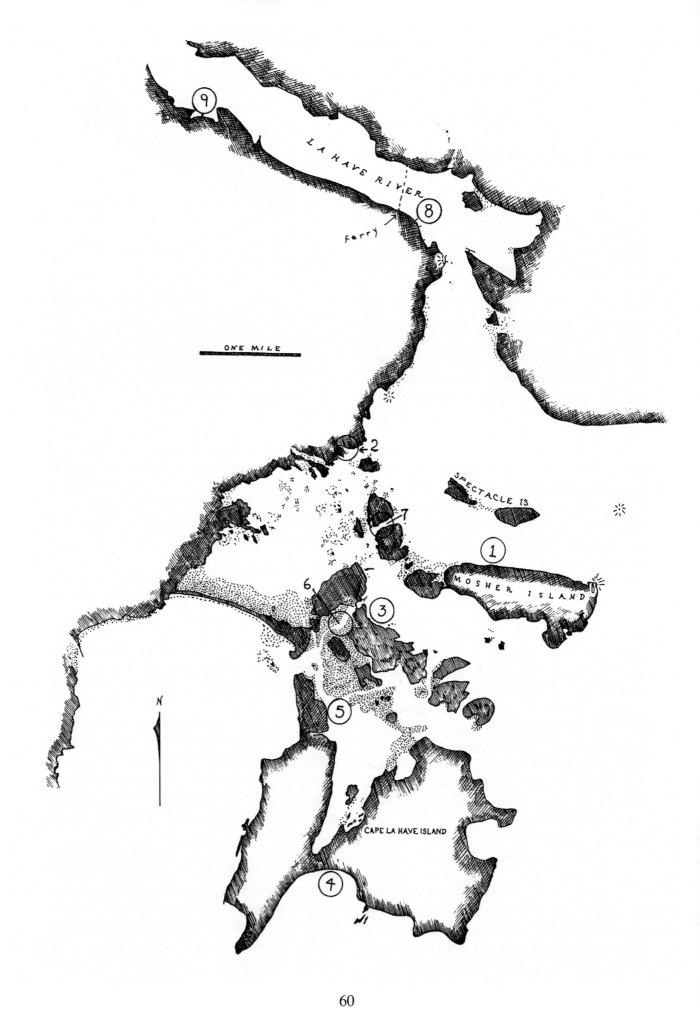

ONE MILE

LA HAVE RIVER

ferry

SPECTACLE IS

MOSHER ISLAND

CAPE LA HAVE ISLAND

N

60

don't attempt to go through here, as a bridge with 13' of clearance was built between Bush and Bell Islands in 1980.

6. It is possible to anchor off the northern end of Tumblin Island just inside **Wolfe Gut***. Wolfe Gut is really worth exploring, even if only by dinghy. Wharves line both sides of the narrow gut and it is really pretty. [Getting out of the main channel and the use of a riding light is highly recommended here -ed.]

7. In **Folly Island Channel*** there is an anchorage between Folly and Outer Hirtle Islands. Although there is little traffic, one must insure that the channel is not blocked. The architecture of the buildings that were part of the Covey Island Boatworks (now moved to the mainland) is very interesting and provides quite a contrast to the neighboring old fishermen's houses.

*Use Chart #4394 for these anchorages.

8. In the **La Have River** there are two anchorages of special interest. Proceeding up the river three-quarters of a mile after the narrows between Fort Point and Krout Point, one comes to two wharves at Lee Point in La Have. The second wharf has a float and is the home of the *LaHave Bakery* which is famous for its fresh-baked products. This bakery has some moorings as well as limited dock space.

9. Three miles up the river from the LaHave Bakery lies **Pernette Cove** where the very friendly **LaHave River Yacht Club** resides. www.lryc.ca

Here are guest moorings for $10.00 (Canadian) and dockside space is usually available for $5.00 (Canadian). One caveat --- the water in Pernette Cove is shallow. One correspondent spent two nights on the end of the dock here drawing 6 feet, without touching, but any more draft would be dicey. (The tide range here is 7 feet.) The Club monitors channels #16 and #68 during regular business hours and is helpful about accommodations.

REMARKS: The Nova Scotia Travel Bureau refers to the LaHave River as "The Rhine of Nova Scotia," a sobriquet it does not deserve. The anchorages here are very pretty, however, and the area provides convenient overnight refuge for those traveling up or down the coast. If a spell of weather is coming through, the river ports provide adequate protection, but if given enough time to get there, nearby Lunenburg would be the more interesting place to get holed in.

FACILITIES: With the possible exception of Bridgewater, there are no repair facilities here. Fuel (at half tide or better), water, a dining room and a bar are all available at the LaHave Yacht Club.

Otherwise, basic supplies are available in South Dublin and at Krout Point.

LUNENBURG

44°22.0'N, 64°18.5'W

Charts: #4384, #4328

Rewritten and condensed from earlier material by J. McKelvy, J.C. Kiley, A. Weld, F.B.M. Jones. Update by R. Michiner.   2002

DIRECTIONS: From the west, steer 36° (mag.) from Pollock Shoal buoy (TC52) located one mile ENE of West Ironbound Island. Leave Point Enrage and Kings Bay to port until Rose Point is abeam. Shift to course 356° (mag.) for Sculpin Shoal bell (E52), leaving Rose Bay and Ovens Point to port. From Sculpin Shoal bell steer 330° (mag.) for the lighthouse on Battery Point.

From the northeast and Mahone Bay, depart East Shoal Light buoy (one mile east of Big Tancook Island) on a course of 183° (mag.) until Little Duck Island is abeam. Shift course to 222° (mag.) for Lunenburg bell buoy (EDA); from Lunenburg bell steer 286° (mag.) for Sculpin Shoal bell* and from Sculpin Shoal bell come to 330° (mag.) for Battery Point lighthouse.

From east and offshore, a direct course from Pearl Island whistle to Lunenburg bell leads directly across Big Duck Island, so the course to Lunenburg must be plotted with a dog leg in it. Once Lunenburg bell is located, the same courses apply as from Mahone Bay.

*Note that there is a wreck marked on your chart just south of the course between Lunenburg bell and Sculpin Shoal buoys. This marks the remains of H.M.C.S. Saguenay, deliberately scuttled here to serve as an underwater park. Vessels drawing 15 feet or less should be able to pass safely over this hulk.

ANCHORAGES AND BERTHS: Berths are available at the Nova Scotia Trawler Equipment Company located at the east end of the harbor and easily identified by their sign. Deep drafted vessels (9 feet and over) should beware of a ledge reported to the west and south of Scotia Trawlers fuel dock. One caveat: This is not a good place to berth in a south to southeast wind, as there is plenty of fetch up Lunenburg Bay.

The best place to anchor is in the west side of the harbor, out of the way of traffic to and from the docks. The bottom is soft mud, however, so anchor with a Danforth or plow, and in any kind of a blow it is advisable to set two anchors.

The Yacht Shop and Marina (902-634-4331) manages the rental moorings off the Town Dock, marked by numbered red floats. It also has some berths just below the shop for rent for visiting yachts. A dinghy float lies between the Adams and Knickle and Fisheries Museum wharves, along the northern perimeter of the harbor. This is a strategic location within easy walking distance of the amenities of the town.

Berths are sometimes available at the Fisheries Museum at the west end of the harbor. A berth here is most desirable because of the privacy it offers when the museum isn't open. However, this museum has so many floating exhibits tied to its docks that there is little space for visiting yachtsman. The public wharf (next to the museum) has berths available as well, but many of these are taken permanently by tour boats, and there is less privacy here.

REMARKS: In June 1749, shortly after the founding of Halifax, Governor Cornwallis visited Lunenburg Bay and found French settlers and considerable land under cultivation. In 1753 the Governor decided to settle there a number of German, Swiss and French persons who had arrived a few years before. The name of Lunenburg was given to this new settlement as a compliment to George II of England, who as Elector of Hanover held the Duchy of Lunenburg in Germany. A town site was laid out and on June first 453 people (about two-thirds Germans, one-third French and Swiss) were transported to Lunenburg.

During early days the settlers suffered from Indian attacks and many were killed and scalped or carried away. During the Revolutionary War and War of 1812, the town had many brushes with privateers. In 1782 when most of the militia were on duty in Halifax, the town was seized and sacked by American privateers, and some prominent private citizens were carried away but later released by command of General Washington.

For many years, schooners and vessels for the Grand Banks fisheries had their principal depot at Lunenburg. Contestants for the International Fishermen's Race came here when those races were at the height of their popularity some 60 years ago. The famous *Bluenose* was built and manned here. Unfortunately the fisheries have gone into steep decline, but Lunenburg has done well to hold on to what inshore fishing there is and has made the town attractive to many tourists.

Over the past decade, Lunenburg (pop. 3000) has made a commendable effort in refurbishing itself to attract tourists. There are many good restaurants and the very interesting Fisheries Museum of the Atlantic with exhibits and several trawlers to inspect. (Alas, the old *Reo*, a rumrunner which operated between Canada and the U.S. in the days of Prohibition, is no longer an exhibit. She died of natural old age.)

There are some local culinary specialties here that one should be aware of. The first is Lunenburg sausage, made from a recipe brought over by the early German settlers. If you like sausage, this with some local sauerkraut makes an excellent meal and is served in most of the local restaurants. Also, salamagundi, a Nova Scotia specialty, is a delicious species of potted herring served throughout the province and available at most restaurants and grocery stores.

While the policy of the Guide is not to mention specific private shops due to their ephemeral qualities, we make an exception here because this one is more of a museum.

The Houston North Gallery, 110 Montague Street, is an exceptional art gallery whether in Lunenburg or New York City, specializing in Inuit and Canadian Folk Art. If you are unfamiliar with these genres, this is a good place to start learning. High prices, but some of the art is very moving and beautiful.

Lunenburg is truly one of the most interesting ports of call on a Nova Scotian cruise.

FACILITIES: Repairs, fuel and water may be obtained at the Nova Scotia Trawler Equipment Company, previously mentioned. Scotia Trawlers always had a good reputation until some years ago when they went through a period of eschewing business with yachts. Most recently they have sent letters to yachting interests encouraging the yachting trade, so all is well for now (1998). They also have a store called the "Yacht Shop" which carries charts, books, wet weather gear, and other items of nautical interest. Food and supplies of practically every nature can be found in town as well.

EAST POINT GUT

44°21.1'N, 64°12.4'W

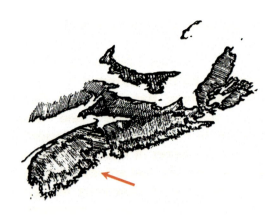

Charts: #4384, #4328

Rewritten and condensed from earlier material by Lt. Cdr. Julian Benoit, Robert J.Cram, Jr., Dr. Edmund B. Cabot, Capt. T.F.T. Morland and Sydney P. Dumaresq. 1995

DIRECTIONS: Proceed along the line between Lunenburg bell (EDA) and Tanner Pass whistle (EA51) until the Gut opens up on a bearing of 290° (mag.). The Gut does not open completely to the water line, but there is a very clear 'V' from the skyline to within a few feet of the water. Alter course to 280° (mag.) which should place the fixed green light at the entrance dead ahead. This course keeps you well clear of the ledges to the north (Green Island Ledges). These ledges extend much further south than the chart indicates. Following this line (280° mag.) will take you to the green can (EC51) off the entrance. Stay at least 50' away from this can and alter course to head a little north of the red cone (EC52). If you proceed on a direct line from the green can to the red cone, you will strike the ledge which makes out from the point on which the green light is located. This ledge also extends out further than the chart indicates. It is safe to alter course towards the red cone when the point with the fixed green light is abeam. Both these buoys are moored in shallow water and have been known to relocate themselves in southeast gales.

Having left the red cone well to starboard, start closing the south shore for about 200 yards. Then proceed to the north shore to avoid a mud bank which comes out from the south shore. Keep a sharp lookout for another mud bank on your starboard which comes out from the north shore. You can now hold the north shore through the remainder of the Gut. Expect to carry 8'-10' through the Gut.

The key navigational buoys at the west end of the Gut have been removed and it is not recommended that you use this entry/exit without local knowledge.

ANCHORAGE AND BERTHS: There is a good anchorage at the west end of the cove, just before the cove closes and the Gut narrows to form the western passage. Be sure not to put mooring lines across the channel as the Gut is often used as a short cut for fishermen heading to or from Lunenburg. There are no wharves available to tie to.

REMARKS: The community at the anchorage is pretty well deserted although some of the houses and fish stages are used seasonally. One local fishermen spoke of up to 30 schooners being moored here in days gone by. On the whole, the Gut is quite tricky, requires a sharp lookout, and is definitely not for the faint of heart.

FACILITIES: None.

TANNER PASS (STONEHURST)

44°22.4'N, 64°13.2'W

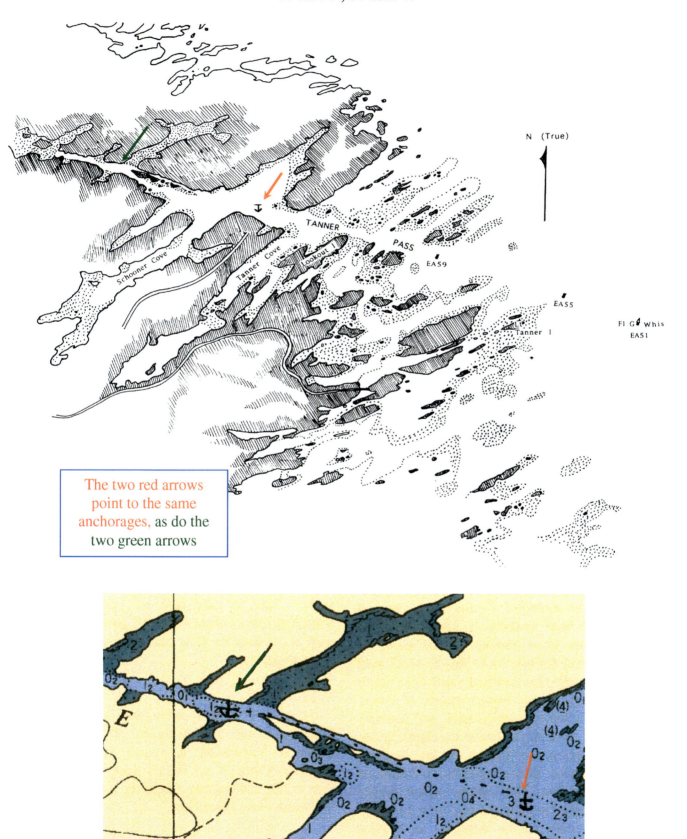

The two red arrows
point to the same
anchorages, as do the
two green arrows

TANNER PASS (STONEHURST)

44°22.4'N, 64°13.2'W

Charts: #4328, #4381, #4384

Rewritten from material by H. Rhude and R. Cram .Update by K. McCurdy 2004

DIRECTIONS: Chart #4328 is preferable for entering this harbor, although it can be done using #4381 or #4384 and with caution.

From the green Tanner Pass whistle (EA51), keep a sharp lookout and steer 313° (mag) toward the mouth of Tanner Pass and green spar EA55, located 0.2 miles distant. (Don't turn toward Tanner Pass coming from the east much north of the whistle because there are ledges not clearly indicated on the charts.) While ledges press in on either bow, the channel itself is deep and unobstructed. Watch for shoals making out from Tanner Island (Gunning Point) where the unmanned light is, and also further in off the next little rocky island. Pass a second green spar (EA59) to port and sail closer to Lookout Island because there are sunken ledges to starboard.

ANCHORAGE AND BERTHS: There is good holding ground in bold water off the point of land between Tanner and Schooner Coves with enough room for four to five medium-sized vessels to swing. Upon reaching the mouth of Tanner Cove, proceed toward the bluff marking the eastern entrance to Schooner Cove making a wide swing to port to avoid the two rocks on the south side of the passage. One hundred yards or so south of the bluff, on the eastern shore, is a lone fisherman's house, outbuildings and a wharf (1969). In front of the house the depth varies from six feet at low tide for the first hundred feet from shore, increasing to 2-2 1/2 fathoms beyond this line. The bottom is soft grassy mud with good holding qualities in a moderate breeze. It may not be adequate in heavier winds.

For the brave there is an alternative anchorage further up the Pass. (See lower chartlet) There is small boat passage from the mouth of Schooner Cove between Heckman's Island and the mainland that is navigable with 6' draft (at low tide) for some distance. The passage is to the north of the small islands (Heckman's Island side) that seem to block the entrance to the cut. Do not try the south side, which looks the easiest, as there is no water. The bottom is shallow (6' and muddy at low tide) as you enter, but deepens out to 10 to 12 feet when you get into the cut. A good lookout at the bow is necessary as there is an underwater ledge half way along the islands, which is easily avoided. Once past the islands the channel opens up into a lovely little bay. Anchor in the center as room is tight. Keep in mind you are in a small boat channel and expect a few small motorboats to pass by. An anchor light is advisable as occasionally fishermen leave before dawn. A lovely spot with no houses in view and well worth the effort to get there.

REMARKS: There are a few houses in Schooner Cove and a dozen or more in Tanner's. Vegetation is sparse and rocks abound. Although no beauty spot, Tanner's Pass is not unattractive. Certainly a visit here is a worthwhile experience.

FACILITIES: None.

MAHONE BAY AND HARBOURS

(Including Heckman Anchorage, Prince Inlet, Island Anchorages, Chester, Deep Cove, New Harbour, and Bandford)

Chart #4381

Rewritten and condensed from earlier material by Frederick H.M. Jones, Walter T. Flower, Jr., Freeric T Rhinelander, Murray Brown, Arthur B. Homer, and Sydney P. Dumaresq. 1998

This fine body of water is approximately thirty miles west of Halifax and is regarded as a superior area of protected water, delightful for cruising, sailing, racing and all yachting activities. Attractive and lively towns dot its shores, and supplies of all kinds are obtainable.

Mahone Bay stretches for some ten miles in a southwest-northeasterly direction, and has a distance between the entrance headlands of Heckman Island (at the southwest) and Aspotogan Peninsula (at the northeast) of about six miles, part of which, however, is filled by islands. Of the islands, Big Tancook is the largest and supports a population of several hundred people. There, local boat-building shops used to exist, and the term "Tancooker" generally applies to a special design of a small schooner. At Northwest Cove on Big Tancook, there is a small basin with sufficient water to tie up inside, and it is a rewarding experience to walk to the top of the island and see the wonderful view. Mahone Bay itself is deep, with few obstructions or dangers --- those that need to be noted are clearly shown on the chart.

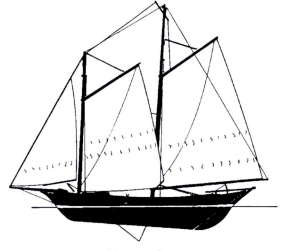

Tancooker

DIRECTIONS: From the southwest, the landfall will normally be Cross Island, which is also the outpost and guide for Lunenburg Bay, harbour and town. A major light and navigational station is shown at the eastern end of this island. Passing on either side of Cross Island, the course leads to the eastward of Little Duck Island, or the skipper as an alternative may choose the passage via the Tanner Pass bell, with general water depths there of two or three fathoms. From that bell or from Little Duck Island lay the course to clear the rocky shoreline to the west and head for Big Tancook and fetch the Mahone Bay (Mo A M) fairway buoy 1 1/4 miles southwest of that island. From here you enter the Bay proper.

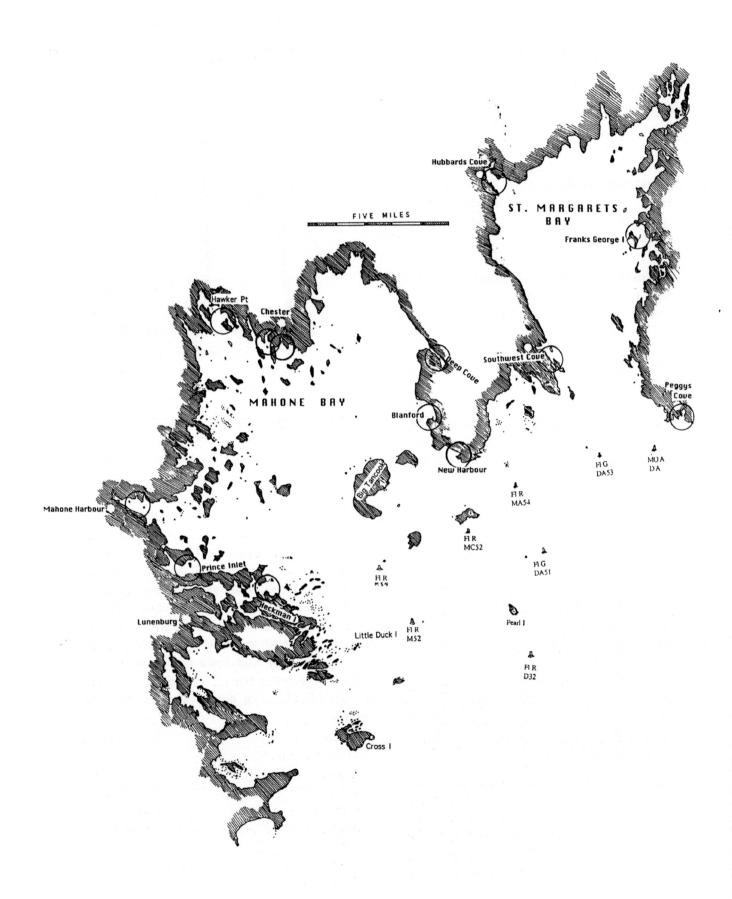

FIVE MILES

St. Margarets Bay

Hubbards Cove

Franks George I

Hawker Pt

Chester

Deep Cove

Southwest Cove

Peggys Cove

MAHONE BAY

Blanford

New Harbour

MO A
DA

Fl G
DA53

Mahone Harbour

Big Tancook I.

Fl R
MA54

Fl R
MC52

Prince Inlet

Fl G
DA51

Fl R
M 54

Heckman I

Pearl I

Lunenburg

Little Duck I

Fl R
M52

Fl R
D32

Cross I

68

HECKMAN ANCHORAGE

44°24'N, 64°15'W

DIRECTIONS: Proceed from the fairway buoy (Mo A M mentioned above) on a general westerly course for Hobson Island and leave that island to port, then picking up the green buoy to the west of it (ME55), round the buoy and set a south by west course for Lucy Island. Leaving Lucy Island to starboard, choose your spot as you please.

ANCHORAGE AND BERTHS: The anchorage is a good one. No berths available.

FACILITIES: None.

PRINCE INLET

44°24.2'N, 64°19.7'W

DIRECTIONS: From Heckman Anchorage, leave by the same route, leaving Lucy Island this time to port, and picking up the green buoy west of Hobson Island. Then set course for the west and proceed along the north shore of the Second Peninsula and enter Prince Inlet.

ANCHORAGE, BERTHS AND FACILITIES: There is a good anchorage off the Lunenburg Yacht Club located on the south side of Herman's Island facing Little Herman Island. The Yacht Club is a very friendly place with a fine restaurant, fuel, water, ice, moorings and attractive surroundings. There are no stores or repair facilities here however.

MAHONE HARBOUR

44°26.9'N, 64°22.5'W

DIRECTIONS: This town in particular is distinguished by the sight of its three beautiful churches which stand side-by-side at the head of the harbor. Ample depths of water are the rule and adequate channel and approach aids to navigation are marked.

ANCHORAGE AND BERTHS: There is reasonable room to anchor off the town and some berths are available at the government wharf. The town maintains about 20 rental moorings and there is a sheltered floating dinghy dock immediately east of the Town Wharf. Located on the Town Wharf are showers, restrooms, and the wharfmaster's office. There is a small Marina just to the west of the Town Wharf. It can get crowded in here at the time of the Wooden Boat Festival (see below).

REMARKS: Mahone Bay (pop. 1,000) is very attractive and a center for craft shops and restaurants. In the last week of July the town celebrates its Wooden Boat Festival which signals a gathering for wooden boats from far and wide. There are races, prizes, and promotions all honoring wooden boats.

In the Revolutionary War and War of 1812 the town was attacked by privateers. On June 27, 1813, a British warship chased an American privateer into the Bay, and a British deserter aboard, fearing hanging, threw a torch into the powder magazine. It is legend that on the anniversary of this event an apparition known as the "fireship" can be seen drifting in the Bay. "Mahone" is derived from an old French word which was the same for a low-lying craft used by pirates, since these waters were once a resort for such gentry.

ISLAND ANCHORAGES

There are more pretty islands in the western portion of these waters than anywhere along the coast. Directly to the north of Mahone is an enjoyable run past Indian Point Village to and among the adjacent islands of Gifford, Rous, Zwicker, Kaulback, Young and Birch Islands. The channels have good water depth, and snug and sheltered anchorages abound.

Referring back to the fairway buoy (Mahone Bay Mo A M, one-and-a-quarter miles southwest of Great Tancook Island) you will see that an alternative route of departure from the buoy might well have been a northwesterly direction toward Mason, Rafuse and Black Islands. Mason Island has a distinctive red bank on the south, in appearance somewhat like the prow of an old-fashioned battleship. At the north end of Mason Island is a semi-circular cove with a fine sand beach, open to

the eastward, and providing a reasonably good anchorage (subject to southwest swells), bathing spot and large areas of sand. An even better anchorage and bathing spot is reported to be between the two Rafuse Islands on the north side of the sand spit.

Beyond the northern islands (Gifford, Rous, Zwicker, etc.) you will find Martin's Point, formerly known as Murderer's Point because of the massacre of a U.S. ship's company by Indians while the crew was ashore foraging. One lone hand survived.

Beyond Martin's Point lies Oak Island where legend has it that Captain Kidd buried a treasure and history confirms that many treasure hunters have tried in vain to find Kidd's original cache.

CHESTER

44°32.2'N, 64°15.0'W

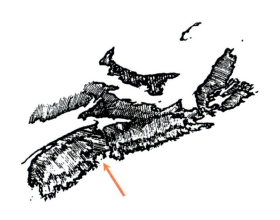

DIRECTIONS: Because of the many light and sound buoys in Mahone Bay, navigation into Chester is easy. From the west, round Little Duck Island, leaving it 1/4 mile abeam to the west and lay a northerly course for East Shoal light buoy (MC55) (due west of Big Tancook Island). From East Shoal light buoy another northerly course should be laid to Quaker Island which has a red flashing light. (Quaker Island is easily identified by its light and is "bald" looking, whereas the other islands are wooded.) Leaving Quaker Island to starboard, one has a choice of threading one's way into Chester Harbour or Back Harbour, each with merits mentioned below. From the east, courses should be laid from the Seal Ledge buoy in a northwesterly direction, passing Little Tancook Island to port to New Harbour and Coachman Ledge buoys, thence to Quaker Island (avoiding Lynch Shoal) and in.

ANCHORAGE AND BERTHS: There is a narrow strip of land between the town and the peninsula. The better-protected anchorage is to the westward in Back Harbour, but beware of the holding ground as it is very soft mud. Sometimes a mooring may be had by inquiring at the Yacht Club or in the town. Some boats lie off the easterly side where the Chester Yacht Club is. You will note that there is a public wharf on the inset map on the chart of Chester Harbour. Don't tie up here; it's the dock for the Tancook ferry. There are some moorings here and you may find one by inquiring at the restaurant nearby on shore. There is good water on both sides of the peninsula as well as up in the back harbor where boat building and repair facilities are situated.

REMARKS: Chester (pop. 1,000) was settled in 1759 by families from New England. A blockhouse that mounted 20 cannon was erected for its defense. The cannon may have kept marauding Yankees out for a time, but in the last century the Yankees have breached the walls and returned in the guise of "summer people." While it still has a majority Canadian population, many of the summercators come from the States --- as far away as New York and Baltimore, and have been doing so for generations. Quite frankly, Chester takes up where Northeast Harbor [ME] leaves off. It has that summerplace look --- sailboat races, little kids, verandas, picnics and good clean fun. There is even a summer theater for intellectual evening entertainment.

The one big summer yachting occasion in the summer is Chester Race Week held over the third week in August. If you are from New England and this editor mentions the Edgartown Regatta as being the equivalent, you will know what I mean. Hard racing, hard living, but also harmless. This editor has nothing but happy memories of his regatta days and even today the sight of 50 or so racing boats splitting tacks or flying spinnakers moistens his eye, but he knows that this is no longer a viable lifestyle at his age.

The people of Chester are the friendliest and generally go out of their way to be helpful.

FACILITIES: Water is available at the Chester Yacht Club dock, but no fuel. On the east side of **Mill Cove**, which is just north of Back Harbour, there is a marina which has diesel fuel, gasoline, water, moorings and some repair facilities.

Comestibles and a liquor store are in town as well as the usual P.O., bank, and interesting shops (particularly one which in 1998 sold local sailboat half models made in wood).

At **Hawker Point** (located between Marriot's Cove and Chester Basin) is South Shore Marine, a full-service yard formerly owned by Christopher (Kit) McCurdy who is a valued contributor to this Guide. South Shore Marine has a travel lift and can supply diesel fuel, gasoline, berths, moorings, showers, laundry facilities, and can handle repairs of any kind Phone # 902 275-3711. There is a first-class restaurant here as well. At **Gold River**, the North West corner of the bay is Gold Water Marine Services, A full service marina. www.goldrivermarine.com . Phone # 902 275-1322

DEEP COVE

44°32.2'N, 64°07.0'W

DIRECTIONS: From the eastern entrance to Mahone Bay, pick up the Blandford Shoal light buoy (MK52) north of Little Tancook Island and steer 30° mag. until you clear Meisner Point and see the conspicuous cliff (marked on chart #4381) ahead. Change course then to head for the cliff and hug the north shore. There is a covered ledge in the center of the entrance marked by three red spar buoys and the channel is to the north of these. The bold north shore at the beginning of the entrance should be followed in, and keeping 30 to 50 feet off this shore should give plenty of water. After passing the ledge, stay in the center of the cove all the way in. The minimum depth at low water is 12 feet, which occurs at the narrows before you reach the basin at the end of the cove.

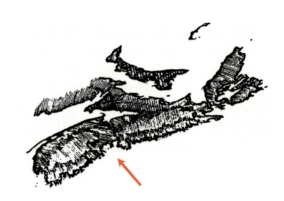

ANCHORAGE, BERTHS AND FACILITIES: The basin has 20-25 feet of water in it with good mud holding ground. Around 1993 a marina was built with slips, fuel, water and a restaurant. The marina is no longer and the buildings are now condominiums.

REMARKS: Ten years ago Deep Cove was magical. No people, few houses, peace and quiet with very nice scenery. Around five years ago a marina was built and there has been a building boom. If you found this harbor on Long Island Sound it would be attractive. For Nova Scotia, though, it is less than perfect. Still pretty, still plenty of room, but not perfect. It offers excellent protection from storms.

NEW HARBOUR

44°28.4'N, 64°05.4'W

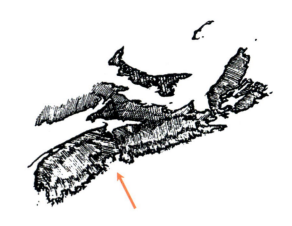

DIRECTIONS: There are practically no obstructions on the way to this harbor.

ANCHORAGE AND BERTHS: Decent holding ground should be found in the middle of this very small harbor, "a delightful and wonderful haven when the easterlies blow," according to one correspondent; however it is open to the northwest. There are two government wharves, one on the north shore and one on the south where berths might be found, (subject to depths alongside and the condition of these wharves).

REMARKS: This is the site of a former whale processing plant (now converted to a fish plant) which earned the area an unsavory reputation among cruising folk. Even today the state of the harbor varies as to the fishing season because of offal which can be obnoxious in the extreme.

BLANDFORD

44°29.6'N, 65°06.7'W

Chart: #4381

Robert S. Carter. Update by L. & M. Bailey.
2001

DIRECTIONS: A well-buoyed channel leads across (well-named) Shoal Cove to the breakwater.

ANCHORAGE AND BERTHS: Anchor behind the breakwater where there are depths of 8-10 feet at low water. The bottom is soft mud and somewhat difficult to get a "bite" on. The floats and quay directly inside the breakwater have less than 5 feet alongside, but the government wharf with smooth plank sides has 11 feet.

REMARKS: The Government Dock has been turned over to the fishing fleet. In 2001 there was no space for visitors.

This is a fishing port with the usual aroma, but conveniently located on the southeast side of Mahone Bay. It has the advantage over Deep Cove in that one can see outside conditions before going out. There is protection from all winds, but a heavy northwester would create a surge.

FACILITIES: None.

ST. MARGARET'S BAY and HARBORS

(Including Southwest Cove, Hubbard's Cove, Franks George Island, Peggy's Cove, Head Harbour/Schooner Cove, and French Village Harbour)

Condensed from earlier material by N.L.C. Mather, Judge Bailey Aldrich, G. Peabody Gardner, C. Boll. Update by R. Michiner.
2002

This bay named "Le Porte Sainte Marguerite" by Champlain in 1631 is often overlooked by cruising folk. Three miles wide at its entrance and ten miles long, it offers a number of pleasant harbors for exploration, many of which are not mentioned here.

DIRECTIONS: From the west, care should be taken to stay offshore of Seal Ledge, Gravel Island Ledges, Gravel Island and Southwest Island (which can be passed inbound either way if the helmsman is paying attention to the two unnamed islands just north of Southwest Island). From the east, wisdom would dictate staying approximately 1/2 mile offshore on a course trending NW from Shag Bay Breaker bell (AT50) to Peggy's Point where a new course should be laid to Crawford Ledge bell (JA56). Horseshoe Ledge is an obvious obstruction to be avoided off the bay's entrance.

SOUTHWEST COVE

44°31.5'N, 64°00.5'W

Chart #4386

DIRECTIONS: From the west, sail halfway between White Point and the ragged tip of Southwest Island and then steer directly towards the high and prominent Owl's Head. Follow the shore of Owl's Head Island (it is an island) where the water is very deep and the shoreline high. The northern tip of Owl's Head Island has a rock, hidden at high tide, so the course should continue towards Horse Island and after approximately 150 yards, alter it to the west where two cabins are built. There a rock is in the center of the channel, but the western shore is relatively deep.

ANCHORAGE AND BERTHS: After the mid-channel rock (mentioned above), there is a pretty, well-protected harbor for deep-keeled yachts. Shallower drafted vessels may proceed nearly up to the level of the small waterfall. (It shallows very quickly south of this landmark.) There is no public wharf.

REMARKS: There are a number of small houses around this small harbor, one of particular interest made of stone which looks like a miniature Medieval castle.

There is a pretty walk available by taking the dinghy to the narrows and following a path to the left across a field, and walking around a cliff to Owl's Head, where there is a beautiful view of St. Margaret's Bay. The lighthouse at Peggy's Cove is directly across to the east.

FACILITIES: None.

HUBBARD'S COVE

44°38.4'N, 64°03.4'W

Chart #4386

DIRECTIONS: There is no obstruction whatever coming up the bay until Slaughenwhite Ledge, located just south of the entrance to the cove. The Slaughenwhite bell (DY52) and nun (DY54) should be left to starboard on entering.

ANCHORAGE AND BERTHS: A pretty, well-protected anchorage is off the town and there may be a berth at the wharf. This wharf is now part of a town park but was formerly the site of the town's fish processing plant.

The Hubbards Yacht Club has moorings marked "HYC" which may be available. There are two dinghy docks: one at the Town Wharf on the north side of the harbor, the other at the Yacht Club just west of the Town Wharf. The Daphinee Inn on the south side of the harbor has floating docks for its guests.

REMARKS: Hubbard's Cove (pop.700) was the sight of a prosperous sawmill in the late nineteenth century and has a summer colony and public beach on its east side. In 1998 Mr. Douglas Robinson operated Pine Cables Craft Studio here and he builds ship models fitted into bottles, certainly a "lost art," and for the nautical buff, something well worth seeing. (We are assured Mr. Robinson and Pine Cables are ready for the '99 season.)

FACILITIES: There is a food market and some restaurants within walking distance. There are no repair facilities and there is no food or water available.

FRANKS GEORGE ISLAND

44°35.8'N, 63°56.5'W

Chart #4386

DIRECTIONS: There is no difficulty getting in, but once you turn the corner from the west, you will see 8 fish pounds with a floating guardian line. Proceed in between these and the eastern point of the island.

ANCHORAGE AND BERTHS: Anchor in 15 feet of water between the fish pounds and the eastern point of the island. There is no wharf here,

REMARKS: The water temperature in this anchorage in the summer of 1968 was 68° F., warm enough to swim in.

This was the site of an aquafarm for raising trout and salmon, run by a marine biologist named Karen Westhaver. Her house is the only one on the island.

In 1986 Mr. Carlton Boll reported that Karen had a number of interesting big fish stories, including some about shotgun fights with local vandals trying to harm her fish.

FACILITIES: None.

FRENCH VILLAGE HARBOUR

44° 38.09'N, 063° 55.03'

Chart #4386

From the Ringdove Shoal Bell (DA58), proceed NE into French Village Harbour, keeping the nun (DA60) off Wedge Island and Davy Point to starboard, and Davy Rock to port. Once past Davy Point, head east toward the cove between Croucher Point and French Village.

On the north shore of this cove is the St. Margaret's Bay Sailing Club building and dock. Visiting yachts are welcome and guest moorings are usually available. The Club can be reached by phone at 902-823-1089.

HEAD HARBOUR (SCHOONER COVE)

44° 40.42' N, 063° 54.92' W

Chart #4386

Schooner Cove in Head Harbour at the NE corner of St. Margaret's Bay provides excellent protection from severe weather.

From Crawford Ledge Bell (DA56), proceed N past Shut-In Island to the Ringdove Shoal Bell (DA58), then NNE toward Croucher Island which has a lighted daymark. When Indian Point is abeam, head NE toward Clam Island. This island may be passed safely on either side.

Keeping the nun (DA68) off Green Point to starboard, head NE toward Mason Point. From Mason Point, proceed north keeping the nun (DA74) to starboard. Turn NW at Slaughenwhite Point, and anchor anywhere in Schooner Cover. Stay clear of a covered rock just NE of the nun (DA78).

The late Peabody Gardner, a renowned cruising man and beloved member of the C.C.A., took his yacht Glide *(49'11" l.o.a., 12'6" beam, 7'2" draft) into Peggy's Cove in 1953. Rather than bend his narration into the standard format, his description appears below, unchanged.*

Peggy's Cove, probably the most photographed and photogenic place in Nova Scotia, should not be missed. It has a picture-book lighthouse on a granite point; a tiny harbor with the most paintable of docks and fishouses; a toylike village --- the whole surrounded with granite ledges sprinkled with huge boulders that look like giant hailstones.

It is possible to negotiate the fantastically narrow entrance to this cove, but this is one of the few places where local knowledge, if not a must, is certainly highly desirable. After scanning it twice from the sea and once from shore, I finally screwed up my courage, in 1953, to enter it.

Conditions were ideal --- a smooth sea, no wind, the tide nearly low, and two friendly fishermen in a small boat to lead the way. To avoid rocks we had to first zig and then zag, and so narrow was the entrance that our bowsprit appeared to sweep over the land. The water was crystal clear and the rest of the crew, who were looking over the side, could easily see the obstacles and were holding their breaths; but I was steering and busy trying to follow the little boat, so I could only sense them.

We tied up at a very small dock where we photographed and were avidly photographed in return. There was no room to turn to get out, so we had to wind the stern around one end of the crowded dock in order not to cause damage to ourselves or to others. *My advice is to anchor somewhere else --- Boutilier Cove or Indian Harbour and visit Peggy by motor.* [AMEN! ed.]

PORT DOVER

(Including Dover West, Dan Blain's Cove and Leary Cove)

44°30'N, 63°52'W

Chart: #4386

Rewritten and condensed from earlier material by Dr. Alexander Forbes, R. MacD. Black, T.F.T Morland, Lloyd J. Marshall, and S. Dumaresq.   *1993*

DIRECTIONS: The route in is fairly apparent in clear weather. However, with poor visibility the safest course (either from east or west) would be to pick up Dover Castle fairway whistle (MoA AT) which is 1 1/4 miles south of Taylor Island. From there proceed on course 72°mag) for 1.4 miles to Shag Bay Breakers bell (AT50), thence on course 351°(mag) to the spar (AT54) at Sand Shoal, leaving it to starboard. Running in, keep the green can (AT51) and Black Rock well to port. Leave the three red buoys (AT54, AT56, and AT60) to starboard. At the red blinker (AT60) you have the choice of turning west into Port Dover or continuing on to Dan Blain's Cove.

The most conspicuous landmark for the general area, from seawards, is the church spire at East Dover, between Dutchman and Leary Coves on the chart; the spire at West Dover cannot be seen from outside. Dover Castle, a high and imposing rock, is also a striking feature.

The outer harbor (marked "Port Dover" on the chart) is convenient and easy of access. It is well protected by the fringe of bold, rocky islands to the south, but a heavy sea rolling in from the SE would rock a boat in this outer anchorage.

There are many good anchorages inside, the nearest being behind Baker Island, rounding it to the north.

PASSAGE BEHIND TAYLOR ISLAND (DOVER WEST)

44 29.2'N 63 52.01'W

K. McCurdy   *2004*

When leaving Dover West and heading west there is a lovely passage inside Taylor and Indian Islands. This passage is challenging and should be avoided if there is any sea running. You round the stake just south of Soi Point and head west, favouring the mainland shore. As you approach the inside on Indian Island you will notice Peggy's Cove Light house directly ahead. Passing inside Indian Island there is a small rock (on the chart) that you leave to starboard, the depth here is over 8' at low tide. A person on the bow would be comforting in this restricted area until you get to open water.

Proceed to the small basin inside Polly Cove Rock and Indian Island where you change directions to south-south east and head for open water. This area has shown 6' at low tide but we were not sure we were reading the bottom or kelp beds. Follow the contour lines on the chart and proceed with caution, especially if there is a swell running and it is low tide. A truly lovely passage showing the ruggedness this coast has to offer.

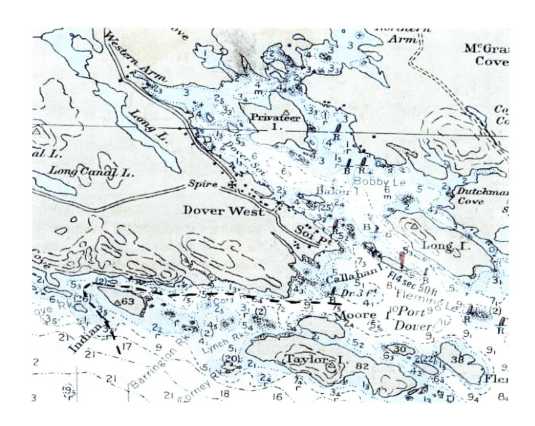

DAN BLAIN'S COVE

44°30.4'N, 63°53.8'W

Dan Blain's Cove is not named on Canadian Chart #4386, but is so named here after the late Dr. Daniel Blain C.C.A., of Philadelphia who was well-known in the area and cruised the waters between Mahone Bay and Halifax extensively in his yacht *Corisande*.

This attractive harbor is located just north of Privateer Island. The southerly course leaving Privateer Island to the east is the easier route.

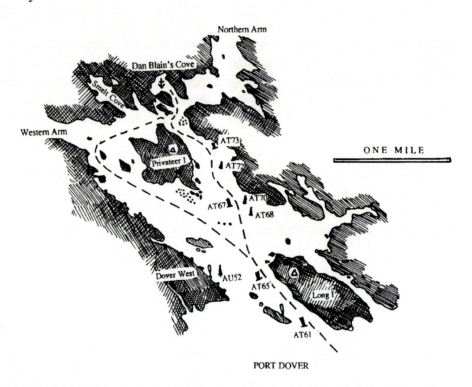

LEARY COVE

(East Dover)

44°29.8'N, 63°53.7'W

DIRECTIONS: The approach is easy, and the deep-water reef at the mouth of the cove is small and has always been well-marked with a green buoy (AX53). Unless one draws 10', there is no way one can be picked up by this shoal.

ANCHORAGE AND BERTHS: The anchorage is open to the southwest. One should be able to tie to the government wharf which has a depth of 8 feet at the outer end.

REMARKS: Leary Cove (pronounced locally as "Larry's Cove") is a very attractive, typical Nova Scotia fishing village. It is much quieter than West Dover which had many dogs and screeching cars at night.

80

PROSPECT

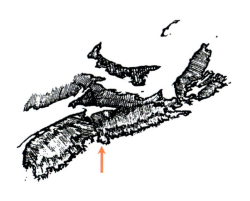

(Including Murphy Cove and Prospect Bay Anchorages)

44°28.1'N, 64°47.0'W

Chart #4386

Rewritten and condensed from earlier material by R. MacD. Black, Alexander Weld, Dr. Edmund Cabot and M.S. Grant.   1998

DIRECTIONS: Prospect is the fishing village behind Saul Island. It is entered through a narrow passage from the east. A white fixed light on a pole on the east end of Saul Island is the port marker; stay in the middle between it and the large rock opposite.

ANCHORAGE AND BERTHS: There is surprisingly good protection. Although swinging room is limited, a spare fisherman's mooring can sometimes be had or a stern line put ashore. There is a small government wharf here with 7 1/2 feet off the end.

REMARKS: Prospect (pop. 130) is a quick place to duck into without a long inside trip.

FACILITIES: Very limited supplies may be had here. No fuel or water is available.

PROSPECT BAY

There are at least two fathoms almost to the north end of the long inner bay. The whole stretch of the approach is wooded and uninhabited until north of Purcell Island. Above this on the west side is a large colony of cottages with attendant outboards to spare.

DIRECTIONS: After leaving Hearn Island, keep pretty well to the middle with the exception of Kelly Ledge, which is well marked, with green buoys (AN57 and AN59) at the north and south extremities; you can leave it on either hand. There is also a green buoy (AN55) marking the shoal off Kelly Point. Leave the two islets south of Purcell Island to port and then favor the island side, which is quite steep-to.

ANCHORAGES: The best anchorage is on the west side of the north tip of Purcell Island; go as far south down it as soundings will permit. This area offers great protection from all winds, including hurricanes. The bottom is very soft, though; good for the plow or Danforth, and not so good for the yachtsman anchor. The enticing little cove to the right, or west is blocked by a large rock at the entrance.

PIG ISLAND

Pig Island offers a beautiful, deep, landlocked and secluded anchorage on its north side, which can be entered from the south without problems, even at half tide despite what the chart may say.

[This information is from Dr. Cabot, whose yacht *Caracole*, draws 5.4 feet. -ed.]

MURPHY COVE

DIRECTIONS: This is a tricky entrance. First, find the two bold, whitish boulders side-by-side on the northwest side of the entrance. Approximately opposite and in the center are two rock patches, quite extensive, but with a channel in between. You can enter either to the northwest or try to twist between the patches, but BE CAREFUL. In 1984 Sandy Weld surveyed the entrance here and at low tide reported 3 feet maximum depth in the northwest channel and 6 feet through the rocks. Caution and reconnaissance in the dinghy are advisable before attempting this.

REMARKS: Once you are in, it is a pretty, wooded and landlocked anchorage. There is a path from the head of the cove to the highway - a fairly long walk. There are no houses or even a fish shed.

ROGUES ROOST
& CUB BASIN

Rewritten and condensed from earlier material by Peter Richmond Dr. Edmund Cabot and Alexander Weld with new information from Walter Wales. *1996*

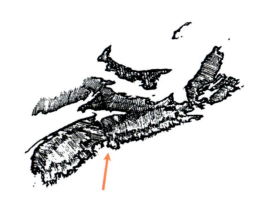

ROGUE'S ROOST

44°28.3'N, 63°45.1'W

Chart #4385

DIRECTIONS: The entrance to Rogue's Roost is between the northern shore of Roost Island and two unnamed islands as shown on the chart. On entering, favor the Roost Island shore and leave the large rock between Roost Island and the first small island to port. Also leave the other rock between Roost Island and the second small island to port. The first of these rocks may be awash; the second is always dry. The minimum depth is generally twelve feet.

Rogue's Roost and Cub Basin are <u>not connected</u> by the channel on the NE side of Roost Island.

ANCHORAGE: Once inside, you may proceed to the left to what is labeled Rogue's Roost on the chart. The preferred anchorage is to the SE down the short narrow channel which opens up on the eastern shore of Roost Island (marked by a 3-fathom spot on the chart). Favor the middle or even the port hand when entering this anchorage. There is a large rock on the starboard side of the entrance.

This last anchorage is tight. Unless you are willing to raft, it will not afford swing room to more than a few boats. The surrounding land is not particularly high. In a heavy blow the combination of windage in a high rig and little room to drag makes this anchorage dicey.

REMARKS: Here is one of the most beautiful anchorages in Nova Scotia, and this editor has two friends who were so inspired by its scenery and location that each named his boat after this harbor. Unfortunately, it has become "discovered." In 1996 Walter Wales reported, "The best of all gunkholes is not to be visited on a Sunday afternoon in the summer. Every small outboard from Mahone Bay and Halifax gather here to picnic and party."

Unfortunately, the *Guide* must take some responsibility for this "discovery." Already this editor has been given information about other gunkholes and secret harbors *on condition that such information not be put into the Guide*. Most harbors in Nova Scotia are outside urban outboard range, but Rogue's Roost is not.

It still remains beautiful, but not as pristine as it once was. Probably it is best to avoid Rogue's Roost on weekends in summer, and even under the best of circumstances, be prepared to move on if the outboard-boombox crowd show up.

A bronze plaque is displayed here in memory of John Snow, 1914 - 1970, a well-known local yachtsman.

CUB BASIN

44°27.8'N, 63°45.0'W

Chart #4385

DIRECTIONS: From the east, steer course 345° (mag) from Grampus light and bell buoy (AM52) south of Mars Head, Mosher Island, leaving Breakfast Island and Bald Rock to port until the southern end of Burnt Island is to starboard. There should be three red buoys just to the east of this course (MA54, MA56, MA58), all to be left to starboard. With the southern tip of Burnt Island abeam to starboard on course 345° (mag), turn sharply toward the southern tip of Burnt Island, avoiding the large rock awash at half tide west of Shannon Island. There is a ledge off the southern end of Burnt Island which should be avoided. After rounding the end of Burnt Island, favor its eastern side, which is bold, thus avoiding a rock to starboard between Roost Island and the unnamed island to starboard. Make a gradual turn to starboard, leaving Roost Island to port and the unnamed islands to starboard.

ANCHORAGE: Continue in to the south and anchor in 3 1/2 fathoms north of Shannon Island. The anchorage is completely landlocked, but the holding ground is rocky, so a yachtsman anchor with a trip line is recommended.

REMARKS: This is a very picturesque harbor and the surrounding land is completely deserted.

RYAN'S GUT

44°26.5'N / 44°27'N • 63°42.1'W / 63°45.4'W

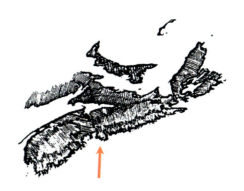

Chart: #4385

Reprinted exactly as Capt. T.F.T. Morland, R.C.N. (Ret.) gave it to the Guide in 1962.

This pretty little channel of about one mile in length, connects Pennant Bay with the channel on the east side of Betty Island. The channel is staked but no details are given on the chart, therefore the markers should not be relied upon absolutely. We have never found less than 7 feet of water at the lowest tide, *but the passage is very narrow in several places and can hardly be recommended unless somebody on board has previously been through it.*

Passing from the east to the west, the red stakes are left on starboard hand and the green on port hand. However, the green stake on Broad Shoal to the south of Woody Island does not belong to the Gut system, and must be left on the starboard side. Likewise, at the western end the red cone buoy and Dollar

Rock (which always breaks) are left on the port hand when leaving.

Arriving from the east one can see the houses to the north of Woody Island. The island itself has smooth sides, grass on top, and a few scraggly spruce trees. The course from Broad Shoal stake is 325° (mag).

The most westerly of the green stakes in the channel is very close to a large dry rock, but you must pass the rock - there is hardly any water to the south of the stake. Passing to the north of Dollar Rock, head for the northeast corner of Betty Island.

Approaching from the west, it is necessary to spot Dollar Rock which can be passed within 100 yards. Just to the north of the first red stake is a flat shelf with a conspicuous square rock perched on it. See the following schematic chartlet

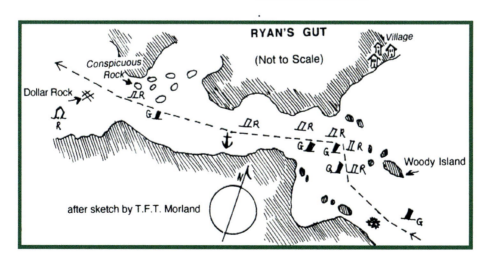

after sketch by T.F.T. Morland

The Canadian Government has threatened to remove the stakes from within Ryan's Gut. Should this occur and you are a stranger to these waters, TURN BACK.. Sailors with local knowledge will still be able to do this, but you won't.

SAMBRO HARBOUR

44°28.6'N, 63°35.9'W

Charts: #4385, #4237

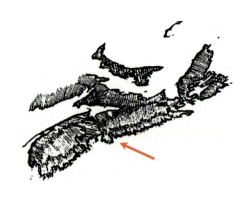

Rewritten and condensed from earlier material by G. Bryant, A. Fowler, S. Campbell and J. McKelvy, with new information by Dr. E. Cabot. 1998

DIRECTIONS: The inner harbor at Sambro Village is in the cove between Powers Island and Bull Point. Using Chart #4237 you should have no problem getting in. The harbor is possible to enter using Chart #4385 in good visibility by using common sense with the channel markers (which aren't on that chart). Don't try to be original when using #4385, as there are a lot of rocks in the area.

ANCHORAGE AND BERTHS: The anchorage is located south of the government wharf and west of a line between Bull Point and Power Island. The holding ground is reported to be poor, as the bottom is covered with kelp. A yachtsman anchor may be in order here. There is also an anchorage with good holding ground north of Powers Island.

The T-shaped government wharf has a depth of fifteen feet on its end. Depending on the season, this wharf can be busy with the comings and goings of local fishermen.

REMARKS: Sambro is an excellent harbor if you are "muzzled in" at Halifax by fog or bad weather and wish to be in a good position for going west as soon as the weather breaks, and you want to eliminate the 10 - 12 miles of getting out of Halifax Harbour.

Sambro (pop. 600) is a typical fishing town. One correspondent recalls discovering an excellent retail fish market here in the summer of 1975 while his vessel was waiting for a pea soup fog to clear. It was the time of the mercury-in-the-swordfish scare and the sale of swordfish was outlawed. He, nonetheless asked the store proprietor if there was any swordfish for sale. After much winking, rolling of eyes, and pledges of anonymity, he and his crew dined on the best swordfish steaks that night they had ever had.

FACILITIES: Basic supplies may be obtained in the village. No fuel or water is available.

KETCH HARBOUR

44°29.4'N, 63°33.1'W

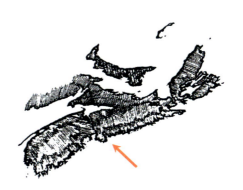

Charts: #4385, #4237

Rewritten and condensed from material by G. Macintosh, G. Bryant, R. Black, R. Richmond, C. Bartlett, and R. Pirie.   *1991*

DIRECTIONS: A course of 348° (mag) from Ketch Harbour whistle (HE19) will bring you to the first pair of buoys leading in a northerly direction up the half mile of harbor.

ANCHORAGE AND BERTHS: Anchor anywhere off the village in 10 - 12 feet of water. Swells often come up the harbor making this an uncomfortable anchorage and it is open to any weather from the southeast.
The government wharf is reported to be in a state of disrepair so tying up is not recommended.

REMARKS: Ketch Harbour's appeal is primarily as a harbor of refuge. It may be useful as a harbor to position yourself for an early start in the morning when going west, but for this, most correspondents prefer Sambro Harbour.

The village has a small fishing population and it is a "bedroom community" for Halifax. It isn't very interesting and has none of the usual amenities.

FACILITIES: None.

HERRING COVE*

44°34.1'N, 63°33.3'W

Charts: #4385, #4203

Rewritten and condensed from earlier material by H. Streeter, C. Bartlett, B. Trembly, J. Moore and M. Grant.

DIRECTIONS: Herring Cove is easy of access. There is a bell (HM1) just south of the entrance and a fixed green light on the shore to port when entering. The cove opens up to starboard. Keep in the center of the channel as you pass the green light. The breakwater at the entrance of the cove and the rocky point are on your starboard hand beyond the breakwater.

ANCHORAGE AND BERTHS: The second wharf on the port hand is the government wharf. It is possible to anchor in the center of the cove just beyond this wharf in two fathoms, BUT use as little scope as possible and a stern anchor to keep from swinging into the wharves. Sometimes a mooring is available.

The government wharf does not have enough water to lie to it at low tide.

This harbor is tight.

REMARKS: Herring Cove generally gets bad press from most correspondents. It is a working fishing harbor, it is congested, and there are numerous reports of boats being stoned by the town's youth.

A former editor familiar with the harbor had this to say: "[Herring Cove] is absolutely tiny, it is crowded with houses all around and the houses look straight down upon the water, and therefore the urge to stone must be irresistible. Many of the houses belong to commuters to Halifax who have little respect for yachts, unfortunately, and likely they supply the marksman. Against this, should one have to shelter against weather I would anticipate receiving only kindness and assistance."

FACILITIES: Basic supplies are available ashore and it is only a short taxi ride to Halifax for anything complicated or exotic. There is no fuel or water.

Caution should be used on entering this harbor as it has not been reported on in the last ten years.

HALIFAX HARBOUR

44°39'N, 63°37'W

Charts: #4237, #4203, #4202
Chart: #4201 if proceeding into Bedford Basin

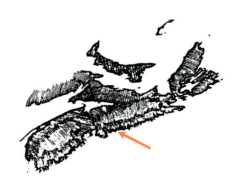

MacCallum S. Grant

Halifax Harbour is best surveyed as a whole on Chart #4237 which demonstrates the "fault" structure which created the harbour in the first place and which is undoubtedly one of the very best in the world - ice-free, protected from prevailing winds and covered from seaward by MacNab's Island.

A similar fault has created the Northwest Arm on the west side of the harbour and the old city of Halifax hangs down like a pear between the two. If one could reverse this pear (i.e. turn it upside down) the mirror image would be the Bedford Basin at the head of the harbour, the assembly and staging area for mighty convoys in both wars - capable of anchoring 100 merchant ships at once in a safe "lagoon" pending provision of escorting warships for Atlantic crossings.

Look closely at the chart again - deep water everywhere for the largest ocean-going carriers, well-marked channels, and for the average yacht, absolutely no hazards in the harbour proper. Which raises an important point. Halifax has two container ports, two refineries, a major Naval presence, a large grain elevator, an auto port, a bulk gypsum depot, and a lot of ancillary traffic such as coastal freighters, pilot boats and so on. These all take the marked channels, with the exception of fishing craft - and therefore all yachts should avoid the said channels like the plague, especially in thick weather, staying on the wrong side of each marker for the sake of safety. However - "Halifax Traffic," monitoring VHF 12 and/or 14, has a total

radar overview of the harbour and its approaches and will have you in sight at all times. If you identify yourself on the air and spot your location for them, they will not only tell you of approaching danger but also guide you directly, if you so wish, right up the harbour. This is a remarkable service and well worth using when in any doubt or feeling pooped.

If you have a spare day while in port, go for a mini-cruise up the harbour as far as Bedford Basin and, if you feel so inclined, stop at Historic Properties for lunch. This is in the heart of the main business area, marked by tall buildings. There are floats to lie alongside, good restaurants and stores, and a very interesting reconstruction of old Halifax. The trip up the harbour is rewarding, offering a wonderful view of the Naval dockyards, and you might spare a glance at the Narrows where the harbour debauches into Bedford Basin. This was the site in December 1917 of the largest man-made explosion prior to Hiroshima - when an ammo ship hit a freighter in the Narrows and was practically vaporized. The entire north end of the city was destroyed and nearly every house elsewhere in the city suffered damage; all rail connections were cut, and the explosion (in keeping with Murphy's Law) was followed by a disastrous blizzard. There were thousands of dead and injured; the roar of the explosion was heard in Truro, 60 miles to the north, and Halifax owes a large part of its recovery through prompt action by Boston and other cities in relief action. (Boston in particular - their most generous response has been remembered on the anniversary each year since.)

ANCHORAGES, BERTHS AND FACILITIES: There are no commercial marinas in Halifax. Instead their services are provided for by yacht clubs. The closest to seaward is the Royal Nova Scotia Yacht Squadron ("the Squadron") which lies in the Northwest Arm about 1/2 mile from the mouth on the west shore. The Squadron, incidentally, has lineage to the Halifax Yacht Club of 1837, picking up the honorific "Royal" later, dropping the Halifax Club for the "Nova Scotia Squadron" later again. But it is still, of course, the same - like grandfather's axe which has two heads and three handles. The squadron dockmaster and launches monitor VHF 68 and you can speak to them a short distance seaward to get a berth, but it might be a fair idea to call ahead a day or two if you can, as space can be short in mid-season. And speaking of which, don't come at all in early July on odd years - this is when the Marblehead - Halifax Race fleet is in town with attending crises and congestion. The old rule seems to work that there's always room for one more - but with the inevitable hassle. After July 10th it's generally safe! But check it.

The Squadron has a good dining room, and a jacket and tie are required in the dining room except at brunch on Saturday. Casual dress may be worn in the wardroom and other parts of the clubhouse. Meals are served in the wardroom and on the patio deck. No breakfast is served.

The dock has excellent water for your tanks, fuel, showers, access to all repair facilities, ice, and so on. The dockmaster will allot you a slip if he has one; he may also let you tie along the dockface or as a last resort give you a mooring. There is a modest charge for these services.

The Squadron is eager to be helpful and will act as a staging area for mail, crew change and re-provisioning. The official address is:

Royal Nova Scotia Yacht Squadron
376 Purcell's Cove Road
Halifax, Nova Scotia
CANADA B3P 4J7

Telephone: (902) 477-5653
www.rnsys.com

Another excellent club is the Armdale Yacht Club, a further 1 1/2 miles up the Arm from the Squadron. They are not quite so organized for visiting yachts if only because of their greater distance from seaward - but they are likewise anxious to be helpful. Limited dock space here is available at $15.00 (Canadian) in 1992.

Their mailing address is:

Armdale Yacht Club
Armdale, Halifax, Nova Scotia
CANADA B3L 4J7

Telephone: (902) 477-4617
www.armdaleyachtclub.ns.ca

This Club, AYC, is situated on the grounds of an old prison in full use for military prisoners during the Napoleonic Wars and the War of 1812. They still have the old cell block (now used for yachting gear) and it is well worth a visit to see how things were then. The clubhouse sits where the governor's house used to be, on a lovely knoll overlooking the Arm.

The Dartmouth Yacht Club in Bedford Basin is located in Wright's Cove, 1 1/4 miles northwest of the MacKay Bridge. They are reported to offer marina service with berths, moorings, ice and fuel, and the staff is most helpful. It is, however, a long way to Halifax from here and even longer to the ocean.

If you are particularly gregarious, you may wish to tie up at the public wharf at Historic Properties (a harbour front renovation similar to Boston's Quincy Market or Baltimore's Harbor Place). This area is very crowded on nights and weekends. You will also be the object of much shore side attention. The wharf is on the west (Halifax) side of the harbour below the Citidal and is easily located because of the number of yachts and "character boats"

tied here. Aside from the lack of privacy, there is also some surge around this wharf. You are, nonetheless, in the heart of Halifax.

On a final note - the Northwest Arm is not much good for gunkholing due to excess yachting activity and lack of privacy. Try behind McNab's Island at Wreck Cove or at the head of Bedford Basin. These are nice little spots and the latter in particular makes a good harbour of refuge in all but a vicious nor'wester. (Wreck Cove, incidentally, is full of decayed wooden hulks at its northwest corner so don't try to anchor there. They are old tern schooners and the like and are largely hidden beneath the surface.)

METRO HALIFAX / DARTMOUTH:
(History, Sights & Services) The peninsula of Halifax, between the harbour and NW Arm, is the Old City of Halifax of some 100,000 now of a total of about 300,000 in the metro area. Halifax is a pleasant place, not unlike Boston in many respects and the parallel has been made many times. Halifax didn't grow from a one-time crossroad or fishing village. It arrived as a package between dawn and dusk on Midsummer's Day, 1749, deposited for the specific purpose as a foil to the great French fortress at Louisbourg on Cape Breton Island — said fortress Louisbourg in its turn being where it was as a shield to the approaches to the St. Lawrence River and the settlements of Quebec.

The choice of the site for Halifax was based on the harbour well known then as Chebucto, and populated only for fishing stages by a scattering of European fishermen. Ironically, the French knew Chebucto only too well. A year or two prior to the founding of Halifax, a large French reinforcing fleet had tried to winter over in Bedford Basin and left 10,000 of their men behind, dead of scurvy, starvation and frost. The ruined fleet is still largely there, in the waters off Bedford, scuttled and sunk.

Halifax, then, was a fortress by design, and the wonderful bastion of Citadel Hill in the center of the town was ringed in its turn by a score of smaller forts and outposts guarding the harbour and the hinterland approaches. Citadel Hill is a fortification in the grand manner enfilading fields of fire from the projecting redans and battlements. A museum now, it is a priceless example of on-going engineering in the military arts of the 18th and 19th centuries, and if you see anything whatsoever of Halifax, give this first priority and make your visit coincide with the firing of the noonday gun by uniformed gunners of the past who put on quite a show.

The yachtsman arriving at the Squadron can get a cab, but it isn't cheap. Alternatively, there is a bus of Metro Transport to the major shopping malls of Sears, Hudson Bay Company and others. Perhaps best of all, every major car rental office is in Halifax, all trying harder and glad to oblige.

Be advised, however, that Halifax is still old-fashioned enough to close most of its stores and outlets on Sunday. If you have errands to run and Sunday gets in the way, you had best inquire by phone first.

The City has, besides Citadel Hill, two fascinating museums. Try the Maritime Museum downtown on Lower Water Street - you'll love it. And while in that area walk 1/4 mile to the aforementioned Historic Properties. Try it again at night - this is where a lot of the action is and it's a great place for dinner overlooking the harbour. Except in fog.

Scholars of every stripe might be interested in Dalhousie University, founded from Customs duties collected when the British captured and ran Castine in Maine during the War of 1812 - (a very civilized form of occupation where life proceeded much as normal but the Customs were siphoned off for the benefit of the youth back home). At present Dalhousie has a student body of some 10,000 and two outstanding faculties, medicine and law. Its rival, particularly in sports, is St. Mary's University, also in the city.

The second museum referred to above is the Nova Scotia Museum, a first-class examination of the natural history of the Province, complete with panoramas of early days, archaeological studies and evincing great imagination.

There are six top-rated hotels in the city and literally scores of good restaurants - and it's worth a good splurge now and again if only so someone else can do the dishes and mop up afterwards. (And think of the food too.)

Yacht chandlery is well and truly available and inquiry should be made from the dockmaster as to which firm might be best able to help. Likewise for engine and electronic repairs. Both the Squadron and Armdale YC have substantial haul-out facilities for the average yacht, but very large cruisers (of, say 100') will have to use commercial facilities in the harbour.

When in Halifax, bear in mind the absence of marinas and fuel docks along the coast, particularly to the eastward. Don't neglect to top up with fuel and water as well as provisions, liquor and spare parts. Halifax should be your principal staging depot for this and crew changes too, if possible, if only for an easy life.

Lastly, inquire for parks and libraries - there are plenty of parks, beautiful public gardens and two good public libraries. Having enjoyed these, try a little of the very active nightlife available.

A good book on the city, probably enjoyable

to all hands, is Thomas Raddall's **Halifax, Warden of the North**, an interesting study by a master historian and one of Canada's top writers. [If you want to read excellent historical novels about the founding of Canada in the C.S. Forester/Kenneth Roberts tradition, carry some of Raddall's books aboard. Perhaps start with **Hangman's Beach** -ed.]

The main Halifax airport is, regrettably, some 25 miles away, though there is a helicopter link from downtown. The airport is served by a major highway, and the time to get there is reasonable enough but better allow an hour to be safe. There are daily flights direct to Boston, New York, London, Bermuda, and of course major Canadian cities inland.

SABLE ISLAND

43°58'N, 60°01.5'W

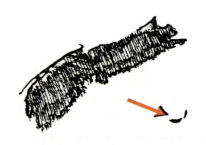

Chart: #4098

Edward C. Brainard and F. Gordon Mack, M.D. Sable island contact info updated   2005

Except for emergencies, no person is allowed to land, visit, or reside on the island without permission from the Director, Marine Programs, Canadian Coast Guard, Dartmouth, Nova Scotia.

Sable Island is more of a phenomenon or an intrigue than an island. It is an object of desire to the zoologist, biologist, geologist, meteorologist, ornithologist, and yet more -ologists whose prefixes and fields have yet to be discovered. Formed by the little-understood, but immensely powerful forces that drive the Gulf Stream and Labrador Current, it lies in a vortex of mysterious physical and gravitational forces. It also lies 150 miles east-northeast of Halifax.

From the time of its discovery in the fifteenth century, it has been known as a treacherous but fascinating place. Private philanthropies and the Canadian government established two lighthouses and some life-saving stations here in 1801. The life stations (virtual communities in themselves) were disestablished in 1958; the lighthouses have become automated, and only a meteorological station sustains year-round residents on the island today.

The wild horses, the Ipswich Sparrow, and all the other flora and fauna are interesting, and a visit should be preceded by some personal research on these matters.

In the early part of the twentieth century, the island had a strategic radio station established by the Marconi Wireless Company which relayed communications from ships at sea to land lines on the American continent. One of these wireless telegraphers was Thomas

Raddall, later to become Canada's most famous novelist. He spent a year (1921-1922) on the island and later wrote **The Nymph and the Lamp**, his greatest novel. This editor cannot recommend reading this book more highly in preparation for visiting Sable. The winter storms, the glistening summer sun on the dunes, the fog are all held together by a fine romance.

From the yachtsman's point of view, Sable was too dangerous and uninteresting to visit in the nineteenth century. To be sure, Dr. Alexander Graham Bell visited there in 1898. However, it wasn't until Dr. Bell's grandson (CCA member Melville Grosvenor) visited Sable on the yawl *White Mist* and wrote a splendid article on Sable for the September, 1965, **NATIONAL GEOGRAPHIC**, that the offshore cruising community became interested in Sable. (This article is also greatly recommended.)

Thereafter, unannounced visits to Sable by yachts became the consternation of the Canadian government, and for a number of years *no* permission was given any yacht to land. In fact, this editor tried to use influence through the U.S. Ambassador to persuade the Canadians to grant such permission to a CCA fleet in 1973. The then Minister of Transport, Jean Marchand, wrote to Ambassador Schmidt, "The sudden increase and easier access to the island have made it necessary to restrict landing to those persons who have legitimate reasons for being there." The Minister goes on to say, "I wish to emphasize that we welcome the Cruising Club of America to Canadian waters and have a high regard for their competence, goodwill and sense of responsibility. I must, however... withhold the requested permission." And so the matter sat for decades.

Recently there has been a change within the Canadian government's attitude toward granting permission to land. Articles have appeared in **BLUE WATER SAILING** (March 1997) and the **CCA NEWS** (December 1997), which outline how to obtain permission to land and sailing directions to Sable Island.

PREPARATION: To attempt a trip to Sable Island your yacht should be well prepared for offshore work. Be prepared for the worst. The weather must be near perfect. The most desirable conditions for landing are a high pressure system with moderate southerly winds which make Sable's north shore a safe lee. Landing on a beach here in a north wind is not advisable. Make sure that your electronic navigation system (Loran and/or GPS) is working perfectly, because the island is low and you probably won't see anything on the approach.

DIRECTIONS: Stay well off the bars at the western and (especially) the eastern ends of the island, because these bars extend out for many miles and surf may build here.

From whatever direction you are coming, position yourself approximately ten miles north of the center of the island. Do not try to "angle in" as tidal current and/or loss of power might ground you on a shoal. Keep an accurate Loran/GPS plot correlated with fathometer soundings. Given proper antenna height and a properly tuned set, you should see the island on radar at five miles. (During the summer months there usually is a night fog which burns off by midday.) The west light tower is an excellent reference point and a good mark to come in on. There is a fairly flat shelf of 20-25 feet on which to anchor.

Before dropping the hook, contact the island's weather station on VHF channel #16 or #8. Presumably you will have secured all your clearances and they will be expecting you.

On the very successful CCA cruise to Sable Island in August, 1998, yachts were given the waypoint 43°58.0'N, 60°01.5'W. From there, you should be able to see the light tower, the shoreline, and the meteorological station, and the beach is two miles south of this position.*

You must now choose how much farther you wish to move into the beach and what ground tackle to use. The bottom (not surprisingly) is soft sand. Then you must make a judgement as to whether to leave an anchor watch aboard. These decisions must be made by <u>you</u>.

Probably inflatables with a good outboard are best for landing, provided they aren't overloaded. A reconnaissance of the shore should be made to determine surf conditions. Find a gently-sloping beach. Remember to pull your tender well up beyond the surf. You must rely on your common sense as to how long to stay. (The Canadian Coast Guard discourages long visits.)

REMARKS: There is a lot of hype about Sable Island; but if you go, it is truly like a safari. Wild horses meet you on the beach or maybe sea lions (avoid landing near groups of sea lions). Take a change of shoes or light boots, as there is a large amount of marshland and sharp grass around the inner ponds.

Environment Canada has the attitude that these animals live in their own wild environment. There are no veterinarians, keepers, shepherds or domestic farmers. You easily come across the carcass of a dead horse or seal, but that's life and what nature is all about.

As you gather your documentation for this safari, you will hear many times: <u>Only take ashore what you intend to bring back</u>.

In the briefing we received at the R.N.Y.S. in Halifax before leaving for Sable, one ornithologist said to us, "You are the beginning of a new service — eco-tourism." And so we were.

A PLEA: We are fortunate the Government of Canada will allow us to land. Don't spoil it. Don't bring back the, "it is necessary to restrict landing to those persons who have legitimate reasons for being there" attitude of the 1970's. Be adult, respectful, and do what you are told. Otherwise none of us will be allowed to land on the island in the future.

To apply for permission to visit Sable Island, both the following offices should be contacted in writing:

Mr. Gerry Forbes
Sable Island Weather Station
c/o Canadian Dept. of Fisheries & Oceans
45 Alderney Drive
Dartmouth, Nova Scotia
CANADA B2Y 2N6
Telephone: (902) 453-9350

Ms. Nancy Hurlburt
 Director Marine Programs
Canadian Coast Guard
P.O. Box 1000
Dartmouth, Nova Scotia
CANADA B2Y 3Z8
Telephone: (902) 426-9022
hurlburtn@mar.dfo-mpo.gc.ca

The officials and telephone numbers frequently change in the Canadian government, so start with these names and numbers. It is best to telephone first to establish contact and make sure you are addressing the correct official and office. Then send in your written request, which should include:

(1) Reason for visit.

(2) Number of people and their names.

(3) Mode of transportation.

(4) Projected dates of arrival and
    departure.

Permission may take some time to be granted, so start this process early.

Nothing is forever. Geologists tell us the island is inexorably marching east, and sandbars shift. This location is only good for awhile.

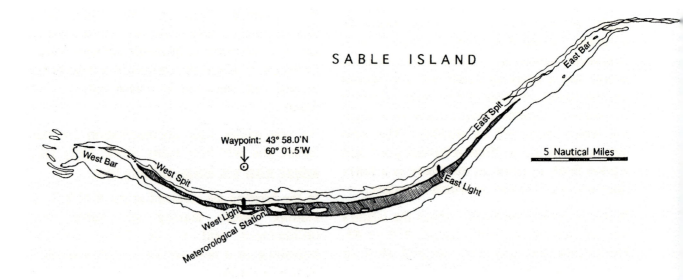

96

THE EASTERN SHORE

(Stretching from Egg Island to Cape Canso.)

Most visiting yachtsmen tend to pass this area in a hurry to get to Cape Breton, even though it is one of the finest cruising grounds in the Province. Of particular merit are the harbors between Egg Island and Liscomb, including such jewels as Shelter Cove, Beaver and Liscomb Harbours.

It is (or was) possible to navigate this coast in relatively sheltered water behind most of the islands, ledges and rocks that girdle this coast. In 1986 the Canadian Coast Guard removed many of the buoys which marked the famous "Inside Passage." Portions of this route are still marked, but unless you are sure your course inside and along shore are well marked, seek deeper water a few miles offshore and avoid the myriad obstacles closer in.

Offshore, a line of whistle buoys mark your progress east or west and the navigation is easy. At night, in clear weather, you are further aided by lighthouses spread out at five- to ten-mile intervals on which you can take bearings for position fixes. However, coming inshore in a fog in this area requires concentration, and you should lay your courses from one sound buoy to the next, even though it may lengthen your course. This is no place to lose your position, and even in the clearest weather, the islands and ledges tend to take on a vaguely similar quality which can cause confusion if you aren't paying attention.

As with most places that are a little difficult to get to, the rewards are great. Here are deserted harbors waiting to be explored and few other boats to inhibit your privacy.

THREE FATHOM HARBOUR*

44°37.9'N, 63°16.4'

Chart #4236

Rewritten and condensed from material by B. Aldrich, G. Lewis and E. Cabot

DIRECTIONS: From Shut-in Island bell (HX) run for one mile at 06° (mag) and leave the two red buoys to starboard.

ANCHORAGE AND BERTHS: Proceed as far north as your draft permits and you dare, leaving Ball Island to port for some protection from the bar that runs northeast from Ball Island, and anchor. A correspondent reports less than seven feet of water here. It is suggested that you use a stern anchor to keep from swinging over even more shoal.

The government wharf here has a reported depth of four feet on its end.

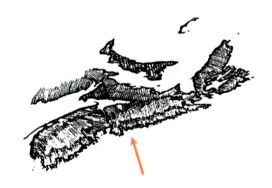

REMARKS: Dr. George Cabot reported in 1975 that, "This is a quaint little village worth a visit for those with shallow draft, but definitely *not a good haven in a southwest blow*. Getting in and out can be hairy, and the outer entrance can have breakers on either side when there's a sea running. There is no good protection from the southwest swell and very little swinging room.

FACILITIES: None.

*Caution should be used entering this harbor as it has not been reported on in the last ten years.

JEDDORE

44°43.5'N, 63°00.5'W

Chart: #4236

Rewritten and condensed from earlier material by Victor Mader, Alexander Fowler, Howard French, Fredrick Rhinelander, Bayard Clarkson, Eric Swenson and Larry & Maxine Bailey.   *2001*
.

DIRECTIONS: Jeddore Harbour is approached by picking up Thorne Shoal flashing bell (YT5) on a course toward the high land on East Head. Favor the east side of the entrance in order to avoid Thorne Shoal which makes out from the land on the west side. There is a succession of green markers to be left to port, and particular attention should be paid to the mud banks at Marsh Point and the west side of the harbor in general.

ANCHORAGE AND BERTHS: There are two reported anchorages in Jeddore: the first between Bakers Point and Marsh Point, and the second off Rum Point. The mud banks on the west side of these anchorages (previously mentioned) are to be treated with caution, though the channel is reported to be well marked with green and red stakes. The holding ground is fair to poor, owing to grass patches on the bottom and a one-knot tidal current through the harbor which may flip your anchor flukes. Plenty of scope and caution is advisable here.

The Government Dock at East Jeddore appears to be in poor condition, with the anchorage near it full of lobster pots.

The channel beyond East Jeddore is buoyed. One can securely anchor at the end of this channel, off Brown Island.

REMARKS: Jeddore receives mixed reviews from cruising folk -- from, "the first good anchorage east from Halifax," to "I don't care much for it." However, many mariners are glad to see it, particularly when cruising east and seeking a suitable harbor for the night.

The name of the place is either a corruption of the name Theodore or it is named for an eighteenth-century Indian named Ned Jeddore. (Perhaps both stories are true.)

FACILITIES: None.

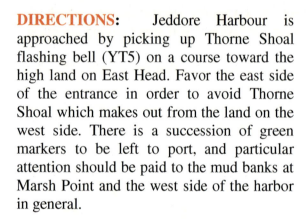

OWLS HEAD BAY*

44°44.2'N, 62°49.7'W

Chart #4236

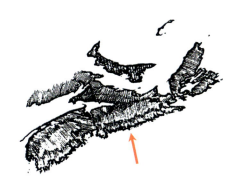

Rewritten and condensed from earlier material by Joseph Guild, Frank and Mary Calderone, Richard Lemmerman, MacCallum Grant and John McKelvy.

DIRECTIONS: Locate Owls Head light and bell buoy; from there steer 339° (mag), leaving Owls Head lighthouse to port and Cable Island to starboard and continue into Owls Head Bay. In foggy conditions the fog tends to scale-up as you proceed toward the light and beyond, owing to the high bluffs just to the west of the light and bay. Once past the light, the shore is bold.

ANCHORAGE AND BERTHS: There are two anchorages, one in Southwest Cove which is small and well sheltered, and one off the wharf on chart #4236 - both of these are located on the west side of the bay. The bottom is reported to be mud and the holding ground good. At the wharf area, the fishermen generally keep their boats on the wharves in settled weather, but maintain moorings for rough (easterly) weather. It is sometimes possible to ask for a mooring for overnight if one is not in use. There is always a slight "bobble" here, and because the harbor is open to the south and east, there can be a very uncomfortable swell. A berth can be had at the dock, but you must remember that if the wind shifts east, you are on a lee shore here.

REMARKS: The problem of easterlies and the swell notwithstanding, this is *an excellent harbor in settled summer weather.* The scenery is pretty, the fishermen are friendly (one offered a Guide correspondent the use of his private telephone), and it is not too long a way in or out when cruising to the east or west.

FACILITIES: None.

*Caution should be used entering this harbor as it has not been reported on in the last ten years.

SHIP HARBOUR

(Including False Passage, Deep Cove and Passage Island)

44°47.5'N , 62°49.5'W

Chart #4236

Rewritten and condensed from earlier material by Judge Curtis Bok, T.F.T. Morland, C.W. Bartlett , M.S. Grant, with new material by R. Nostrand, and W.Cook 2004

DIRECTIONS: Coming from offshore, the dangers in the entrance to Ship Harbour are (from west to east) Friar Ledges, Bear Rock, and the ledges south of Borgles Island. There is also a back passage in from the west called False Passage which skirts the NW side of Wolfes Island and is described below. Once past the outer hazards, the entrance between Beach and Black Points, though narrow, is reasonably clear except for Black Rock which lies south of Black Point. Inside the harbor, the channel is well marked. Going to the head of the harbor, care should be taken between White Rocks and Garret Ledge just short of Eisans Point.

ANCHORAGE AND BERTHS: A good anchorage is reported just west of Beach Point and east of Whale Island. Another good anchorage is reported to be in Siteman's Cove (see Chart #4236 inset), halfway between

Whale Island and Garret Island in 6 feet. The cove on the south side of Borgles Island is adequately protected by a row of small islands. Bill Cook found low water depths of 8' or more as far as the east end of these islands and good holding. The ledge on the south side of the entrance appears to extend further than shown on chart #4236 and is not visible at more than half tide. There is a government wharf east of Salmon Point with 12 feet of water on the end.

REMARKS: Charlie Bartlett described Ship Harbour in 1971 as, "nothing but a long estuary with a couple of government wharves, very few houses and almost no fishermen or activity. This harbour is 11 miles from the Ship Harbour whistle buoy. Unless the weather is threatening or time is unimportant, you will probably do better in Deep Cove or Passage Island, both described below.

FACILITIES: None

FALSE PASSAGE

DIRECTIONS: Passing from E to W, leave Passage Island close on the starboard hand and head for Cable Island. When past the rocks south and west of Passage Island, swing to the S and head for Little Shag Rock. At half tide there is a minimum of seven feet over this bar which is composed of smooth, hard sand. When abreast of Cable Island, keep well to the east side, running down halfway between Wolfes Island and Little Shag Rock. When the latter is abeam, head for Shag Rock (resembling the Rock of Gibralter). The reef on Wolfes Island appears to extend farther towards Cable Island than the chart says. When about 3 cables (3/10 mile) from Shag Rock, alter for Owls Head lighthouse.

DEEP COVE

This cove is located on the northwest side of Borgles Island, and it is described as "the best available anchorage in this area without going well inland." Anchor halfway between the 2-foot ledge and the apex of the cove.

PASSAGE ISLAND

This is a secure and snug little stopover anchorage in the mouth of Ship Harbour. It has good holding ground and perfect protection from wind and surge all the way from south through the west and including north-northwest. The island is easily found from seaward by simply skirting Wolfes Island, leaving it to port. The anchorage has no nasty surprises - just enter the bight which opens to the east.

SHOAL BAY AND TANGIER HARBOUR

44°47'N, 62°45.4'W   44°47.8'N, 62°42.4'W

Chart #4236

Rewritten and condensed from earlier material by T. Morland, M. Grant, V. Spooner, A. Weld and R. Carter.   1991

DIRECTIONS: **Shoal Bay** may be entered via the approach to Ship Harbour. Going north, bring Bear Rock close to port, then head for Tuckers Head on the western tip of Borgles Island. Then head for Round Island on the north side of Borgles island; it is wooded, and soon appears at the far end of the passage. To the right of Round Island is a conspicuous high white rock which is on the beach of Borgles Island, about 1/4 mile east of Round Island. Leave Little Island (just south of Round Island) and Round Island close to port and progress into Shoal Bay.

Alternatively, you may enter Shoal Bay through the passage between Borgles Island and the Baltee Islands which presents no problems in clear weather.

Tangier Harbour may be entered from Shoal Bay through the marked channel (indicated "Channel Buoyed" on Chart #4236) between Inner Baltee Island and Indian Point on the mainland. Coming from offshore, stay 1/4 mile east of Tangier Island, and feel your way NNW up the harbor for 1 1/4 miles to green buoy YK1 which must be left to port. Now steer NW for Hog Island, being sure to leave Shad Ledge (the dot over the "G" in "TANGIER HARBOUR" on Chart #4236) to port.

ANCHORAGES AND BERTHS: In **Shoal Bay** there is an anchorage in the extreme northwest cove west of Carters Point, with 25 feet of water and good mud holding ground. Here is reported to be a government wharf (condition unknown) with 9 feet on its end. There is also a good anchorage in the area of Beaver Bluff, where you must be careful to avoid Mercury Rock.

In **Tangier Harbour** there is a good anchorage just to the north of Hog Island in 15 feet. Another anchorage is off the fish dock in the northeast corner of the harbor by Mason Point. The government wharf in Tangier Harbour is in very poor condition (1991) and has a depth of 18 feet off its end.

REMARKS: Both Shoal Bay and Tangier are beautiful anchorages with numerous uninhabited islands covered with dense stands of spruce and inhabited by curious seals.

The one-mile walk on the road east from Tangier Village brings you to the *Willie Krauch Smokehouse* where salmon and mackerel are smoked for export. If you like smoked fish, these are delicious.

POPES HARBOUR

(Including Harbour Island, Shelter Cove, and Gerard Passage)

44°47.8'N, 62°39.3'W

Chart #4236

Rewritten and condensed from earlier material by T.F.T. Morland, E. Cabot, M. Grant, J. McKelvy and N.McKelvy 2004

DIRECTIONS: Popes Harbour refers to the body of water bounded on the east by Gerard Island and on the west by the peninsula which contains Porcupine Hill and Shelter Cove (and it shouldn't be confused with the town of Popes Harbour which lies north of Gerard Island on the mainland).

Coming from the east, steer 306°(mag.) for 6.5 miles in from the red whistle buoy (X26) west-southwest of Geddes Shoal past the bell (YA2) south of Redman Shoal. From the west, find the Mo A (YJ), two miles SE of Tangier Island, then steer 85° (mag.) for 1.5 miles to the can (YE1) SE of Horse Rock. From the Horse Rock can (HE1) steer 359° (mag.) for 1.7 miles to the bell (YE2) off Popes Head. From the YE2 bell, proceed on course 324° (mag.) which will take you past the green Buoy southeast of Schooner Rock and bring you up on Grum Point opposite the red buoy and light on **Harbour Island**.

In fog the green buoy off Schooner Rock is sometimes hard to see, though the fog should scale up as you head inland behind the peninsula. If bound for **Shelter Cove**, wait until the cove visually opens up on a bearing of 265° (mag.), then turn to port thus avoiding the rock. On entering the cove, favor the south side of the entrance to avoid the shallow spot off the unnamed island to the north.

ANCHORAGE AND BERTHS: In the **Harbour Island** area, proceed past the red buoy and light, around to the north side of the island and anchor practically anywhere. If this isn't snug enough for you, move further around the island to the cove on its east side and anchor in 15 feet with a mud bottom. In **Shelter Cove**, anchor anywhere but the extreme southwest end.

There are no wharves in any of these anchorages.

REMARKS: **Shelter Cove** is a beautiful and fairly secluded anchorage (even though some sporadic camping exists on its shoreline). In 2004 Nancy McKelvy noted that new Chart # 4236 did not show enough water to enter the cove. (As charts are rationalized regretfully detail is lost – hence the importance of sketches –ed)

At one time Shelter Cove was called Molly's Cove, and during Prohibition (yes, the Canadian's had a Prohibition too!) it was a rumrunner's rendezvous. Apparently schooners would secure spruce trees to their topmasts and blend in with the scenery.

For a pleasant walk, row your dinghy to the west end of the cove, tie it to some bushes or rocks, and walk over the marshy grass patch to the beach facing west. If desired, cross this same marshy patch at its southern end (there are trees and bushes here) and walk southeast to the beach facing — a good place for a picnic on a nice day.

A primitive road has been cut down to the cove's northern side. Otherwise the shores are wild and secluded.

FACILITIES: None.

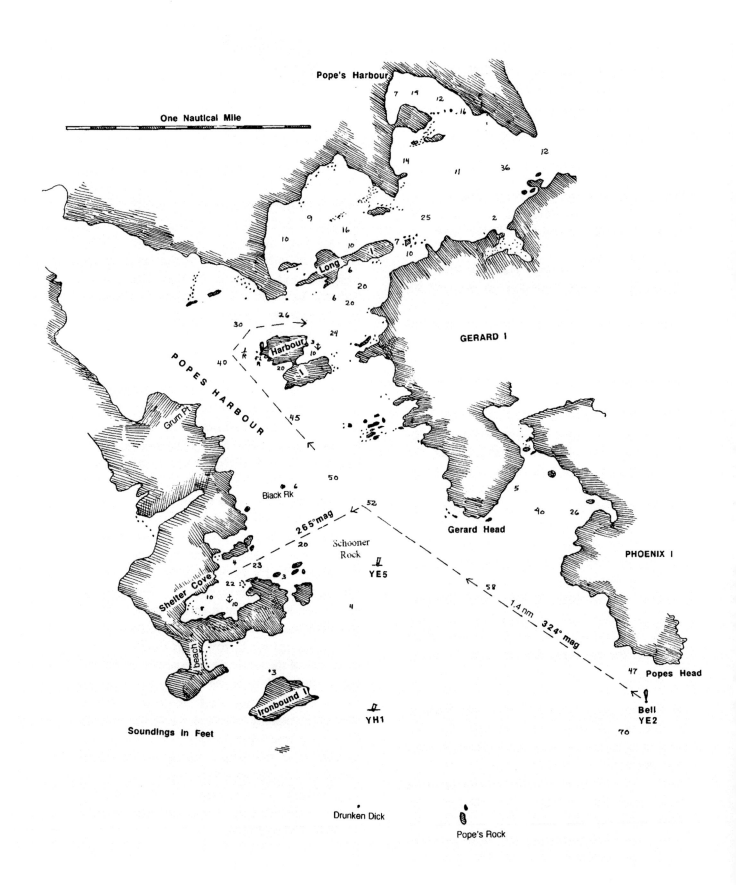

One Nautical Mile

Pope's Harbour

7 19   12
14
11   36
9   25   2
16
10   10   7
Long   1   10
6   20
6   20
26
30   24
40   Harbour   3
10
20   1
45

POPES HARBOUR

GERARD I

Grum Pt.

Black Rk   6
50
52
20   Schooner
Rock
4   23
YE5
22   3
10   4
Shelter Cove
beach   3   Ironbound I

265°mag

5
Gerard Head

40   26

PHOENIX I

58   1.4 nm   324°mag

47 Popes Head

Bell
YE2
70

YH1

Soundings in Feet

Drunken Dick

Pope's Rock

104

GERARD PASSAGE

From the anchorage behind Harbour Island, there is a beautiful waterway through to the head of Spry Harbour, between the mainland and Gerard Island.

Bound east from Harbour Island and nearing the west end of Long Island, leave the one fathom spot to port. Nearing the east end of Long island, keep close to the point of the island to avoid some rocks off the islet in the middle of the channel (8' to 10' can be carried through here). You are now in a completely enclosed bay 1/2 mile across with 3 to 5 fathoms throughout. On the north side is a small cove (the town of Popes Harbour) containing some fishermen's wharves with 2 fathoms; when entering it, leave the rock in the middle of the entrance to port. [This is reported to be a decent anchorage, but uninteresting and noisy due to the traffic on the nearby highway -ed.] The channel out to Spry Harbour has a minimum depth of 25'. Pass 50 yards from the end of Dutchtown Point and keep parallel to it for the next 300 yards to avoid the shallow patch between it and Gerard Island.

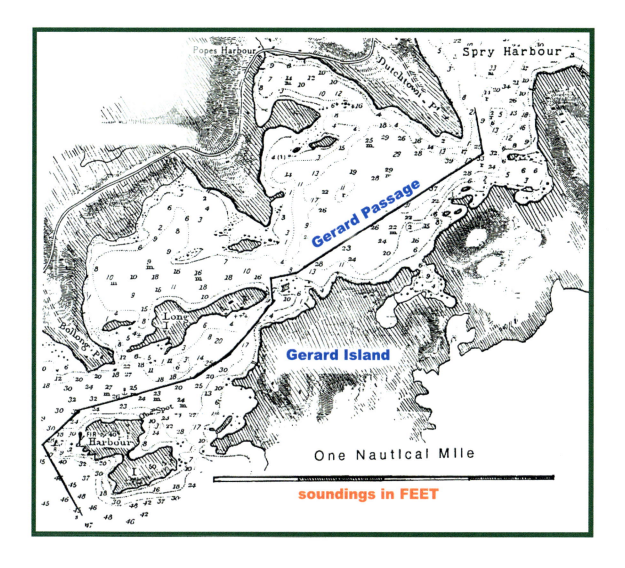

One Nautical Mile

soundings in FEET

SPRY HARBOUR*

44°49.1'N, 62°38.9'W

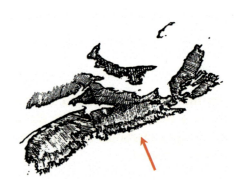

Chart #4236

Rewritten and condensed from material by P. Richmond.

DIRECTIONS: Find the red Spry Bay bell buoy (YA2) just south of Redman Shoal and proceed on course 000° (mag.). This course will lead you past Mad Moll to starboard and Maloney Rock to port; after 3 miles you will come to Bald Rock, visible at any tide. From Bald Rock, swing to course 315° (mag.) and proceed into Spry Harbour.

ANCHORAGES AND BERTHS: Anchor anywhere to the east of Dutchtown Point in good (mud) holding ground. This anchorage has excellent protection from every wind but the southeast.

FACILITIES: None.

*Caution should be used entering this harbor as it has not been reported on in the last ten years.

MUSHABOOM HARBOUR*

(Including Malagash Cove)

44°50'N, 62°34.3'W

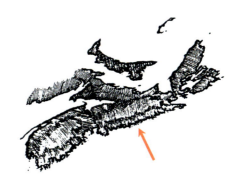

Chart: #4236 for Mushaboom Harbour
Chart: #4235 for Malagash Cove, The Gates, and MacPhee Passages

Rewritten and condensed from material by T. Morland, H. Franch and F. McRoberts.

DIRECTIONS: Coming from the west, if you take the inside passage from Popes Harbour via Gerard Passage, it is necessary to make an excursion to sea around Taylor Head. Mad Moll Reef extends 3/4 mile southwest and is marked by a red cone (YA4). Course 100° (mag.) from this buoy will take you 1/4 mile off Taylor Head, and when it is abeam, come to 45° (mag.) which will take you east of Psyche Island. Midway between Psyche and Salisbury Islands, alter to 324° (mag.), a course which will take you under Bull Beach in Mushaboom Harbour.

MacPhee Passage from Mushaboom Harbour between Salisbury and Carroll Islands has 25 feet of water in it and takes you toward Sheet Rock and the entrance to Sheet Harbour.

Going east, after passing the south side of the islet in the eastern end of the passage, a course of 65° (mag.) will take you between Western and Danbury Islands. Abreast of Roach Island you will pass between two visible piles of rock about 400 yards apart, but there is over 30 feet of water here.

The Gates passage, from Mushaboom Harbour between Gibbs and Malagash Islands north of MacPhee Passage, provides a short cut to Malagash Cove and Sheet Harbour.

Going east, pass north of the islets showing in the mouth of the channel, then round down a little to the south to avoid a 4-foot patch about 400 yards inside the eastern entrance. Minimum depth through here is 20 feet.

ANCHORAGE AND BERTHS: In **Mushaboom Harbour,** anchor off Bull Beach.

In **Malagash Cove** there is a good anchorage southwest of the rock in the middle of the cove. This location is well-protected from all winds except the northeast.

In **The Gates** there is great temptation to anchor in the area just north of Gibbs and Roach Islands. In spite of what appears on the chart, this passage carries 10 fathoms through most of it right up to the islands, making it too deep to anchor comfortably. The only place to anchor here is in the little cove on the northwest side of Gibbs Island, BUT you will share this anchorage with a large rock jutting offshore which one correspondent reports to be very disquieting.

REMARKS: All these anchorages are scenic and very pleasant.

FACILITIES: None.

*Caution should be used entering these harbors as they haven't been reported on in the last ten years.

The withdrawal of Chart #4361 from the Canadian Catalogue of Nautical Charts has greatly reduced the detail of knowledge of the Malagash Cove-Gates and MacPhee Passages area. To assist those who wish to transit or anchor in this beautiful area, the Guide presents the following chartlet for your reference. We believe this chartlet is reasonably accurate, but cannot assume responsibility for any mishaps that may occur to anyone relying on this chartlet.

SOUNDINGS IN FEET

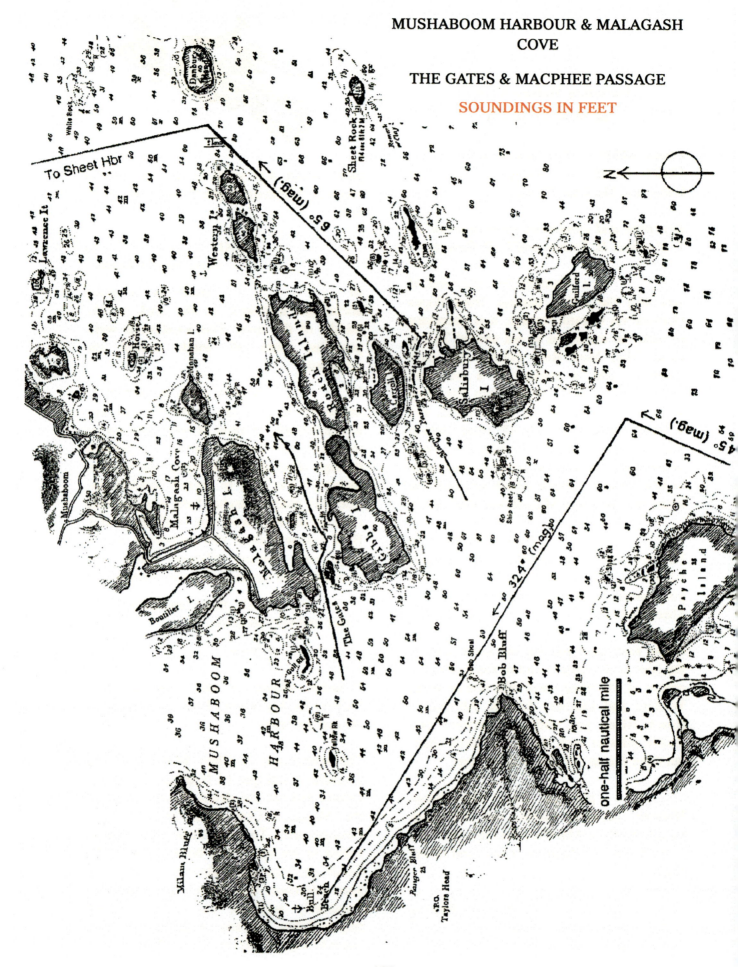

SHEET HARBOUR

44°54.9'N, 62°32.0'W

Chart #4235

Rewritten and condensed from earlier material by Frank and Mary Calderone, Bailey Aldrich, T.F.T. Morland, Francis Moore, Arnold Forrest, W.F. Close and Alvin Zink.

DIRECTIONS: The key to entering Sheet Harbour is to locate Sheet Rock, an easy matter in good visibility, but difficult in fog. (Sheet Rock lighthouse once was manned and had a foghorn, but man and horn are now gone making fog navigation here difficult.)

Inside courses from the west through the Gates and MacPhee Passage from Mushaboom Harbour are discussed in the "Mushaboom and Malagash" section.

From the east it is necessary to locate buoy XP7 (formerly Sheet Harbour Passage light and bell) off Fishery Point; then continue on a westerly course so as to avoid the ledges off Fishery Island and MacDonald Rock, both of which should be kept to the north of your course; then shift course gradually north for Sheet Rock.

It is best to keep Sheet Rock to the west on entering as there are rocks south and west of it. From Sheet Rock, steer 10° (mag.) between Danbury and Western Islands—one of which is sure to be visible in thick fog.

Inside these islands, proceed up the harbor carefully from buoy to buoy. Sometimes these small buoys may be difficult to see, in which case prudence would dictate keeping in the middle of the channel.

ANCHORAGES AND BERTHS: This area abounds with pleasant anchorages. The first is behind **East Gibbs Island**, which regrettably is open to easterlies. In finding your way into this anchorage, do not be seduced into anchoring in the bight in the northeast side of West Gibbs Island unless you enjoy sharing this tight anchorage with a large rock across which you may swing. Further to the north is **Malagash Cove** (noted previously), also open to the east. If the easterlies do blow, however, there is **Hurd Cove**, which is best entered from the north, leaving Gull Ledge (which doesn't show at high tide) to starboard and Coomb Point to port.

In days gone by, Hurd Cove marked the western end of Sheet Harbour Passage, a back entrance north of Sober Island into Sheet Harbour, now effectively blocked by a bridge with 4' of clearance. This blocked passage affords an excellent snug anchorage north of **Sober Island** which is protected from all quarters but must be entered from the east. Two lights form a range clearly marked on the chart to guide you in from the south. Inside, beware of the shallow bar between the two islands in mid-harbor. Fresh water enters this anchorage from the northeast via a small reversing falls.

Up in Sheet Harbour proper, beware of the bar by Church Point which extends well out from the eastern shore. There is a good anchorage above Church Point marked "SHEET HARBOUR" on chart #4235.

There is a government wharf in the Northwest Arm as well as some private wharves where one may lie with permission. A good government wharf is on the north side of Sober Island in the Sober Island anchorage mentioned above. The government wharf in the Northwest Arm is reported to be in poor condition.

REMARKS: Sheet Harbour (pop. 600) is considered by many to be the best harbor east of Halifax in terms of supplies, and one of the best for protection. Until recently this was a mill town, but the pulp mill burned down and times are hard. This coupled with a six-mile run in from Sheet Rock, makes it less appealing unless you have a great need for supplies or shelter.

FACILITIES: No dockside fuel or water is available. There are: a gas station, a motel (with a restaurant), and more importantly, an R.C.M.P. detachment, a hospital and a liquor store.

BEAVER HARBOUR

44°54'N, 62°25.3'W

Chart #4235

Rewritten and condensed from earlier material by C. Bok, P. Richmond, T.F.T. Morland, H. Jones, D. Fuller, J. McKelvy; update by A. Weld. 2001

DIRECTIONS: An inside passage runs from Sheet Harbour through the Bay of Islands; however, this is not recommended because several correspondents have reported an uncharted ledge SE of Round Island (at 44°50.8'N, 62°24.6'W— right where there is supposed to be good water). Also, the Canadian Government, due to a changing pattern in the fisheries, no longer maintains some of the buoys critical for a stranger to navigate this passage.

For peace of mind, find the bell (XK3) east of Beaver Island, then come to course 336° (mag.) which will bring you past Horse and Sutherland Islands and Beaver Point to port, as well as Harbour Rock (visible on a clear day) to starboard. Inside Beaver Point there are several anchorages.

ANCHORAGES AND BERTHS: One mile northwest of Beaver Point there are two green buoys (XK17 and XK19). Rounding these buoys to port and turning south, you enter a tiny bay that resembles an upside-down horse's head. This narrow entrance has 8' to10' in it; proceed slowly. **"Horse's Head Harbour"** (as it was named by Judge Bok in the 1953 Guide) is a tight anchorage with good holding ground and is lovely under the right circumstances (see REMARKS below).

Another attractive anchorage is at **the mouth of the Salmon River at Port Dufferin**, where the holding ground is excellent, but the area is somewhat exposed to the southwest. The Government Wharf is gone.

One can land a dinghy on the private wharf below the church on the east side of Port Dufferin, as well as at the small wharf owned by the motel north of the church.

The wharf at Factory Cove is now privately owned.

REMARKS: Horse's Head Harbour is one of the prettiest on the coast. You can easily anchor among the local boats moored here, but in 1986 half this harbor was sealed off by wire lines on floats for an aquaculture project. One Guide correspondent got tangled in these lines, became disabled and had to be towed out! These aquaculture projects tend to come and go, and in future years this harbor may be totally clear. In any event, be prepared to move on to Salmon River or perhaps the town of Beaver Harbour if it looks too dicey.

FACILITIES: None in Horse's Head. There is a general store in Port Dufferin for basic necessities.

NECUM TEUCH

(Felker Cove)
44°55.9'N, 62°15.9'W

Chart #4235

Rewritten and condensed from material by M. Grant, R.Lemmerman and A.Campbell   2003

As **Felker Cove** isn't marked on Chart #4235, for fast identification purposes, it is the cove just south and west of Moose Head which is approximately 3 miles southwest of the town of Necum Teuch on Chart #4235.

DIRECTIONS: There once was a marked inside route from Beaver Harbour to Felker Cove, but the Canadian Coast Guard has removed some of the key buoys, so don't try to do this.

From seaward, steer for Harbour Rock, then on to Ship Island. Leave Ship Island close to port and come to course 295° (mag.) for 1.2 miles, and pass Moose Head and the rock off it to starboard, and proceed into the cove.

ANCHORAGE AND BERTHS: Anchor at the head of the cove in 10 feet of water. The holding ground is good mud, and the anchorage is protected from all winds except southeast and all seas except a southeast swell. A.Campbell touched an uncharted rock at dead low water just about where the "18" is marked on the chartlet. He recommends a more southerly course than shown on the chartlet using the headland as a steering point and turning north close to the shore when the soundings fall below 20ft.

REMARKS: Felker Cove is a pretty place and once had a shingle mill at its head. Necum teuch is now blessed with foul smelling seaweed which spawns very active flies! A beautiful place but only for the nasally challenged!

The withdrawal of Chart #4355 from the Canadian Catalogue of Nautical Charts has greatly reduced the detail of knowledge about Felker Cove. To assist those who would visit this beautiful area, the Guide presents the following chartlet for your reference. We believe this chartlet to be reasonably accurate, but cannot assume responsibility for any mishaps that occur to anyone relying on this chartlet.

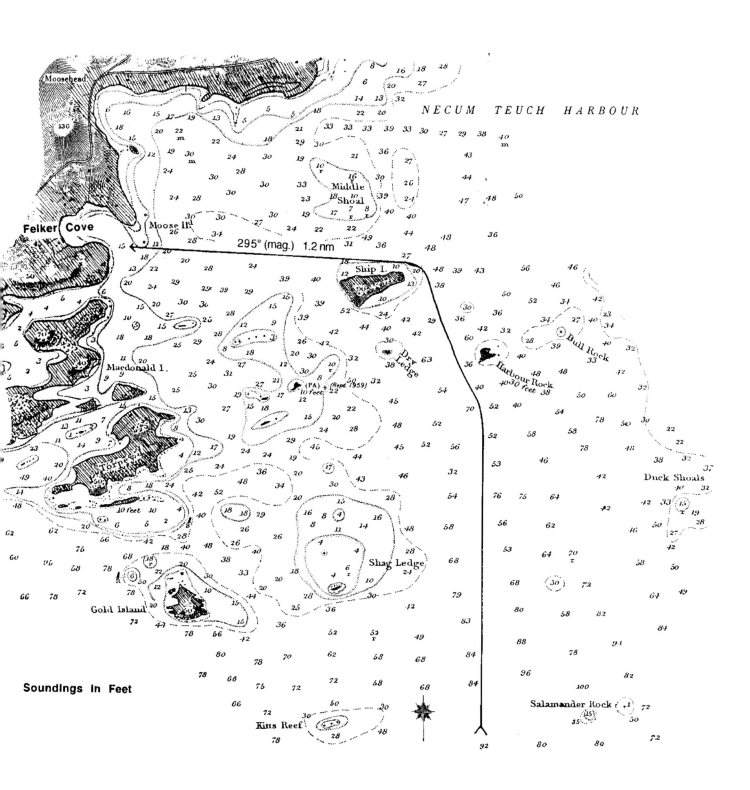

Moosehead

NECUM TEUCH HARBOUR

Middle Shoal

Felker Cove

Moose Id

295° (mag.) 1.2 nm

Ship I.

Dry Ledge

Bull Rock

Harbour Rock
30 feet

Macdonald I.

(PA) (Repd. 1959)
10 feet

Torpe

Duck Shoals

10 feet

Shag Ledge

Gold Island

Salamander Rock

Soundings In Feet

Kins Reef

113

MITCHELL BAY

44°56.7'N, 62°11.4'W

Chart #4235

John H. Harries   1993

DIRECTIONS: *From the east*, proceed into Necum Teuch Bay and then into Mitchell Bay by using the entrance between Hartings Island and High Island. <u>Be</u> <u>very</u> <u>sure</u> <u>you</u> <u>have</u> <u>the</u> <u>correct</u> <u>entrance</u>, since all the islands look the same. *If coming west* from the inland passage: from Deepwater Island run a course of 38° (mag.) between Calf Island and the second rock southwest of Mitchell Point. [The area around Deepwater Island looks pretty shallow to me. -ed.]

ANCHORAGE: There seem to be many options in this cove as the chart indicates. Be very wary of Barney Ledge in the middle of the Bay and the rocks off Barney Point on the east side. Two good anchorages are: **(1)** in the small cove just north of Barney Point, and **(2)** in the cove on the northeast end of Hartlings Island.

REMARKS: This is a pretty harbor with only a few small cottages on the northeast shore.

WHITE ISLANDS

44°53.2'N, 62°07.5'W

Chart #4235

From Robert S. Carter

DIRECTIONS: Approach the most western of the White Islands from the north.

ANCHORAGE: There is a shelf at the west end of Long Island where one can anchor with good holding ground in fair weather, but it is open to the north and west.

REMARKS: *This is a luncheon stop only*, but the island and adjacent Camp Island form a natural breakwater with attractive walks on the most magnificent sweep of rock you will find. These islands are a bird refuge.

ECUM SECUM

44°57.6'N, 62°08.2'W

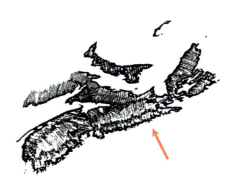

Chart: #4235

Rewritten and condensed from earlier material by G.P. Gardner, T.F.T Morland, R.M. Love, R. Lemmerman, V.C. Gray, M.S. Grant, S. Dumaresq and R. Carter.   *1993*

The *harbor* of Ecum Secum refers to Ecum Secum Inlet. The *town* of Ecum Secum is located on Back Cove, one mile east of the inlet. Both are reported to be pleasant harbors, though the inlet is more protected from the south.

DIRECTIONS: In days of yore there was an "inside passage" behind many of the off-lying islands and ledges between Halifax and White Head at the entrance to Canso Bay. Ecum Secum was more popular then because of its convenience as a stopover en route. Unfortunately, many of the key buoys on the inside passage have been removed, and today safety dictates clearing and entering many Eastern Shore harbors from offshore. (The inside passage still exists, but we recommend you have local knowledge to use it.)

From offshore, locate White Island bell (VV1) and steer a northerly course. Leave Little White Island, Hubbub Rock and Frenchman Rock to starboard, and Tuffin Shoal to port. From Harbour Rock there is a choice of proceeding to Ecum Secum Inlet between Hardwood Island and Necum Point, or going into Back Cove (being careful to avoid Ballast Shoal). This is the clearest approach to Ecum Secum.

ANCHORAGE AND BERTHS: There are two anchorages in the area, the most obvious being in Ecum Secum Inlet behind Hardwood Island. Here you may anchor north of the government wharf in 14'-18' of water. The bottom is soft mud and it is difficult, though not impossible, to get a good bite here. Back Cove offers the other anchorage, less desirable because it is exposed to the south. The Guide has no report as to the condition of the holding ground.

A government wharf with seven feet of water on the end is located in the southwest corner of Ecum Secum Inlet. Another government wharf is at the head of Back Cove with five feet of water on the end. There is also an open-ended breakwater protecting the wharf at Back Cove and it has been suggested that you may tie up to this, but no soundings are presently available.

REMARKS: Ecum Secum is apparently the Indian name for "red bank." The inlet is charming and you can pick berries on Hardwood Island in season. The Ecum Secum River (said to be stocked with salmon) marks the division between Halifax and Guysborough Counties.

FACILITIES: In Ecum Secum Inlet, no fuel, water or supplies are available.
In Back Cove, groceries and basic supplies are available, but again, no fuel or water.

MARIE JOSEPH HARBOUR*

44°58'N, 62°04.6'W

Charts: #4234, #4235

Robert S. Carter

The entry from offshore and the west is hampered by having the entry courses divided between chart #4235 and #4234. The chart for the harbor itself is #4234.

DIRECTIONS: From offshore from the vicinity of the White Islands, steer in a northerly direction for the west side of Crooks Island, leaving Little White Island and The Hubbub to starboard, Tuffin Shoal and High Ledges to port. Keep Frenchman and Siteman Rocks to starboard. Swing to an easterly direction and pass between Ram Island and Hapes Point. Leaving Hapes Points to port, there is a choice of entering Marie Joseph Harbour by leaving Round Island either to port or starboard. The west entrance (leaving Round Island to starboard) is partially blocked by a large rock, whereas the east entrance (leaving Round Island to port and Turners Island to starboard) is the safest route, subject to the note below.** Once in Marie Joseph Harbour, proceed northeast between Turners Island and Lobster Point into Hawbolt Cove. From the east the channel in between Barren Island and Smith Point is well-buoyed.

ANCHORAGE AND BERTHS: In **Hawbolt Cove**, anchor north of the government wharf in 10' of water. The holding ground is mud and good. The government wharf has 8' on the end at low water.

REMARKS: Hawbolt Cove offers good protection from all winds, though a southeaster would make the harbor rough, given the two-mile fetch that such a wind would have.

FACILITIES: Neither fuel nor water is available. A general store is across the street from the fish wharf, selling basic provisions.

*This harbor should be entered with caution as it has not been reported on in the last ten years.

**In August 1988 the passage between Round and Turners Islands was choked with aquaculture nets marked by very low (radar-proof) buoys, making this a very dangerous area. Be alert here!

The withdrawal of Chart #4356 from the Canadian Catalogue of Nautical Charts has greatly reduced the detail of knowledge of the Marie Joseph Harbour area. To assist those who wish to transit or anchor in this beautiful area, the Guide presents the following chart for reference. We believe this chartlet is reasonably accurate, but cannot assume responsibility for mishaps that may occur to anyone relying on this chartlet.

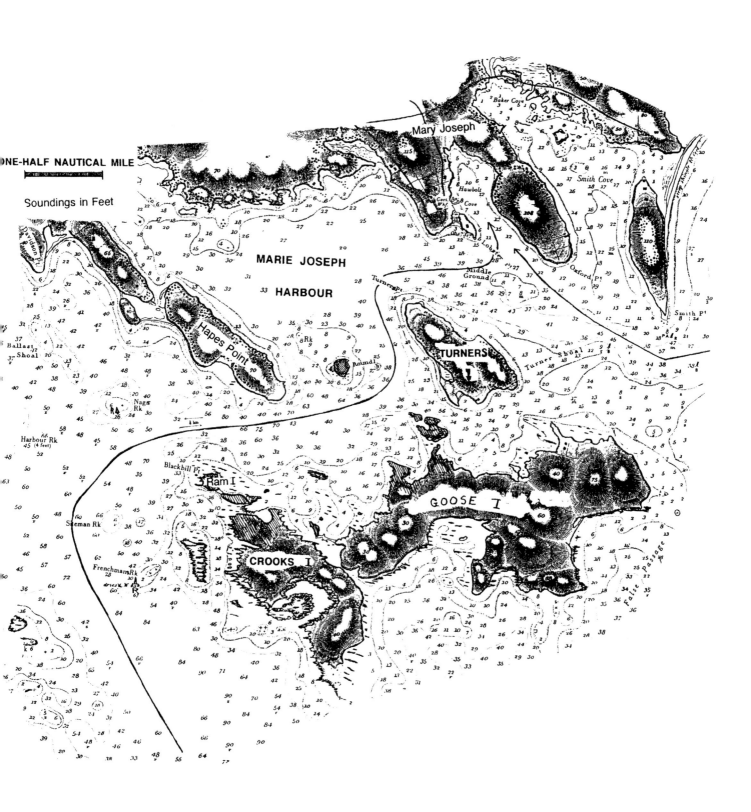

ONE-HALF NAUTICAL MILE

Soundings in Feet

MARIE JOSEPH

HARBOUR

Mary Joseph

Hapes Point

TURNERS

GOOSE I

Ram I

Blackbill Pt

CROOKS I

LISCOMB

45°00.4'N, 62°06'W

Chart #4234

Rewritten and condensed from earlier material by G Whitely, M.S. Grant, J. Schroeder and J. McKelvy. Update by Steve Taylor.   2002

DIRECTIONS: The name "Liscomb" means almost any place along the four miles between Little Liscomb and Liscomb Mills, though most cruising folk think of Liscomb Mills when you mention the name.

There is a strong horn at Cranberry Point on Liscomb Island to guide you in from offshore. Once under Smoke Point, any fog should begin to scale up, and the shores being bold, you should see any danger before getting into trouble.

ANCHORAGE AND BERTHS: At **Liscomb** there is a pleasant anchorage known as "Gaspereau Brook" (not labeled on the chart) in the little inlet northwest of Hemloe Island, west of the 100' hill. It is a pretty, landlocked basin 1/4 mile up the narrow estuary from Little Liscomb Harbour. On the west side of Liscomb Harbour there is a government wharf with a reported depth of 9' on the end.

At **Spanish Ship Bay**, enter slowly, favoring the east side, and leave all buoys to port. Once inside, anchor anywhere; the holding ground is good. There are no wharves here.

Liscomb Mills may be found by proceeding west across Liscomb Harbour to Riley's Island which you must leave to port. Pass north of this island, then turn north up the buoyed channel in the Liscomb River. Favor the west side of this channel, as mud banks build out from the east side. You may get the feeling there's nothing up here, but as you turn the final corner, you will find a dock and float (usually with several cruising boats tied to it). This is a tight but very adequate area in which to tie up (often alongside another boat). Sometimes a mooring is available in this little basin to which you will be directed, providing your boat is small enough to have swing room. For those who find this area too tight, anchor in the river's elbow and row the 1/4 mile up river to the dock.

REMARKS: For peace and quiet, anchor in Spanish Ship Bay. There probably won't be anyone there but you.

For pleasant contact with civilization, however, go to Liscomb Mills. The dock here is run by *Liscomb Lodge*, one of the hotels owned by the Province of Nova Scotia— these are generally considered to be hotels of standard good quality. There will be a wharfage fee which will cover the use of the facilities including shower and electricity.

Older Nova Scotia hands will recall Liscomb Lodge when it was owned and operated by Commander "Trigger" Wadds, one of the saltier characters of the coast. Since 1976 the province has run this lodge, only a short walk from the dock, which consists of a number of cabins (called "chalets") and a main dining room with a craft shop and reception area. The crafts for sale (particularly the quilts) are most attractive. The food and service are also very good (try the "planked salmon," specialty of the Lodge). This is a great place to hole in for a spell of bad weather, avoiding cabin fever with an occasional walk and good food cooked by someone else.

FACILITIES: At Liscomb, no facilities are reported.

At Spanish Ship Bay, you can row ashore, stumble through some thickets to the road where, after a short walk, you will find a general store with very basic supplies. At Liscomb Mills (Liscomb Lodge) there is electricity, fuel, water, ice, laundry and showers, a nice pool and a game room. As noted, there is a good restaurant here and the lodge will give you a ride in their microbus to the local shopping center for supplies.

New Chart #4234 is so lacking in detail that one is discouraged from entering Liscomb Harbour from the east through the passage north of Liscomb Island (between Liscomb and Henloe Islands). The following chartlet shows that eight feet can be safely carried through this passage by positioning yourself midway between Hog and Liscomb Islands, then avoiding Gravel Point and favoring Hemloe Island when westbound into Liscomb.

Soundings in FEET

119

GEGOGAN (JEGOGAN)*

45°03.1'N, 61°57'W

Chart: #4231

Condensed from earlier material by W.G. Barker, E.B. Cabot and V.C. Gray.

DIRECTIONS: Find Little Liscomb lighted bell (VM3), two miles south-southeast of Tobacco Island, and lay a course for the center of Redman Head, which is high and easy to find; avoid Robar Rock (which is marked by red cone VM6) and Shag Ledge. Follow the shoreline in, avoiding the ledge just inside Redman Head (clearly visible), but maintaining a close proximity to the western shore. Just above Brig Point, cut diagonally across to the eastern shore. The passage past Coot Head and Rae Island is clearly marked.

ANCHORAGE AND BERTHS: Anchor off the **northeast shore past Rae Island**. Here is a good mud bottom and excellent holding ground. The anchorage shallows considerably to the north. There are neither wharves nor berths.

REMARKS: The shoreline is pretty—wooded with some open fields. Good clamming is reported to be on the eastern shore on the way in (1976).

FACILITIES: None.

*Caution should be used entering this harbor as it has not been reported on in the last ten years.

ST. MARY'S RIVER

&

SONORA

45°03.5'N, 61°54.3'W

Chart #4234

Rewritten from earlier material by R.M. Black P. Richmond and update A. Campbell 2003.

DIRECTIONS: Locate St. Mary's bell (Mo A VK), two miles southeast of Wedge Island, and come to course 345° (mag.). This course lies between Cape St. Mary's and Barachois Point (not to be confused with Barachois Head at Port Bickerton). Pass Barachois Point bell (VK3) 2.2 miles in, and continue on to the green can (VK5) off Black Head. By this point any fog should have scaled up on a normal summer's day. Thread the channel between the green and red buoys past the fixed light, 20' high on the end of Horse Shoal. (The light is easily distinguished as a pyramidal tower on a massive foundation with a fluorescent red stripe on its seaward side.) Beyond this light there are one green, and two red, buoys. The village of Sonora with two government wharves lies to starboard. **BEWARE** - the buoys may be moved to mark the best channel. In 2003 A.Campbell reported that the river seemed to have silted up some. He would not recommend yachts drawing over 6ft to enter St Mary's, and all yachts to navigate on a rising tide after half tide.

ANCHORAGE AND BERTHS: The St. Mary's River carries a strong and deceptive current. Anchoring off Sonora is not recommended because of this current and a foul bottom. The better anchorage is north of the first red buoy above the village, where the channel is broad and the current less (though you should be wary of breaking your anchor out when the current reverses). You must anchor with short scope to stay in the narrow channel.

There are two government wharves in Sonora. Logic would dictate that the best berth would be on the S side of the upper wharf, but in reality, the N side of the lower (south) wharf is best, because eddies will fend you off this wharf during all tides. This wharf is reported to have 13 feet on it toward the outer end.

REMARKS: This is a port of necessity and not a place one seeks out. The upper reaches of the river are reported to have good salmon fishing.

Also, if your boat is shallow-drafted enough, you may wish to visit Sherbrooke Village further up the river.

FACILITIES: Only very basic supplies can be found in Sonora.

SHERBROOKE VILLAGE

42°08'N, 61°59.1'W

Chart #4234

Sydney Dumaresq   *1995*

The directions for entering the St. Mary's River from seaward are already given in the St. Mary's River & Sonora section just before this entry.

DIRECTIONS: The sail up the St. Mary's River is a delightful run, especially in a west or southwest wind. The buoys mark the channel extremely well, and the chart is quite accurate. *Surprise* draws 6 feet and we never recorded less than 7 feet on the sounder which equates to 9 feet of water. This was on a rising tide both up and down the river. If the stakes are followed, there should be no surprises.

From the last pair of buoys to the little wharf just upstream from Mill Cove, the best course found was a pretty straight line. We found lots of thin water to port of this straight line.

ANCHORAGE AND BERTHS: Tie up to the little wharf or anchor in the stream just off the wharf.

REMARKS: A short walk up the road from the wharf has the beautiful Sherbrooke Village Restoration — a Canadian (smaller) Williamsburg. Lots of wildlife (particularly birds) here. Also, because of the Restoration, many Canadian crafts are sold here.

FACILITIES: There are some grocery stores—nothing else.

PORT BICKERTON*

45°05.7'N, 61°42.6'W

Chart: #4234

Rewritten and condensed from material by D.S. Byers, P. Richmond, E.B. Cabot, A. Fowler and V.C. Gray.

There are two harbors at Port Bickerton— Port Bickerton to the north and Mouton Harbour to the west (not to be confused with Port Mouton west of Halifax). Port Bickerton itself is not recommended as an anchorage because of uncharted rocks in the harbor. These directions refer to Mouton Harbour.

DIRECTIONS: From offshore and from the west in good visibility, locate the Nixonmate whistle (VH2) south of Nixonmate Shoal, and come to course 54° (mag.) for 2.7 miles until Castor Rock is abeam. Shift to 80° (mag.) and proceed to the Mo A bell (VCA) southeast of Bickerton Island and you are ready to enter. From the east or in poor visibility, find the Port Bickerton Mo A (VC) two miles south of Pollux Rock, and follow course 356° (mag.) to the Mo A (VCA) southeast of Bickerton Island. There are obviously other ways of approaching inside from the east, but Nixonmate and Castor Shoals make this maneuver a little risky coming from the west. From the inner Mo A, the chart suggests a course of 320 1/2° (t.) or 342° (mag.) which will bring you close to the green flasher north of Bickerton Island. As the chart indicates, swing to 286° (mag.) after the green flasher, toa red flasher, and after the red flasher, come to 322° (mag.) to the end of the breakwater in Mouton Harbour. To the north of the breakwater is a marked ledge (not on the chart). Favor the ledge side, as an uncharted rock is in the channel between the breakwater and the ledge.

ANCHORAGE AND BERTHS: Anchor to the west of the breakwater near the buoys, making sure to leave room for the fishing boats to turn around. Berths may be had at the government wharf south of the breakwater, or at the breakwater itself which also serves as a wharf. (At this breakwater/wharf, you will probably have to tie outside one of the fishing boats.)

REMARKS: Though the people here are most friendly, this is not an attractive harbor, especially when the fish factory is emitting odors of *pisces mortissimi.*

FACILITIES: Basic supplies are available here, and recent reports indicate that you can arrange to get water and fuel at the fish factory, though the availability of this service can change from year to year.

*Caution should be used entering this harbor as it has not been reported on the last ten years.

COUNTRY HARBOUR

(Including Fishermans Harbour, Mount Misery Cove,
Stormont, Isaacs Harbour, Drum Head and Harbour
Island Cove)

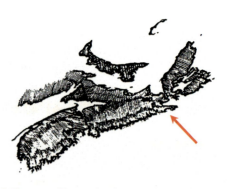

45°08'N, 61°38'W

Chart #4234

*Rewritten and condensed from material by
W.L. Saltonstall, J. Norwalk, P. Richmond, J.
Wickersham, W.T. Tower, C. Bok, H.B.
French, A.R. Fowler, S. Dumaresq, D.C.
Drinkwater and A. Weld   1998*

Country Harbour is a long, narrow river mouth. It contains two good harbors (Mt. Misery Cove and Stormont), flanked by several other good harbors (W to E: Fishermans Harbour, Isaacs Harbour, Drum Head and Harbour Island Cove).

DIRECTIONS: In good visibility there are obvious back passages: from the west between Cape Mocodome and Rose Shoal, and from the east between Drum Head to the south and Harbour and Goose Islands. In a fog, however, the best approach is to find Isaacs Harbour Mo A (TT) south of Tom Cod Shoals, and come to course 348° (mag.) which will bring you into Bear Trap Head. There the visibility should improve so that you may choose whether you will go into Isaacs Harbour or up into Country Harbour.

ANCHORAGES AND BERTHS: Southwest of Country Harbour, **Fishermans Harbour** offers a good anchorage roughly on a line between the light on the narrow spit of land which forms the anchorage basin and the government wharf. You may also tie to the wharf where there is reported to be 12' of water.

Mount Misery Cove is located up Country Harbour 1 1/2 miles northwest of Harbour Point, just to the north and behind Mount Misery. Anchor in 12-15 feet of water with a mud bottom, noticing Carding Mill Brook which flows into the southwest corner of the cove (see REMARKS). **Stormont**, located 3 miles up Country Harbour from Mt. Misery, is reported to have a good anchorage near the government wharf (but be sure to anchor toward shore out of the tidal current). There is also a T-shaped government wharf with 20' of water on the end (but again, beware of the tidal current which can be as fast as 2 knots).

Isaacs Harbour has two anchorages: **(1)** In Webb Cove, just east of the entrance, you may anchor in 8-10 feet in a good mud holding ground. This anchorage may be unsuitable, however, in a hard northerly or in a hard southerly, because the bar connecting Hurricane Island is just underneath the surface at high water which would allow heavy seas to come in. **(2)** Anchor in front of the church in Isaacs Harbour Village, about halfway between the two green cans about 100 yards offshore. Here is good holding ground in 25 feet.

Drum Head is a tiny, but well-protected harbor. Anchoring is not recommended, but you may tie up to the breakwater (10' at the outer end) which is also a wharf.

Harbour Island Cove is located on the north side of Harbour Island facing Drum Head. The anchorage in this cove is reported to be well-protected during normal summer weather.

REMARKS: Most of the anchorages mentioned here are pleasant and remote. Special mention should be made of **Mt. Misery Cove** where hollows are gouged out of the rocks about 1/4-mile up Carding Mill Brook which flows into the southwest corner of the cove. This is a great spot for a bath, and there's usually privacy if you wish to bath "in the full Monty," but as you pack your bathing kit with soap, towels, etc., don't forget some "Cutter" or "Off" to discourage the midges.

FACILITIES: Basic supplies may be obtained in **Isaacs Harbour**; there is also a gas station. At Drum Head there is reported to be a general store 1/2-mile down the highway from the wharf. Water and fuel are unavailable on the wharves except in Fishermans Harbour where fuel was reported available (1997).

NEW HARBOUR COVE*

45°10.2'N, 61°27.2'W

Chart: #4233

From earlier information by N.L.C. Mather and C.W. Bartlett.

DIRECTIONS: There is no difficulty finding your way in.

ANCHORAGE AND BERTHS: There is shelter behind a 300' breakwater, with an anchorage and a government wharf that offers 11' on its end where you may tie up.

REMARKS: This harbor is wide open to the southeast and there is a terrible roll in here in any kind of weather. This place should be used only for shelter and not for a snug anchorage.

FACILITIES: A general store is reported to be 1/2 mile up from the dock. Otherwise there is nothing.

*Caution should be used entering this harbor as it has not been reported on in the last ten years.

THE HARBORS OF TOR BAY

(Including Webber Cove, Port Felix, and Cole Harbour)

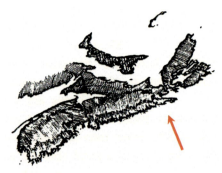

Chart #4233

Rewritten and condensed from earlier material by N.L.C. Mather, C.W. Bartlett, T.F.T. Morland and R.S. Carter with new information by J. Margolin and P. Travis.
1997

DIRECTIONS: Tor Bay is easily entered, even in poor visibility. The entrance buoys are bells, and while the buoys in the bay are small, they are closely-spaced and show on radar at one-mile range or less. The shoreline is also clearly delineated on radar, especially at low water when exposed shore rocks give a good return echo.

WEBBER COVE

45°12'N, 61°21.3'W

ANCHORAGE AND BERTHS: For a lee from southerly winds, the anchorage north of Webber Cove is suitable. Green buoys lead around Webber Shoal which is reported to be able to carry 7' over it. Anchor inside the 10-meter line as your draft permits. The bottom is kelp and mud, offering good holding ground once the hook is set. (Perhaps the use of a fisherman anchor would be wise here.) There are adequate shore lights to check your anchor bearings at night. Strong southerlies may create some motion in the anchorage, but it should be comfortable under most conditions. [Looks shallow here. Better check the state of the tide when you set the anchor. -ed.]

FACILITIES: None.

PORT FELIX

45°14.7'N, 61°13.3'W

DIRECTIONS: From the whistle buoy TA4, steer 22° (mag.) for the green bell TA7, and from there directly to the lighthouse on Hog Island. When you are next to the lighthouse, come to starboard and bear for the red nun TA12, leaving it to starboard, then swing north and leave green can TA15 to port. Proceed north to nun TA18 and leave it to starboard (even though the chart may lead you to believe there is more water east of the buoy). You may round the little island with the 12 on it (formerly Patate Island) on either side.

ANCHORAGES AND BERTHS: There is a good anchorage north of Boudreaus Island (formerly Mattee Island) on either side.

FACILITIES: None.

COLE HARBOUR

45°15.4'N, 61°17'W

DIRECTIONS: Cole Harbour has been properly buoyed so there is no problem entering; follow the buoys indicated on the inset on Chart #4233. Obviously one should stay away from the southern portion of this harbour.

ANCHORAGE AND BERTHS: The whole northern and central portions of this harbor are reported to be a good anchorage, and there is a particularly pleasant spot next to the wooded islet just off the south shore.

FACILITIES: None.

WHITEHEAD

45°14.3'N, 61°11'W

Chart #4233

Rewritten and condensed from earlier material by S. Campbell, W. Holcombe, C. Schutt, H. French, C. Bartlett and M. Grant. Update by A. Weld. 2001

DIRECTIONS: The main entrances (Western Passage, Southern Passage and Eastern Passage) are clear of obstruction, and most of the island shorelines on the way in are bold. Even in fog, if cautious, you should see something before you get into trouble. Once inside you have a choice of anchorages.

ANCHORAGES AND BERTHS: Yankee Cove offers an excellent anchorage with good protection northwest of the 5-meter island in the center of the cove, between the island and the unnamed point of Harbour Island. Yankee Island and the bar to the east of it dampen most of the seas. The ledge off the southeast corner of Yankee Island is farther south than the chart indicates. Beware of this danger, as a number of correspondents have fetched up on these rocks. There is no wharf here.

Marshall Cove provides an anchorage in about 7' of water with good holding but limited swing room, between the end of the government wharf and the pier to the northeast. Anchoring farther out is questionable because of exposure to seas from the south, a bottom with lots of kelp, and a steady stream of boat traffic from Marshall Cove to Kelp Shoal buoys. The government wharf has a reported depth of 11' on the end.

Northeast of **Prices Island**, is an excellent anchorage in 12' of water. Unfortunately, it is said to contain an aquaculture operation now, but it may be worth a look. There are no wharves.

The **Northwest and Northeast Arms** are navigable, but caution should be used at both entrances because of ledges. In September of 2001 the water temperature in the Northwest Arm was reported to be 69 degrees. This Arm is beautiful and protected. The Arms are sometimes used by the locals in severe storms, but prolonged high winds change the water levels here. The Prices Island anchorage is adequate for riding out most storms.

REMARKS: The scenery is beautiful in Yankee Cove and at Prices Island. There is reported to be good clamming on the bars between the islands southwest of the Prices Island anchorage.

Numerous areas within Whitehead have been taken over by mussel farms—an extensive one to the south of the entrance to the Northwest and Northeast Arms, and another to the NE of Prices Island.

FACILITIES: There is a general store near the government wharf in Marshall Cove. Otherwise, nothing is available.

PORT HOWE*

45°14.3'N, 61°05.2'W

Chart #4233

Rewritten and condensed from earlier material by C.W. Bartlett, V.C. Gray and S. Dumaresq.

DIRECTIONS: There are no navigational marks south or west of the entrance to Port Howe. With a variety of rocks and ledges, entering from south or west in a fog should not be attempted unless you have radar.

A swell from the south and west makes the ledges off Whale Island, and Whale and Snorting Rocks, look forbidding, but they can easily be cleared. Black Rock off Fluid Point is readily identifiable and can be passed close aboard. From there, the run into Port Howe is straight and clear on course 354° (mag.). Coming from the east through Dover Passage the entrance is simple.

ANCHORAGE AND BERTHS: The **westerly cove** provides good protection behind the two islets barely discernable on the chart.

The **northern arm** also provides an anchorage in the small cove, on the east side about 1/3 mile from the entrance in 15-20 feet of water. There is some controversy about the protection here, however, as the arm is wide open to the southeast. It's probably safe enough *in settled summer weather*.

There are no wharves.

REMARKS: This is a pretty place with no habitation. In the western cove, a few small streams, one with a tiny waterfall, come from a lake up above. The lake, unfortunately, has a wide variety of stinging and biting insects. A good mussel bed is at the mouth of this stream. An Osprey nest was reported to be in the north arm in 1986.

FACILITIES: None.

*Caution should be used entering this harbor as it hasn't been reported on in the last ten years.

DOVER PASSAGE AND LITTLE DOVER RUN

45°14.1'N, 61°03.2'W   &   45°16.3'N, 59°59.7'W

Chart #4233

Rewritten and condensed from material by T.F.T. Morland, C.W. Bartlet, A. Fowler. Updates by A. Weld and W. Feldman.   2001

EXPLANATION: **Dover Passage**, **Little Dover Run** and **Andrew Passage** provide inside passages along the route between Canso and Whitehead. Dover Passage and Little

Dover Run straddle Louse Harbour and Dover Harbour. Little Dover Run has two anchorages in it (see ANCHORAGES AND BERTHS below). The entrance to Dover Harbour is straightforward, with buoys clearly shown on Chart 4233. One sailor anchored near the fish plant in 35 knots of wind, then was directed to tie to the Government Wharf which provided a good lee and quiet night.

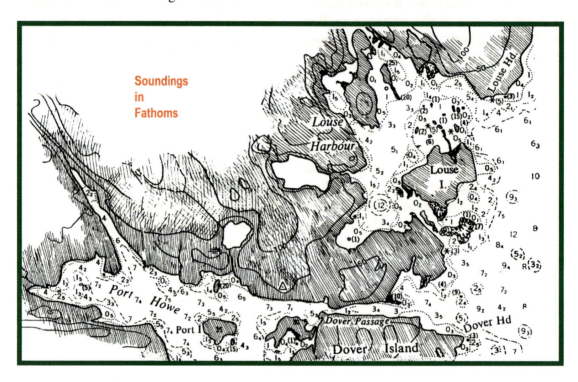

DIRECTIONS: **Dover Passage** runs from Dover Bay to Port Howe inside Dover Island and just south of Louse Harbour. Minimum width is about 50 yards, and in the narrowest part the depth at L.W. is only 12 feet. There are no buoys at either end, but the rocks on the chart are easily identifiable.

The withdrawal of Chart #4280 from the *Canadian Chart Catalogue of Nautical Charts* has greatly reduced the detail of knowledge about the Port Howe-Dover Passage-Louse Harbour areas, which are navigable. To assist those who wish to transit or anchor in this beautiful area, the Guide

presents the chartlet above. We believe this chartlet to be reasonably accurate, but cannot assume responsibility for any mishaps to anyone relying on this chartlet.

Little Dover Run *from east to west*: From the Little Dover green bell (PP1) at the south entrance to Andrew Passage, steer 308° (mag.) for a little less than a mile, where a red buoy and green buoy should be found leading into the run, a mile-long passage between Little Dover Island and the mainland. Although the narrowest part is only 30 yards wide, favor the northern shore where the minimum depth is three fathoms. At the west end there are green and red buoys between the northwest point of Little Dover Island and the small island to the minimum depth of three fathoms. At the west end there are green and red buoys between the northwest point of Little Dover Island and the small island to the west of it. Alter south between the buoys, then leave the small, rocky island to port and the green buoy on the 1.1 fathom patch to starboard.

The withdrawal of Chart #4280 from the *Canadian Chart Catalogue of Nautical Charts* has greatly reduced the detail of knowledge about Little Dover Run, which is navigable. To assist those who wish to transit or anchor in this beautiful area, the Guide presents the following chartlet. We believe this chartlet to be reasonably accurate, but cannot assume responsibility for any mishaps to anyone relying on this chartlet.

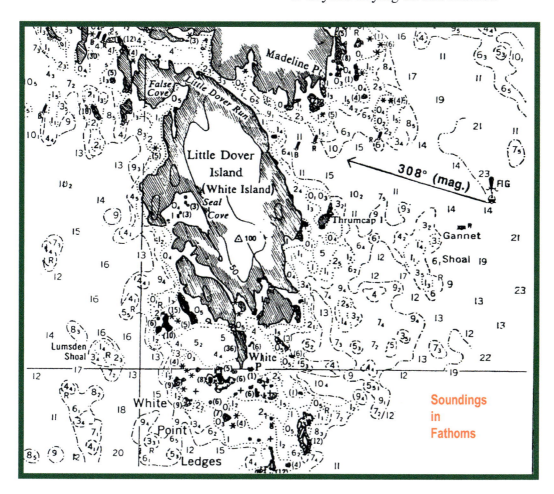

ANCHORAGES AND BERTHS: If anchoring in Port Howe is not desired, there is a small cove on the southern side of the western end of **Dover Passage**. There are sunken boulders around the edges of this little cove but they are plainly visible and there is 20' of water in the center. It offers good protection from all wind directions.

There are two coves in **Little Dover Run** in which you can anchor, located on the north side of the passage. The westerly one is preferable, as it is less subject to swell. Beware that this passage can be very busy in the early morning, as the fishing fleet of Dover exits through the run at high speed. Set an anchor light, stay out of mid-channel and watch stowage of loose articles. There are no wharves in this area.

REMARKS: The scenery here is delightful.

FACILITIES: None.

LOUSE HARBOUR

45°15.2'N, 61°03.5'W

Chart: #4233

Rewritten and condensed from material by C.S. Cooke, C. Bok, F. & M. Calderone, P. Richmond, W. Britton, G.P. Gardner ,E. Cabot, R. Lemmerman, J.N. Newman, and T.S. Casner, with additional material by S. Dumaresq.   *1993*

DIRECTIONS: Although these directions can be followed on Chart #4233, they would be more easily followed on the Dover Passage chartlet in the previous "Dover Passage & Little Dover Run" section.

Approach Louse Head on an approximate course of 330° (mag.). There are five ledges that you should leave to port on entering (though all of them may not be visible due to the state of the tide). After passing Louse Head, watch for a ledge near the shore to starboard that shows at half tide. This is not one of the five ledges that must obviously be left to port; it must be left to starboard. Proceed slowly and use your fathometer. The anchorage is north of the words "Louse Harbour" on the chartlet.

ANCHORAGE AND BERTHS: On entering the anchorage cove, favor the west shore to avoid the first rock shown on the sketch chart as well as a ledge on the east shore.

When the cove opens up, head towards the easterly shore to avoid the rock in the middle of the cove.

A ledge stretches across the cove from a bold granite cliff, but there is good water on the west shore and an excellent anchorage behind the ledge in the west area of the cove.

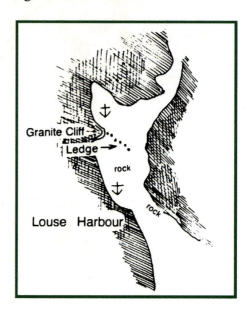

REMARKS: In spite of all the caveats about entering, many correspondents agree that this is one of the quietest and prettiest anchorages in the province.

South of the anchorage a substantial fresh water stream enters the harbor, and if you follow the animal path next to the stream, it will bring you to a beautiful pond where you may swim. There are mussel beds in the stream inlet and scallop beds in 6' of water at the south end of Louse Harbour. The water in the anchorage is warm enough to swim in and there were harbor seals reported living there in 1979.

FACILITIES: None.

ANDREW PASSAGE

45°18'N, 60°58.4'W

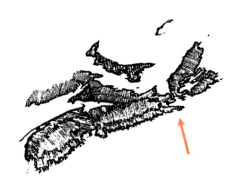

Charts: #4233, #4281

Rewritten and condensed from earlier material by C.W. Bartlett, C.H. Vilas, J.H. Wickersham, G.G. Kirstein, B. Trembly, O. Gates, A. Weld, and T.S. Casner, with new information by J.R. Chandler   1995

DIRECTIONS: Do not attempt this passage without Chart #4281, and if faint of heart, don't attempt it in a fog. In 1972 George Kirstein wrote, "The curious thing is that the buoys are located where they appear to be located on the chart. However, if you take off compass courses, you don't end up running the channel.... It is possible there is some magnetic disturbance here... [and] I would say it is virtually impossible to run this channel in a fog." If in doubt with evening coming on and/or bad visibility, Glasgow Harbour north of the passage or Portage Cove south of the passage offer harbors of refuge (see below).

In good weather this is a relatively easy passage in either direction. Coming from the north, pay particular attention to the Charlotte Island-Coles Point (Barse Point) area, as it is tight and shallow. Coming from the south, Pea Island is clearly outlined by its cap of dark trees above a wide, rocky base, and it stands out from the background. Black Island appears quite large and low and is also tree-covered.

ANCHORAGES AND BERTHS: Glasgow Harbour can easily be entered from the east; it affords good protection from all winds except easterlies. A yachtsman anchor is preferable to a Danforth here because of kelp. This is an isolated, barren anchorage.

Portage Cove may be entered cautiously through the opening north of Pea Island and south of Haulover Ledge. The best place to anchor is in 3 fathoms with a good mud bottom just south of the reef.

Another anchorage to consider is to the north of the reef where there is more water than shown on the chart and three ways to moor. A bow line can be carried ashore to the point marked, with a stern anchor set to the southeast; bow and stern lines could be carried ashore with the boat lying NE-SW; or a boat of quite deep draft could be safely secured with lines ashore in the cut just to the north. There appear to be 10 feet of water (DLW) all the way into this spot. A cut-stone face at the north end suggests that it has been used at some point (Beware though, a rock is just to the south of it).

This anchorage would also be uncomfortable in an easterly. It is a wild, lonely place of granite hills, bare or covered with low bushes. There are fascinating inlets to explore in the dinghy at high tide with a liberal application of mosquito repellent. Deer are said to visit here, and a good clam bed is rumored to be in one of the estuaries.

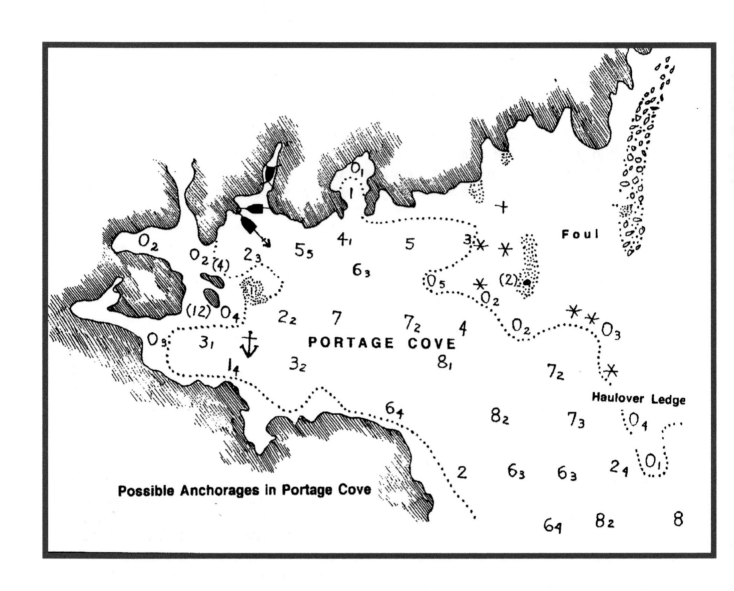

Possible Anchorages in Portage Cove

CANSO

45°20.3'N, 60°59.8'W

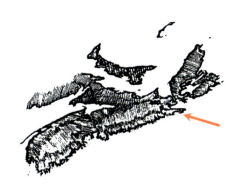

Charts: #4233, #4281

Rewritten and condensed from earlier material by P.P. Chase, R.J. Kerry, M. Grant, H. Villard, H. French,G. Kirstein, J.P. Kendall, A. Weld, and W. Feldman, with new material by S. Dumaresq and R. Nostrand. 1995

DIRECTIONS: You might get away with using Chart #4233 and common sense on entering, but this chart doesn't have many of the buoys, and has little shoreline detail. Strongly recommended for this harbor is Chart #4281.

Entry from the east is straightforward. Entry from the north is a little more complicated because there is a main entrance and another entrance through "False Passage." The main entrance is the one you should use because False Passage has an overhead cable (67' clearance); the harbor buoys south of False Passage are confusing, as some of them mark the way into the Tickle and not the way out of False Passage Channel.

ANCHORAGE AND BERTHS: You may anchor in the harbor, and possibly the best spot is in 18' along the shore midway between the Grave Island breakwater and the wharf area. It can, however, be noisy here.

The preferred anchorage is in the basin between Piscataqui and George Islands, directly in the center of the four-fathom spot, in firm sand. It is best to have a man spotting

from the spreaders on the way in, as the channel is tortuous. You should also take a number of soundings once in, so that when you anchor you are unlikely to swing over a shallow spot when the tide goes out (as one correspondent did).

Berths are available at the government wharf which has 14' of water on it, and there is comfortable berthing at the L-shaped wharf on entering the Tickle (6' at low water).

There is a new floating dock 1/4 mile farther in the harbor from the government dock. This new (1995) pressure-treated wooden dock is at water level which makes it easier to go ashore. It is easier to tie up to, in a more protected area, and cleaner than the government dock.

A new marina is located at the breakwater. The marina basin (8' depth) is enclosed by the breakwater and extends out to Grave Island shown on Chart #4281. It is well clear of the new L-shaped breakwater not shown on the chart. Keep well clear of the Grave Island end of the old breakwater because of shoaling. A course from RGR buoy PCA to the outer end of the new breakwater provides plenty of water.

The marina has excellent floating docks for transients, and it also maintains two moorings off the museum dock.

The docking fee in 1995 was $17.00 Canadian which included shore power (110V or 220V), shower and toilet facilities. There is a coin-operated washer and dryer, and a local company will deliver fuel to your boat.

REMARKS: Over the past decade, Canso has made enormous strides in terms of courtesy to strangers, as well as physical amenities.

Bill Duggan reported in the summer of 1994: "All dock space was occupied by two dozen tuna boats, many of which hailed from Prince Edward Island. All the folks we met were friendly and helpful."

As to points of interest, Sydney Dumaresq writes: "The Grassy Island Interpretive Center, run by Parks Canada, has a very interesting description of the fishing and merchant community located on the island 200 years ago. It is easy to identify, as it is a modern wood and glass building with a distinctive tower on the town waterfront. It is located between the Grave Island breakwater and the fish plant."

FACILITIES: Fuel is available at the government wharf. The pump has a large hose spool capable of reaching a long distance. Ice can be obtained from a large commercial ice machine at the end of the government wharf when it is open. There is no water here.

Fuel can be delivered to the marina, and water is available.

GUYSBOROUGH

45°24.7'N, 61°30'W

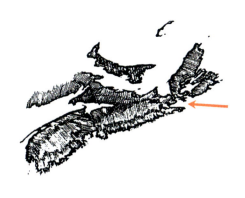

Chart #4335

Robert D. Thompson   *1991*

DIRECTIONS: From either side of the offshore flashing red buoy (CV12), head directly for the lighthouse north of Toby Point. Approach within 75 feet of the shore in front of the lighthouse prior to making a starboard turn. This avoids Stony Patch which is awash at low tide and marked by a small nun.

Stay 50-60 feet off the west side of Hadley Beach Point. At the point, then follow the channel markers. There is a lot of deep water.

Note the rocky shallows between Birch and Byron Islands. You cannot run straight from McCaul Point to the west end of Birch Island. Steer for the center of Birch Island prior to swinging to port, then to starboard to leave Birch Island to starboard.

The chart shows a lighted range into **Mussel Cove**. The lights have been removed, but day markers will guide you in.

There is a "club dock" in Mussel Cove with 8 feet of water alongside. A government wharf is available in Guysborough town with 5 to 15 feet of water alongside (the shallowest area being on the south corner).

There are a number of anchorages available, the most popular being in Mussel Cove or off the town itself.

REMARKS: This area is beautiful, with a multitude of quiet anchorages; it is navigable

for 3.5 miles until obstructed by a bridge. Mussel Cove makes a perfect hurricane hole and is lovely.

FACILITIES: A public golf course is next to Mussel Cove, and a restaurant and laundromat as well. The liquor store is 3/4 mile from the golf course. There is a shopping center 3/4 mile from the government wharf. There is now a small marina with berths for visiting yachts

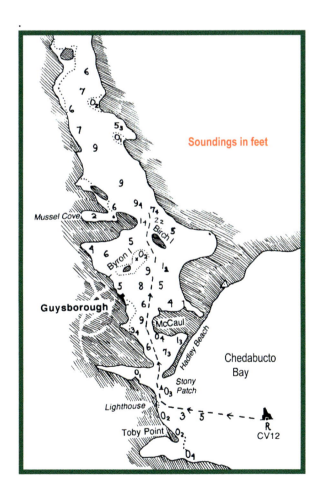

Soundings in feet

STRAIT OF CANSO, LENNOX PASSAGE & CHEDABUCTO BAY

(Including Port Hawkesbury, and Lennox Passage)

45°30'N,45°42'N • 61°30'W,61°52'W

Charts: #4306, #4308, #4335

Rewritten and condensed from earlier material by C.W. Bartlett, M. Grant, G.E. Hall, V. Spooner, and J.P. Fantasia ,with additional information by R. Pietrazak and S. Dumaresq.   1993

The construction of a causeway and lock across Canso Strait in the 1950's has eliminated the tricky tidal currents, which once made navigation across Chedabucto Bay challenging, especially in a fog. This lock is designed for ocean-going ships which use the strait as a "back door" to Prince Edward Island and the Gulf of St. Lawrence. On the east side of the strait are a pulp mill, oil refinery and heavy water plant (makes the stuff you put into atomic reactors). The refinery and heavy water plant are presently inactive, but the pulp mill is still going.

PORT HAWKESBURY

45°37'N, 61°22'W

Chart #4306

Updates by S. Taylor, P. Wick, R. Barton. 2001

ANCHORAGE AND BERTHS: The government wharf at Port Hawkesbury has 22' depth on the outer end, and you can anchor off the Yacht Club. The Club dock has hook ups for 20-amp electricity and water.

REMARKS: This is a good stopover port when bound to and from the Gulf of St. Lawrence or Northumberland Strait. It is an especially good spot to wait out bad weather before proceeding north through the lock.

FACILITIES: Banks, restaurants, motels and a supermarket are here. Bus service runs up and down the coast. Fuel, water, ice, and showers are available at the Yacht Club, where barbecue grills ashore are open all guests.

Laundry is a few blocks up the street, and a very complete mall is less than a mile uphill from the dock.

LENNOX PASSAGE

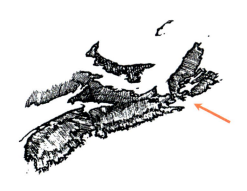

Charts: #4308, #4335

DIRECTIONS: The best chart for Lennox Passage is #4308. You may use Chart #4335 (which doesn't show the marks) as long as you observe the buoys properly.

A causeway and swing bridge connect the mainland with Isle Madame, but you can carry 12' draft through the opening at the bridge. The bridge operates from 08:00 to 17:00 (and Sydney Dumaresq would like us to know, "and not a minute sooner or later").

ANCHORAGES: A number of correspondents feel this area hasn't been discovered by cruising folk yet and you are encouraged to explore places in this protected waterway for yourself. The following three anchorages are highly recommended, the first two being in the Inhabitants Bay area, and the third on the eastern end of Lennox Passage before the causeway. Good harbors are on the south (Isle Madame) side of the passage also, and these are discussed in the Isle Madame section.

Seacoal Bay: Follow the range lights up to the 2-3 fathom area and drop the hook. Here is excellent holding ground in mud, though exposed to the south and east.

The Basin: Leave Rabbit Island and Evans Island to starboard going north and east. Swing south and enter the anchorage between Freeman Island and Round Island, and anchor in 2-3 fathoms with a mud bottom. Here you can find protection from all winds.

Bourgeois Inlet: This harbor is marked by a white lighthouse; it is easily spotted from a distance by the very prominent, large "Chapel" on the hill east of the inlet. The entrance, a very narrow cut in the beach, is easily navigated using Chart #4308; it can be negotiated using #4335 if you leave the marks in proper order. This is a snug anchorage, and there are two towns nearby where some basic supplies may be obtained.

Knife Island: (45°37'N, 61°01'W) provides a nice anchorage with excellent protection from all wind, except possibly northeast, but even then the fetch is short. There are some cottages and fishermen's houses on the shore, but otherwise it is isolated.

The island provides delightful exploring.

There is active mussel farming (1991) northeast of the island.

Grand Anse: Chart #4308 presents the area accurately. The sand island at the entrance is almost entirely under water at high tide; by staying close to the eastern shore it can be passed safely. There are numerous anchorages depending on wind direction. Mussels and clams are abundant on the round of the western shore, northwest of the sand island. A highway borders Welsh Cove, but the noise is not bothersome.

Indian Island: Chart #4308 presents the area accurately. The area between Indian Island and False Bay provides excellent protection. The best entrance to this anchorage is to the west of Indian Island. There was mussel farm aquaculture in 1991 between Indian Island, Savage Point and the 52-foot island.

139

ISLE MADAME

(Including Petit-de-Grat, Arichat and D'Escousse)

45°35'N/45°27'N • 60°53'W/61°08'W

Chart #4308

Rewritten and condensed from earlier material by R.E. Gorton, C.W. Bartlett, T.F.T. Morland, T.D. Cabot, S. Dumaresq, and G. Walters, with new material by R. Martel. 1993

Isle Madame has not received good press since it was first reported on by G.P. Gardner in 1956. The soundings on the chart are sometimes questionable, and it is best to make these harbors (especially on the south side of the island) in clear weather on a rising tide. Reports of groundings where the chart shows reasonable depths are common.

The harbors on the north (Lennox Passage) side get higher marks. This section will start with Petit-de-Grat and go west covering the harbors in a clockwise direction.

PETIT-DE-GRAT

There are two harbors at Petit-de-Grat bisected by the bridge which connects Isle Madame to Petit-de-Grat Island. The **north harbor** at Petit-de-Grat is no longer recommended, as the channel has silted in to 3' at low water, and a power cable with 29' clearance has been strung across the inner harbor.

DIRECTIONS: The channel for the **south harbor** at Petit-de-Grat is well marked beyond the lighthouse on Mouse Island, and it is reported that 10' can be carried up to the bridge.

ANCHORAGE AND BERTHS: Forget about anchoring here. There is no swing room and the bottom is foul. A government wharf is to port just short of the bridge with 8' of water on its outer face where you may tie up.

ARICHAT

45°30.5'N, 61°01'W

Dr. Robert Martel   *1992*

DIRECTIONS: Arichat is easily located by the Cathedral Church which has two spires. Entry is easy, either through Crid Passage, north of Jerseyman Island, or through the passage between Cape Auget and Jerseyman Island from the south.

ANCHORAGES AND BERTHS:
Anchorages are numerous even though the harbor is deep. The two most popular are located:
/

(1) 200 yards east of the bight in Jerseyman Island.

(2) at the south side of the harbor by the newly-constructed wharf of the Arichat Boat Club where guest moorings are also available (1992).

In an easterly blow there is good holding ground deep inside Arichat Harbour in a location called locally, "Head of the Harbour." Wharf space is available at the government wharf just under the spire of the Anglican Church, or at the Arichat Boat Club wharf on the south side of the harbor.

REMARKS: Do not be misled by West Arichat and Le Blanc Harbours. They are reported to be very shoal.

There is pottery and folk art available in Arichat, as well as Acadian cuisine at the local hotel.

FACILITIES:
Basic groceries are available in the village. Members of the Arichat Boat Club are willing to assist in the procurement of fuel, water, ice, and a mechanic for basic repairs.

D'ESCOUSSE

DIRECTIONS: The channel is well marked and there is no problem entering.

ANCHORAGE AND BERTHS: There is a snug anchorage behind the spit (as indicated on Chart #4308) and there may be a guest mooring maintained by the local yacht club.

There is a government wharf where you may tie up with a depth of 12' on the end.

REMARKS: The Lennox Passage Yacht Club has leased the government wharf, which is in excellent condition, and the members "bend over backwards" to accommodate transients.

There is a spectacular view from the road 1/4 mile east of the dock.

FACILITIES: The Yacht Club has showers and a laundry machine. Water is available on the wharf; there are two general stores and a post office.

ST. PETER

(Including Bay, Canal, Inlet, Lions Club Marina, Corbetts Cove and Damions Cove)

45°39.2'N, 60°52.4'W

Charts: #4275, #4308

Rewritten and condensed from earlier material by G.K. MacIntosh, C. Bok, R. Stephens, Jr., C.H. Vilas, T.D. Cabot, B. Trembly, H.B. French, J.H. Wickersham, D. Fuller, H.F. Field, E. Swenson, H. Anderson J.F. Young, and A..O'Grady   2004

DIRECTIONS: The best chart for St. Peter's Bay is #4275. Chart #4308 will do but <u>DO NOT</u> <u>attempt</u> <u>to</u> <u>use</u> <u>Chart</u> <u>#4335</u> <u>by</u> <u>guessing</u> <u>where</u> <u>the</u> <u>channel</u> <u>buoys</u> <u>are</u>. Even in the clearest weather, these channel buoys can be confusing and hard to find, necessitating the use of compass courses.

ANCHORAGES AND BERTHS: There are three suitable anchorages in St. Peter's Bay within a mile or two of the canal. They are from east to west:

Grand Greve: About a mile southeast of the canal, this harbor is preferable in an easterly blow. It is also a good anchorage in light westerlies in settled summer weather, but some correspondents have found it to be "windswept." This would be the editor's first choice, but it's best to look things over and if you get a windswept feeling, move on to one of the following.

Anse de Loup: About 3/4 mile west of the canal, there is good protection from all winds except easterlies. There is a fairly consistent bottom at 3-4 fathoms with good holding

ground. In days of yore some correspondents complained of the noise made by trains on the nearby track, but trains here are a pretty rare phenomena these days.

Tillard River: Located about one mile southwest of the canal. This was preferred by those who were bothered by the trains (mentioned above). While this anchorage offers good protection from winds south and west, there is a current here due to the river, and one must be careful not to swing onto the mud flats if a long anchor rode is used.

For a place to tie up, go to the canal entrance and make fast to the bollards on the west side of the cement wall. Here you are well-protected, and this is probably the best idea if you are too late to get through the canal into the lakes or if you have come through the canal going south at day's end.

An evening here can be very enjoyable. Nobody will bother you, a stroll through the town of St. Peter's is pleasant, and you don't have to haul and stow an anchor when you leave.

Be aware, however, that if a big ship or tow is coming (which will be unlikely) you will be asked to move. For this reason it is best to ask the lock tender's permission before lying alongside.

ST. PETER'S CANAL

The St. Peter's Canal was blasted through a solid granite hill. It was originally opened in 1869 and improved in 1917. This canal provides a "back door" into the Bras d'Or Lakes. Otherwise, it is necessary to go halfway around Cape Breton Island to enter the lakes via the Great Bras d'Or.

Because of differences in the water level of up to 4' in the lakes, the canal has a lock with double doors. The lock is 300' long, 48' wide, and 17' deep. There is also a swing bridge at the north end of the canal with a clearance of 20' when closed.

Canal hours of operation for the summer season (mid-June to the first week in September) are traditionally 08:30 to 20:30. Mid May to Mid June and Labor Day to the end of October 0800-1630

Because the lock tender doesn't have a good view of the north end of the canal, it may be necessary to tie up when coming from the lakes and inform him of your presence. **Contact the lockmaster on VHF Channel 16 or (902) 535 2118**

Customarily, *a fresh water* hose has been at the lock, and this affords an excellent opportunity to top off your tanks. (In 2004 it was not in evidence. –ed)

Heading through the St. Peter's Canal from the lock towards the swing bridge.

ST. PETER'S INLET

This body of water connecting the canal with the Bras d'Or proper, is practically landlocked; about five miles in length, it varies in width from 25 yards to 1 mile. It is buoyed, lighted and well-charted, but the narrowness of the channel and abrupt turns in the southern portion, particularly, discourage catnapping on the part of the navigator and the helmsman.

Sailing through this inlet without power is one of the most delightful features of a visit to the Bras d'Or. A fair breeze and extremely smooth water offer a rare combination, and this, with a swift passage through the beautiful countryside which at times practically touches either side of the craft, affords a thrilling experience.

The main channel of the Bras d'Or Lakes is buoyed as entering at Great Bras d'Or and continuing south to St. Peter's as the head of navigation. Accordingly, when entering the lakes from St. Peter's, Leave the green buoys to starboard and the red buoys to port.

ANCHORAGES AND BERTHS: At the north end of the canal, berths are available on the west wall, but the area is usually crowded with small fishing craft. The only other berths available in the inlet are at the Lions Club Marina (see below).

LIONS CLUB MARINA

45°39.7'N, 60°52.4'W

DIRECTIONS: This marina is located in the bight west of the main channel just north of the canal and southwest of Handleys Island.

REMARKS: This marina is reputed to be kept spotless by dedicated young employees who are also eager line handlers and fuel dispensers.

FACILITIES: Diesel, gas, lube oil, water, ice and stove fuel are available here. It is a short walk to town for groceries, liquor and a restaurant (*MacDonald's*) which stays open late (22:00). The marina will take messages - **Telephone: (902) 535-2792**.

Public internet access is available, and the marina has newly upgraded laundry and showers.

CORBETTS COVE

45°40.2'N, 60°49.2'W

Just turn east off the main channel away from Beaver Island. This is a great favorite for pretty scenery, but you must come well into shore to find a depth of 25' for anchoring.

DAMIONS COVE

45°42.2'N, 60°48.7'W

Enter off the channel through the openingbetween MacNabs Island and MacNabs Point. Favor thepoint side of this entrance, and proceed slowly, as therehas been an uncharted rock reported on the island side.

NOTES ON THE BRAS D'OR LAKES

Rewritten and condensed from earlier material by C. Bok , D.S. Byers, R. Stephens, C.W. Bartlett, W. Britton, H.H. Tucker, P. Richmond and J.F. Young.

In summer the water temperature in the Bras d'Or Lakes is so warm (65°-70°) that fog is rare. It is not uncommon to sail through a beautiful summer day in the lakes and observe banks of fog lying across the land, hugging the Atlantic shore of Cape Breton Island.

There is a tidal range of six to nine inches in the lakes and a noticeable current, especially in the narrow passages at Barra Strait (Grand Narrows) and in the Great Bras d'Or.

Special mention should be made of Barra Strait and the highway and railway bridges at Grand Narrows. On one day it can be a pleasant sail through the bridges. On another, there may be strong winds against the current and you will experience conditions you won't forget, featuring eight-foot-high "square waves." For lack of traffic the railroad bridge remains open these day. The highway bridge usually opens when they see you. If not, call the bridge operator on Channel #16. Under no circumstances should you get close to either bridge if it is closed. These bridges are manned 24 hours a day from July 1 to September 1.

Baddeck (population 1,000) is the largest town on the lakes and about the only place where all supplies and repair facilities may be found. It is wise to stock up here because most other ports of call in the lakes have very limited supplies.

The Great Bras d'Or is divided, from Baddeck to the eastern entrance, by Boularderie Island, twenty-two miles long. The southern arm thus formed, known as St. Andrew's Channel and the Little Bras d'Or,

has a narrow, crooked entrance to the sea and a fearsome current so dangerous that the government no longer opens the bridge across it; this entrance is therefore closed to navigation. The northern entrance has an entrance to the sea only 200 yards wide and a current of at least five knots in diminishing degree as far west as Barra Strait; boats under sail should plan to enter and leave on a fair tide only. (Canadian ***Tide and Current Tables, Vol. 1, Atlantic Coast and Bay of Fundy***, carries the vital information for this area.)

The whole lake system is about sixty miles long, but there are many long arms that provide a maze of snug harbors that could not be exhausted in a month's cruising. The region is surprisingly wild and sparsely settled. The Cabot Trail runs along the western side.

To capture the flavor of the area, carry aboard a copy of Neil MacNeil's ***The Highland Heart in Nova Scotia*** (reissued in paperback in 1983 and available in Baddeck stores). MacNeil, an expatriate turned New York City journalist, recalls his boyhood in Washabuck before World War I. Devoid of the gooey sentimentality associated with such reminiscences of this area, he humorously and graphically portrays the farmer-crofter-fisherman society of the time (so graphically he is still remembered with some pain by a few of the older people living in the area today). And if it's the sound o' the pipes you're wanting and the gathering o' the clans, plan to be in the Lakes the first week in August for the numerous Gaelic festivals.

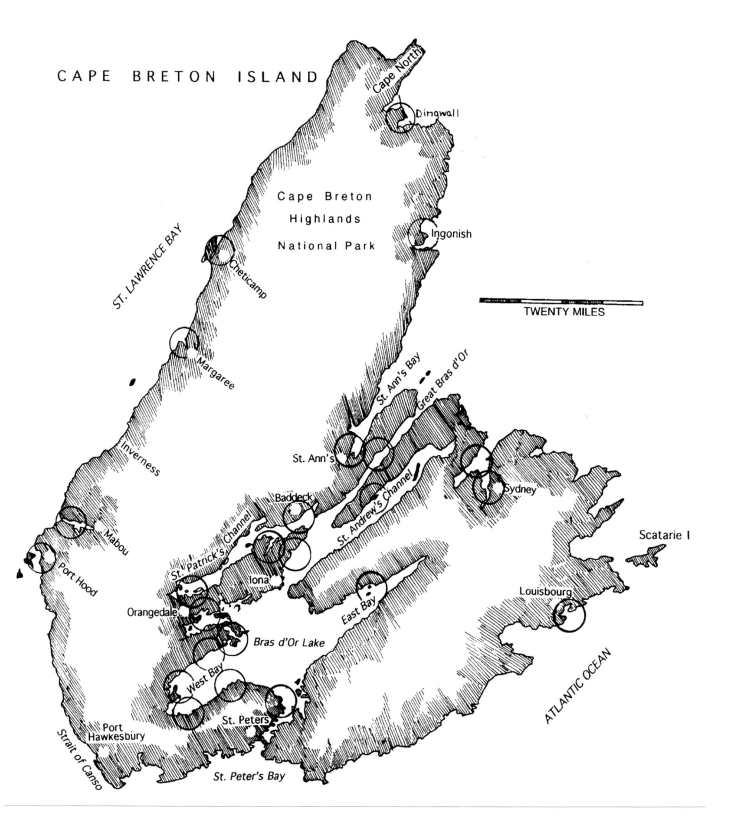

St. Paul I

CAPE BRETON ISLAND

Cape North

Dingwall

Cape Breton
Highlands
National Park

ST. LAWRENCE BAY

Ingonish

Cheticamp

TWENTY MILES

Margaree

St. Ann's Bay

Great Bras d'Or

Inverness

St. Ann's

St. Andrew's Channel

Sydney

Baddeck

Scatarie I

St. Patrick's Channel

Mabou

Iona

East Bay

Louisbourg

Port Hood

Orangedale

Bras d'Or Lake

ATLANTIC OCEAN

West Bay

Port
Hawkesbury

St. Peters

Strait of Canso

St. Peter's Bay

CAPE GEORGE HARBOUR & EAST BAY

(Including Johnstown Harbour & Indian Islands)

Rewritten and condensed from earlier material by C.W. Bartlett, T.D. Cabot R.E. Gorton, T.F.T. Morland , A.F. Chace, Jr. Update by A. Weld. 2001

CAPE GEORGE HARBOUR

45°43.7'N, 60°49'W

Charts: #4275

DIRECTIONS: Chart #4275 is best for this harbor. On entering, there is a sand spit to starboard. Turn to starboard and go behind this sand spit or continue in and enter the arm that goes northward.

ANCHORAGES AND BERTHS: Anchor either behind the sand spit or in the northern arm in 12-14 feet of water. You may not think so, but there is just as much swinging room and water behind this sand spit as there is at Maskell's. There are no wharves here.

REMARKS: This is an excellent harbor. Homes have been built mostly along the southern entrance. The spit has become storage for boats on the beach.

JOHNSTOWN HARBOUR

45°45.8'N, 61°45.5'W

Charts: #4275

DIRECTIONS: A buoyed channel leads into this harbor from the north. <u>DO</u> <u>NOT</u> attempt to enter Barachois Harbour (located between Sheep Island, Evans Island and Hay Cove), as this harbor is completely blocked by sandbars (as indicated on the chart). **ANCHORAGE AND BERTHS:** Good anchorages can be found in 2-3 fathoms. There is reported to be a government wharf here in very bad condition.

INDIAN ISLANDS (ESKASONI)

45°57.2'N, 60°33.8'W

Charts: #4279

DIRECTIONS: Because of the confusion over the names of these islands, a chartlet is provided below with the names of the islands *as they are known locally* (not as they appear on Chart #4279). Directions hereafter refer to the chartlet and not Chart #4279.

ANCHORAGES: There is a good anchorage between Big Island and McPhee Island which may be entered from the north by staying midway between the islands. (However, be careful of the shoal water that extends to the west of Big Island.)

There are anchorages west-northwest and east of the largest of the "Indian Islands" as indicated. Take the channel around this large island either to the east or to the west to either of these anchorages. There are no other navigation marks in this area, so proceed with caution because uncharted sandbars and aquaculture cables and cages may be in these channels.

You should be able to carry ten feet through to the anchorages, however.

REMARKS: The land here is on an Indian reservation and has been the site of much oyster aquaculture. It was also an area where the Indians sold artifacts (sweetgrass baskets and the like) to tourists. The artifacts are gone, but the oyster farms— maybe not. Be careful.

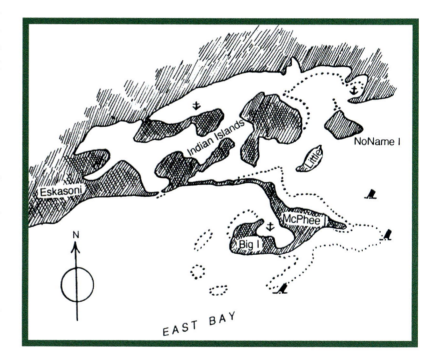

149

WEST BAY ANCHORAGES

(Pringle Island, Morrison Head, Ballams Point, Ross Pond, and Crammond Islands)
Rewritten from earlier material by R.E. Gorton, T.F.T. Morland, D. Begg and R.L. Hart

Chart #4279

PRINGLE ISLAND

45°45.4'N, 60°59.1'W

DIRECTIONS: Located between Pringle Island and the mainland, this harbor may be approached from east or west, provided you remain midway between the mainland and the island. The east end of Pringle Island is distinguished by a grassy knoll joined to the island by a sandy beach.

ANCHORAGE AND BERTHS: When the center of the island bears north, drop the anchor in three fathoms. Do not go beyond this bearing because there are sandbars farther to the west. This is an excellent harbor except in strong east or west winds. The government wharf here is in ruins.

REMARKS: Blueberries grow in profusion on the island. There are several farmhouses on the mainland, as well as the old cemetery of the Pringle family.

MORRISON HEAD

45°45.8'N, 60°54.2'W

DIRECTIONS: This is a little bight about four miles to port as you come out of St. Peter's Inlet.

ANCHORAGE: Tuck into the bight behind Morrison Head and anchor in 8-10 feet. This anchorage is wide open to the east, so you may not wish to spend the night.

REMARKS: This is a delightful place for a lunch stop (perhaps on the way from the inlet to Clarke Harbour). It has clear water, sandy beaches and rising hills behind it.

BALLAMS POINT

(Dundee Resort)

45°42'N, 61°05.1'W

Updated by C. Weaver   2005

DIRECTIONS: Leave the large green buoyand large yellow Marina buoy off MacRae Island to port and round Ballams Point to starboard. The channel into the marina is buoyed with lighted markers.

ANCHORAGE AND BERTHS: The marina, a sister operation of Baddeck Marine, is a full service yacht yard with transient berths and moorings. The entrance channel has a twelve foot depth, but false depth readings are caused by the eel grass in the channel. Depth at the berths is 15 to 20 feet.
Tel. (902) 345 0555, VHF channel 68
www.dbmarina.com

REMARKS: Dundee Resort with conference rooms, restaurant, swimming pool, cottages and an 18 hole golf course, is within 2 km of the Marina.

FACILITIES: Fuel, water, electricity, showers, laundry, ice, and pump-out facilities are available, as well as an eighteen-hole golf course, swimming pool, wading pool, thirty-nine cottages for rent, conference rooms, a restaurant and grocery store--all close at hand.

ROSS POND

45°45.3'N, 61°08.5'W

Chart #4279

DIRECTIONS: From a point one-half mile north of Floda Island, steer 284° (mag.) for 2 3/4 miles, past the north ends of Dumpling Island and Widow Point. Turn south and enter the pond, keeping over to the west side of the entrance. There are several low, grassy sand spits, quite conspicuous against the spruce woods, and these being shallow, they necessitate a swing to the opposite side of the channel where you should find 15 feet of water.

Do not enter MacLeod Creek, as it is very shallow.

ANCHORAGES: There is a good anchorage in the body of water which connects Ross Pond and MacLeod Cove.

An alternative anchorage can be reached by proceeding past the entrance to Ross Pond, then altering your course south, leaving the small island to starboard and entering North Cove (as indicated).

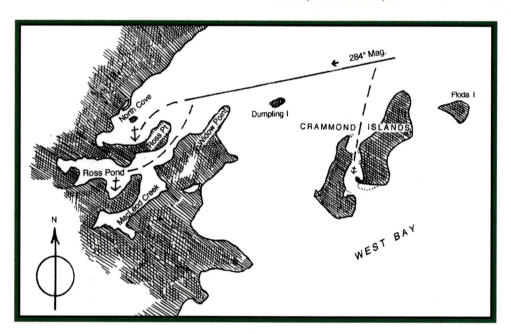

CRAMMOND ISLANDS

45°45.2'N, 61°05.6'W

Chart #427

DIRECTIONS: Enter the channel dividing the islands preferably from the north. It is narrow and not staked, but there is at least 15 feet of water for some 500 yards. Entry or exit from the south can be done, but there is less water here.

ANCHORAGE: Anchor in 15 feet of water inside the entrance.

CLARKE COVE (MARBLE MOUNTAIN)

45°49.3'N, 61°02.2'W

Rewritten and condensed from earlier material by G.K. MacIntosh, T.F.T. Morland, R.C. McCurdy, F.S. Cruickshank,.Jr., R. Prouty, S. Taylor, and B. Clark. 2000

Chart: #4279

DIRECTIONS: This harbor is easily distinguished from miles away by the large stone face in the hill over and to the right of the town (this face showing the remains of a once prosperous marble quarry). The customary entrance from the east is between Cameron Island and MacKenzie Point (In 1982 there existed an entrance range based on two lighthouses on the hill bearing 294° [true]. These lighthouses are no longer lit, but the range carries you past all dangers from Paddle Shoal into the harbor entrance.) Otherwise, a course of 315° (mag.) from the red flashing buoy (WB2) south of Paddle Shoal will take you past the lighthouse on the northeast end of Cameron Island to the red spar (WB10) on the southwest corner on MacKenzie Point. From this spar, steer more to the north, leave MacDonalds Point to starboard, and enter the harbor between MacDonalds Point and the mainland.

ANCHORAGE AND BERTHS: Once past MacDonalds Point, head northeast into the harbor and look for a "fishhook" of sand to appear to port. Follow the 1 3/4 fathom curve into the cove behind the fishhook and anchor in the center in 9'-10' of water. There are other anchorages in this harbor.

The following method of anchoring bow tot he beach on the fishhook sand spit is suggested by Stephen Taylor:

"Drop your stern anchor three boat-lengths away from the beach and drive your boat onto the beach. Carry your bow anchor in your arms 20 feet onto the sand spit and dig it in. You will have four inches of water under your bootstripe, approximately 10 feet under the keel, and 15 feet under the rudder. (This applies to a forty-foot boat.)" A small government wharf with about eight feet of water on its end is approximately 1/2 mile southwest of the harbor entrance, just south of an active (in good weather) bathing beach.

REMARKS: There is a path from the government wharf up to a small museum. Another path leads to the top of the mountain. (Leave plenty of time to walk up).
Alas, the "fishhook" has been discovered, and there are cottages in the cove and quite a bit of motorboat traffic. This mountain and piles of marble "nuggets make an astounding sight however.

Anchor with stern anchor north , bow on beach (literally), facing south. Keel will be in 10-12 feet as bow touches the beach. Cool breeze, no bugs, no waves. Great spot

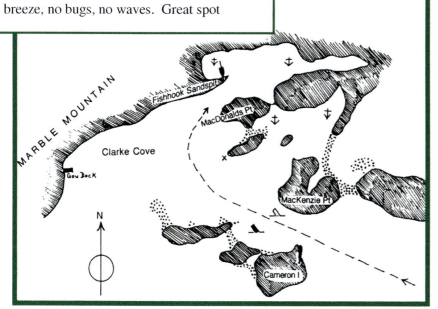

LITTLE & MALAGAWATCH HARBOURS

Rewritten and condensed from earlier material by C. Bok, F.S. Cruikshank, Jr., T.F.T. Morland, D.S. Byers, C.W. Bartlett, C.H. Vilas and J.F. Young.   *1993*

LITTLE HARBOUR

45°51'N, 60°57.3'W

Chart #4279

DIRECTIONS: The entrance to this harbor runs due north between two sandbars barely twenty-five yards wide, but you can carry three fathoms through it. The harbor opens into a lagoon half a mile wide.

ANCHORAGES AND BERTHS: Anchor in one of the coves on the east or west side of the harbor. The cove on the east side is known as "Karen's Cove." It is completely uninhabited and offers great privacy. Both offer complete protection from all winds.

There are no wharves.

REMARKS: This editor recalls a rendezvous sunflower raft in the eastern cove here on August 3, 1993, held by members of the CCA for 43 boats. There was plenty of room for everyone. The raft broke up at 19:30 and most boats anchored singly, yet the harbor looked mostly empty.

This is a pretty spot enclosed by hills with mellow memories.

MALAGAWATCH HARBOUR

45°52.3'N, 60°59.2'W

Chart #4279

DIRECTIONS: The entrance to Malagawatch is between Sheep Island and Gillis Shoal (over which there is 10 feet), and there are no buoys or stakes. There is 30 feet through the narrows in the entrance and 15 feet in the channel around Campbell Point.

ANCHORAGES AND BERTHS: The inner harbor (bounded by Campbell Point, River Cove, Nills Point and Cribwork Cove) affords many anchorages. The most popular is behind Campbell Point, a little south of Nills Point in 20 feet with a mud bottom, but beware that the shoal building north of Campbell Point builds further north than either Chart #4279 or *Cruise Cape Breton* would indicate.

There are no wharves here.

REMARKS: This is a charming harbor...if you like bald eagles.

MCKINNONS HARBOUR

45°55.45' N, 60°56.84' W

Chart #4279

Jurgen Kok   2000

DIRECTIONS: The entrance is no longer where it is shown on Chart #4279. It has been moved to the northwest, and there is now a man-made channel (eight feet deep) with stone embankments, lights, and buoys.

ANCHORAGES AND BERTHS: This is one of the largest harbors on the Bras d'Or and offers many coves and bays, including an excellent anchorage behind a sandspit over which one can look at Bras d'Or Lake.

REMARKS: McKinnons Harbour is a lovely place to explore and is a convenient harbor to stop before or after Barra Straits, or in conjunction with running up The Boom.

FACILITIES: None.

THE BOOM & MORRISON COVE

Rewritten and condensed from earlier material by T.F.T. Morland and C.W. Bartlett.

Chart #4279

THE BOOM

45°54.9'N, • 60°57.6'W

DIRECTIONS: "The Boom" refers to the passage north of Boom Island into North and Denys Basins. Coming from the east, the safest entrance is between Campbells Island and Lighthouse Point (just southeast of McKinnons Harbour which is now closed to navigation). Continue west midway between the mainland and Cranberry Island. To the west of Cranberry Island is an islet easily identified by a stand of trees on it. Leave this islet to port and steer southwest midway between the islet and the mainland. Swing west again as the channel opens up between Boom Island and the mainland. There may or may not be buoys to aid you on this passage.

On entering North Basin, note that a shoal stretches 1/2 mile west of Martins Point going away from Boom Island. Do not alter course south until a single conspicuous rock, lying on the beach on the north side is abaft of abeam. Then swing slowly south across the basin and proceed on a reverse course parallel to MacLean Point. There may or may not be a buoy marking the end of the shoal off Martins Point. Even so, make sure you leave the conspicuous rock, previously mentioned, abaft of abeam before turning. There is usually a red stake off MacLean Point marking the end of the shoal there.

MORRISON COVE

45°54.4'N, 61°02.4'W

DIRECTIONS: Continue west beyond Martins Point (see directions for the Boom above) and Morrison Cove will open to starboard. Just inside the entrance there is a low grassy point to port and another a little further in to starboard. These are steep-to with 10 feet of water within 30 feet of the shore. Favor the starboard (south) side of this entrance. Proceed slowly, and sound your way in.

ANCHORAGE AND BERTHS: Anchor in 10-12 feet of water at the head of the cove. There are no wharves here. Be sure to sound around your anchorage with your dinghy, for you may swing into very shallow water.

REMARKS: This is a "tight" place, and chances are you may be sharing it with some aquaculture oyster rafts, so be prepared to move on if you think it's too tight.

GILLIS COVE

45°54.6'N, 61°03.3'W

Chart #4279

John McKelvy   *1991*

DIRECTIONS: Follow a line 30° (mag.) from 1/4-mile offshore directly to the entrance of the cove. (Do not turn northeast until the 30° line can be used.) Except for a shoal spot of 9 feet offshore on this course, you can carry 10-12 feet into the anchorage, being careful to stay in the middle of the channel on the way in.

ANCHORAGES AND BERTHS: Anchor where the channel turns into the miniscule bay. There is a dock here, but it is private.

REMARKS: This was formerly an aquaculture area for raising oysters. The viscissitudes of the Canadian fisheries have forced the disuse of this place as an aquaculture area (1991). Enter with caution and make sure there is no aquaculture here before dropping the hook.

This is a delightful place to swim and explore the bays by dinghy. Occasionally you can hear the wail of a train on nearby tracks, recalling the balmy days of regular passenger service between Halifax and Sydney (with a whistle stop in nearby Orangedale).

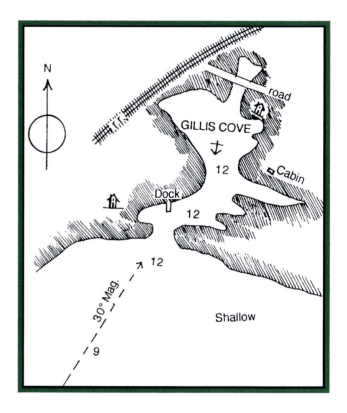

ORANGEDALE

45°53.9'N, 61°05.3'W

Chart #4279

Rewritten and condensed from earlier material by M.S. Grant, W.O. Apthorp, and H.H. Anderson, with new material by P. Travis.1993

DIRECTIONS: Proceed west through the Boom past Morrison Cove. Continuing west, leave Martins Island to starboard, passing halfway between it and the shore. On entering Blues Cove, favor the starboard (northern) shore to avoid a mud bank which has recently built up on the south side of the entrance.

ANCHORAGE AND BERTHS: Blues Cove provides a good anchorage in about 12 feet of water. The government wharf has ten feet of water on its end. There is also another well-protected anchorage in MacDonald Cove, just northeast of Blues Cove.

The little town of Orangedale (pop. 75) is charming. MacDonald Cove, somewhat less interesting as a place, has a bold shoreline and is bordered by high woods which makes it a very safe anchorage in strong westerlies.

The old train station has been restored, and the various spaces fitted with appropriate equipment and furnishings from the glory train days; afternoon tea is served in the stationmaster's quarters. (This station is celebrated in the popular song "The Orangedale Whistle" by Cape Breton Composer Jimmy Rankin.)

In a nearby building there is a small museum which features local memorabilia c. 1860-1930. A small art gallery is in the old hotel.

FACILITIES: There are two small markets in the town. There is no fuel or water.

MASKELLS HARBOUR

(Boulaceet)

46°01.3'N, 60°47.1'W

Rewritten and condensed from earlier material by C.H. Vilas, T.F.T. Morland, C.W. Bartlett, R. Stephens, Jr., J.R. Schaefer and H.H. Anderson, with new material by D. Russell. 1993

DIRECTIONS: Leave the green spar (GB23) to port and enter the harbor, leaving the lighthouse and Gillis Point to port and the sand spit to starboard.

ANCHORAGE AND BERTHS: Anchor just north of the center of the harbor. Do not venture too far west, as this end of the harbor is shallow, and do not go too far inside the sand spit to the northeast, as this area shoals rapidly as well. There is no public wharf here, and the boathouse and dock inside the sand spit are most definitely private.

REMARKS: This harbor, known to the older generation as "Boulaceet," had its name changed to Maskell's Harbour by the Canadian Hydrographic Service in the 1960's, and it's one of the prettiest anchorages in the lakes. The surrounding land (including the oysters found below the high-water mark) is privately owned. The land-owners here are cruising folk and pleased to see yachts in the harbor (as they discovered this harbor themselves on cruises from far away). A walk ashore to the lighthouse or a row down to the marine caves at the western end of the harbor is encouraged, but please remember to treat this property with the same respect that you would treat your own.

The name Maskell's Harbour was successfully promoted by Mr. Edward Russell, one of the early summer residents of this area. In fact, Mr. Russell was responsible for getting the name "Boulaceet" changed to Maskell's Harbour. We are indebted to Diana Russell (Mr. Russell's daughter) for the following story by her father:

"Mr. Maskell, after whom Maskell's Harbour was called by the people in the area, owned a house and forge near the shore. Early one winter morning, he went out in his nightshirt and cap to get some firewood, slipped on the frozen snow, and slid down the hill to the edge of the harbor. Because of the ice, he was unable to climb back up the hill to his home. So he decided to walk along the shore towards Gillis Point Lighthouse where the ground wasn't as steep. When the lighthouse keeper saw this apparition approaching in the dim morning light, he decided to lock his seven daughters in the lighthouse tower before offering assistance. (Then, I guess, everybody ended up "happily ever after.") This is offered by way of substantiation of the origin of the name of Maskell's Harbour. I'm sure my father embellished the story a bit more for fun, but he couldn't have made the whole thing up."

FACILITIES: None.

WASHABUCK RIVER

46°02.7'N, 60°50.8'W

Chart #4278

Rewritten and condensed from earlier material by R.E. Gorton, C.H. Vilas and J.F. Young.1993

DIRECTIONS: When approaching the river entrance from Baddeck, be sure to leave the spar (SP17) off Murphy Point to port. Observe the two spars in the entrance religiously, because the red spar has a ledge behind it, and the green one has some pinnacle rocks behind it. Immediately behind the spars, beware (especially at night) of some aquaculture nets just west of the entrance. There is fairly deep water from here all the way to the inner red spar off Campbells Cove (where there is nine feet of water). Incredibly, to the west beyond this red spar, the bottom drops to 135 feet, making the innermost basin unsuitable for anchoring.

ANCHORAGE AND BERTHS: There are numerous good anchorages in the area. Anywhere in the first basin is suitable, but if you prefer to be snug, try Indian Cove or Deep Cove which are to starboard as you go in. There is a good place just north of the inner red spar as well. As noted above, don't attempt to anchor west of the inner red spar, as the water is too deep.

There once was a government wharf at "Washabuck Center" which is somewhere between Upper and Lower Washabuck as shown on your chart. This wharf is in ruins and therefore there is no wharfage in the area.

REMARKS: This is a wild and unspoiled place where most of the land is owned by some of the more venerable members of the Cruising Club of America, and they have held this land in its natural state to be a joy to all visiting cruising folk. In return, they would appreciate your respect for the land and natural beauty of the area.

After some exploration in the dinghy, this is the perfect place to read MacNeil's ***The Highland Heart of Nova Scotia*** (mentioned in "Notes on the Bras d'Or"). Here is where MacNeil's non-fictitious grandfather had his farm, where owning an outhouse was considered "upity" by the neighbors, and where young men dreamed of getting rich in a far-off place called "the Boston States." A chapter of the book and a dram of usquebaugh before dinner would be a fitting end to a day spent here.

FACILITIES: None.

MCNAUGHTON'S COVE

(formerly McLeod's)

&

LITTLE NARROWS POND

Rewritten and condensed from earlier material by G.B. Bryan, H.H. Tucker and J.H. Young.

Chart #4278

MCNAUGHTON'S COVE

46°03.4'N, 60°55.3'W

DIRECTIONS: Proceed north through the entrance equidistant from both sides. This entrance is very narrow and daunting, but you should carry 10-12 feet all the way in. Once inside, continue north to the center of the basin before making any turns. On leaving, proceed to the center of the basin again until you can see open water in the entrance before turning south. This procedure avoids a rock shoal that extends 60 to 70 feet north on the west side of the entrance inside the basin.

ANCHORAGE: From the center of the basin, turn to port (southwest) and proceed to the center of the western arm and anchor in ten feet. The eastern arm is too shallow to anchor in.

REMARKS: This was once a beautiful place, but some fairly ugly buildings have been erected on the shore here prompting one subscriber to remark, "The harbor is more attractive on the chart than in real life."

LITTLE NARROWS POND*

45°59.7'N, 60°59.4'W

DIRECTIONS: Proceeding southwest through Little Narrows, leave the red spar (SP48) to starboard and go into the entrance into Denas Pond.

ANCHORAGE: Just north of the second peninsula on the port side, drop the anchor in 12 feet. Do not go past this peninsula as the channel shoals rapidly.

Caution should be used entering this harbor, as it has not been reported on in the last ten years.

WHYCOCOMAGH

45°58.1'N, 61°07.8'W

Chart: #4278

Rewritten and condensed from earlier material by G.C. Fraser, R.S. Gillette, and J.F. Young.

DIRECTIONS: Go to the extreme end of St. Patrick's Channel. This village lies about 18 miles from Baddeck by water.

ANCHORAGE AND BERTHS: Anchor off the government wharf in 12-15 feet. At night the noise of the trucks on the nearby highway can be unpleasant, in which case, anchor in West Cove behind McInnis Island where there is peace and solitude.

The government wharf has eight feet on its end.

REMARKS: This is a pretty place with some hospitable sailors who moor their 30-foot sailboats off the government wharf. One correspondent bought four dozen of the best oysters he ever ate for $7.00 (Canadian) at the nearby Indian reservation in 1986. This harbor is worth a visit if one has the time.

FACILITIES: A few basics are available at the general store.

BADDECK

46°05.9'N, 60°44.8'W

Chart: #4278

Rewritten and condensed from earlier material by G.K. MacIntosh, W. Britten, E.B. Cabot, R.C. McCurdy, B.P. Bogert, C. Vilas, G.C. Rockwood, J.F. Young .and Charles Weaver   2005

DIRECTIONS: Baddeck Harbour, just north of Kidston Island presents no difficulty entering from east or west inside Kidston Island.

ANCHORAGE AND BERTHS: The preferred anchorage is just southeast of the Baddeck Community Wharf, but it is open, and when stormy, it is best to move into a dock or go elsewhere for more protection. There are moorings available in the cove inside Kidston Island. These are rented by Baddeck Marine and are serviced by a launch.

One has a choice of three docks to lie to in Baddeck. The most prominent is the Community wharf. West of this are the docks of Baddeck Marine, and well West of Baddeck Marine is a series of docks in a cove owned by Cape Breton Boatyard. All docks have a wharfage charge and you should call ahead for space. (telephone number listed below) (VHF channel 68).

REMARKS: Baddeck (pop. 1,000) is the capital of the Bras d'Or Lakes. Nearby *Beinn Bhreagh* was the summer home of Alexander Graham Bell whose descendants still summer here. In 1956 the Canadian government opened the Alexander Graham Bell Museum in Baddeck. This striking building, in its beautiful landscape, overlooks Baddeck Bay in the direction of Bell's old summer home.

One thinks of Bell only as the inventor of the telephone, but inside this museum are displays of Bell's many other interests which include devices to bring sound to the deaf, and the kites and gliders he used on his many aeronautical experiments. The museum is a splendid example of government funds wisely spent and is a tribute to Canada, as well as to Dr. Bell.

FACILITIES: **Baddeck Marine [Tel: (902) 295-2434]** www.dbmarina.com is a full service yacht open year round and open seven days a week in peak season. The Marina is located just west of the Community Wharf and has full repair and restoration services as well as haulout and storage, shore power, water, fuel, ice, showers, pumpout, and many chandlery items.

Cape Breton Boatyard [Tel: (902) 295-2664] Another full service yard is located at the west end of the harbor, with water, storage, pumpout and repair facilities.

Baddeck Community Wharf [Tel: (902) 295-8110] Restaurants, grocery stores, banks (ATM), yacht club, post office, a liquor store, laundromat, and gift shops abound in town, as well as taxis and a car rental agency. The Sydney airport is 1 1/2 hours away by car.

BADDECK BAY HARBOURS

Chart #4278

Material supplied by Willard C. Butcher and Priscilla Travis.   *1991*

THE HARBOUR

46°07.6'N, 60°42.9'W

DIRECTIONS: Chart #4278 shows six feet or less inside the long bar; however, eight feet can be carried into the large basin just below the word "Harbour" on the chart. [Proceed with caution as depths change over the years. - ed.]

ANCHORAGES AND BERTHS: Anchor anywhere. The basin is uniformly 12-16 feet deep and serves as a storm anchorage for local yachts. There is good holding ground and five private moorings (1991). Boats drawing six feet or less can continue further south to the head of the cove.

REMARKS: This is a hurricane anchorage with total isolation. The bar is used for swimming and water skiing, but these activities are not obtrusive. Eagles roost on nearby trees.

FACILITIES: None.

HERRING COVE

46°07.4'N, 60°42.3'W

DIRECTIONS: As the chart indicates, the water is deep the further southwest you go (60 feet). Six feet of water can be carried just inside the point of land below the word "Cove" on Chart #4278.

ANCHORAGE AND BERTHS: Anchor in the above-mentioned cove, being careful not to anchor over the submerged wreck near the shore on the southwest side of the cove.

REMARKS: The wreck mentioned above is that of the schooner *Yankee*, once owned by Captain Irving Johnson (not to be confused with a later brigantine named *Yankee*, which Johnson owned after the Second World War and sailed around the world several times). Rumor has it that her owner after Johnson deliberately scuttled her.

This is a beautiful harbor.

SAINT ANDREWS CHANNEL

Chart: #4277

Rewritten and condensed from material by R. Carter and A. Chace.

St. Andrews Channel runs in a NE-SW direction from the southwest tip of Boularderie Island to Little Bras d'Or Harbour, a distance of approximately 20 miles. Both shores are rolling hills with many broad fields and farms, making this arm of water scenically attractive, and the waters therein are almost wholly devoid of submerged dangers. The following anchorages are of interest:

ISLAND POINT HARBOUR

46°07.7'N, 60°33.3'W

DIRECTIONS: Sail northeast up St. Andrew's Channel for approximately six miles. Note "weirdly eroded" gypsum cliffs in the vicinity of Island Point. Round Island Point, and reverse course to the southwest and proceed well up into Island Point Harbour.

Coming from the south it is easy to miss finding the entrance if you aren't paying attention.

ANCHORAGE: Anchor in 12 feet at the harbor head.

REMARKS: This is fascinating scenery. Years ago mussels and oysters were reported present if you explored the shoreline. The northeast end of St. Andrew's Channel is very beautiful, but water shallow enough to anchor in is hard to find.

Any northerly wind funnels right in here (as well as northerly seas) making this a poor anchorage under these conditions.

FACILITIES: None.

LONG ISLAND

46°09.9'N, 60°25.3'W

There is a small sand spit (mostly under water in 1986) at the southern entrance between Long Island and the mainland. Anchor to the north and behind this sand spit in 12-15 feet of water, making sure you have a good bite in the sandy bottom. The sand spit should stop any seas from coming in.

FACILITIES: None.

165

GEORGES RIVER

46°12.6'N, 60°20.5'W

There is an anchorage in 12-15 feet of water in the mouth of Georges River, just to the east and south inside Almons Point. This is a poor anchorage from any wind from the north.

REMARKS: Georges River Barachois (just west of the anchorage) is reported to be unattractive "with shacks and outboards," and the anchorage itself is in sight of a (not very active) railway bridge, which does not make the surroundings idyllic.

FACILITIES: None.

BRAS D'OR HARBOUR

46°14.6'N, 60°20.5'W

On entering, turn out of the channel to the east when opposite the prominent white church, and continue to turn south around the sand spit on Burchells Point (a/k/a Chapel Point). There is eight feet of water as far south as the ruins of an old private wharf. In 1986 there was a mooring that you could pick up (after inquiring and receiving permission to do so ashore).

Boats drawing less than five feet can use the cove on the west side of the channel.

There is protection here from all winds, and the holding ground is reasonably good in mud and grass.

REMARKS: This is the head of navigation in St. Andrews Channel for sailing boats, as the Trans-Canada Highway crosses the head of this harbor on a 21-foot (vertical clearance) fixed bridge.

The village is 1/2 mile from the anchorage at Burchells Point. This may be a convenient place to exchange crews, by arranging to get a taxi to Sydney Airport from the village.

Otherwise, the dinghy landing at Burchells Point is inconvenient, and the surroundings, not particularly attractive.

FACILITIES: Basic supplies are available at the general store in the village where there is a post office and restaurant as well. No fuel or water is available.

THE GREAT BRAS D'OR

Chart #4277

Rewritten and condensed from earlier material from G. Fraser, H. Streeter, T.F.T. Morland, J. Wickersham, C. Hastie A. Chace, M.K. Jordan. And new material from W. Tobin 2003

The Great Bras d'Or runs in a northeast-southwest direction from the southwest tip of Boularderie Island to the navigable entrance to the Gulf of St. Lawrence, over a distance of approximately 20 miles. It is spanned by the Seal Island Bridge, which has a vertical clearance of 119 feet. In the narrow northern end of the Great Bras d'Or, the maximum flood and ebb tidal currents run at six knots, and when these currents are contrary to the wind, a considerable confused sea develops. When caught in adverse conditions, the two safe harbors of refuge are Otter Harbour and Kellys Cove.

The Canadian tide book does not say how to estimate fair currents in the great Bras d'Or. In settles conditions the current turns south 3 hours after low water at N. Sydney and North 3 hours after high.

OTTER HARBOUR

46°13.2'N, 60°31.8'W

DIRECTIONS: Enter Otter Harbour from the northeast, being careful to avoid the shoal (11 feet) northeast of Otter Island.

ANCHORAGES AND BERTHS: Anchor anywhere near the island in the center of the harbor with the sectored light on it, being careful not to foul the moorings here. It is also possible to anchor in a spot northeast of Otter Point, and inside Otter Island in settled weather with westerly winds.

REMARKS: This is a good area out of the tide, seven miles southwest of the entrance to the Gulf of St. Lawrence, to wait for a favorable tide before proceeding into the Gulf or into the Lakes.

An interesting lagoon lies north of the anchorage to explore in the dinghy, and there is reported to be a fresh-water spring on the lagoon's northern side good enough for drinking. [I could never find said spring. -ed.]

FACILITIES: None.

KELLYS COVE

46°17.3'N, 60°26.4'W

Anchor in 12-15 feet of water well inside this cove out of the tide. Unfortunately this anchorage is exposed to southerly winds, and it is probably best to tie inside the government wharf here which is reported to have 12 feet on its outer end.

REMARKS: This is a good refuge if caught in a foul tide or bad weather transiting between the Lakes and Gulf of St. Lawrence.

FACILITIES: None.

PORT MORIEN*

46°08'N, 59°52.3'W

&

MAIN A DIEU*

46°00.4'N, 59°50.5'W

Charts: #4375, #4377

Rewritten and condensed from material by C. Vilas.

DIRECTIONS: **Port Morien** on Morien Bay is easy to enter because there are no obstructions going in.

The entrance to **Main a Dieu** off Main a Dieu Passage is tricky, and it is best to have Chart #4377 aboard for this, although it can be done on Chart #4375 with reasonable visibility and caution, observing the channel buoys in proper order. The main channel runs from Mad Dick red bell in a westerly direction to a green flasher, then in a northerly direction, observing the channel buoys into the small harbor.

ANCHORAGE AND BERTHS: In **Port Morien** there is plenty of room to anchor near the government wharf, though the holding ground is unknown. This government wharf will accommodate boats with a draft of six feet.

Main a Dieu Harbour is so small that anchoring isn't advisable. There are several private docks with six feet of water on the ends where you may be able to negotiate a berth.

REMARKS: Both these harbors should be considered as harbors of refuge. Port Morien is the better of the two in northerly or westerly winds, but it is very open to the east.

FACILITIES: None.

*These harbors should be entered with caution, as they have not been reported on in the last ten years.

LOUISBURG

45°55'N, 59°58'W

Charts: #4375, #4376

Rewritten and condensed from earlier material by P. Sheldon, J. Wickersham, C. Bartlett, A. Weld and J. McKelvy. 1993

DIRECTIONS: It is possible to enter this harbor using Chart #4375 which shows the ranges and most of the buoys, although large-scale Chart #4376 is preferable.

The entrance here is easy. Coming from the east, the lighthouse and large water tank behind the town are clearly visible, not to mention the ramparts of the restored fortress once you get close. The channel is clearly marked, and there are two ranges to get you past any off-lying dangers.

ANCHORAGE AND BERTHS: On entering the Northern Arm (site of the modern town), one encounters (going southwest to northeast on the western shore) the fish plant wharf (the fish plant is obvious with a large chimney behind it), the L-shaped government wharf, and two small wharves just northeast of the government wharf. The first small wharf is designated by the locals as the "small craft wharf," and the next small wharf, for unloading fish from the smaller fishermen.

Berths may be had at the government wharf or the small craft wharf — the latter being preferable to the government wharf which has many boats tied to its lee. There is 12-feet of water at the end of the small craft wharf.

A delightful anchorage is under the restored fortification in the Southwest Arm, <u>but</u> the bottom is rocky and full of kelp, so a yachtsman anchor with a trip line is recommended. Anchor in 20 feet northeast of the "Frederick Gate" (the fortified gate on the shore leading to the restored

town and fortress). There is, however, a slight roll in this anchorage and it is suitable only in settled weather.

Use a yachtsman anchor and trip line in any other part of this harbor as well, as the holding ground is reported to be universally rocky and full of kelp.

REMARKS: The Canadian government has spent millions of dollars restoring this great French Fortress of Louisbourg. Captured twice by the British — once in 1745, and the last time in 1758, most of the fortress and garrison town have been restored by Parks Canada to its (supposed) appearance in the summer of 1744. If you anchor under the fortress as recommended above, you will be anchoring where the British fleet, bearing General Wolfe on his way to Quebec and the destruction of the French Empire in North America, anchored in 1758.

It is not considered cricket, however, to simply row ashore and look things over. You must walk or take a taxi from the modern town to the visitors' entrance center, where, after paying a fee, you will board a park bus that will convey you to the main gate of the restoration.

169

This harbor is ideal for those returning from Newfoundland who wish to exchange crews via Sydney, but who do not wish to be slowed down on their passage west by the allure of the Bras d'Or Lakes.

The modern town, once a swordfishing port, has become very dependent on the tourist trade and lacks charm.

FACILITIES: The modern town offers most of the amenities, including grocery stores, a laundromat, liquor store, and some restaurants. The restaurants are of the beanery variety, but if you want a really interesting meal, try the restored restaurant in the old fortress village called L'Epee du Roi (lunch only; the entire fortress is closed at night).

Water is available on the wharf east of the small craft wharf, and fuel may be had (at some expense and time consumption) by arranging for a truck to come down to the government wharf.

SYDNEY

46°08.3'N, 60°12'W

Chart: #4276

Rewritten and condensed from earlier material by C. Bok, C. Bartlett, G. and R. Waters, with new information by M.K. Jordan and B. Dalton.   *1995*

DIRECTIONS: There are no navigational problems entering Sydney, a large, well-buoyed commercial harbor. At Point Edward, the harbor is divided into the Northwest Arm leading to North Sydney, and the South Arm which leads to the Sydney River past the industrial, business and commercial districts of the city.

ANCHORAGE AND BERTHS: An anchorage (and sometimes a mooring) is available at the **Royal Cape Breton Yacht Club**, located on the Sydney shore just south of the government docks, across from Dobsons Point on the Westmount side of the harbor. We suspect the wharf (which was missing for several years) has been replaced, because Brian Dalton reported that they had tender service in 1995.

The Dobson Yacht Club at Dobsons Point in Westmount has a small basin in which you may tie up temporarily for fuel or water, but there is no anchorage.

The Northern Yacht Club is located in North Sydney on the north shore, 1.9 miles beyond (southwest of) the C N ferry dock, where the Newfoundland ferries berth. In mid-summer the N.Y.C. basin can be crowded, in spite of a 500-foot bulkhead with recessed ladders. It is too exposed to anchor outside the Yacht Club

basin, but there are moorings, one of which may be available for a vessel of less than 35 feet. Otherwise, the moorings are too close together. It might be wise to call ahead and reserve a space if you know you are going in here. **N.Y.C. telephone: (902) 794-9121**.

REMARKS: Sydney (pop. 30,000) is a large industrial city which, until very recently, specialized in the production of steel. It remains a major transportation center, with a commercial airport nearby, and the ferry link to Newfoundland.

Being so unlike the picturesque harbors so typical of Nova Scotia one would probably avoid Sydney unless in need of supplies or for a crew change.

FACILITIES: Fuel and water are available at the Dobson Yacht Club in Westmount or the Northern Yacht Club in North Sydney. The Northern Yacht Club can provide ice, showers, and a bar (which some correspondents report operates at irregular hours).

The Royal Cape Breton now has tender service, so one speculates whether they have other amenities as well. (They never had fuel or water in the past.)

Almost any kind of food, drink or supply can be found in Sydney. There are no boatyards capable of handling a yacht, however.

ST. ANN'S BAY*

46°15'N, 60°35'W

Charts: #4277, #4367

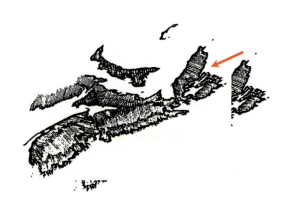

Rewritten and condensed from earlier material by G. Fraser, H. Streeter and A. Chace.

DIRECTIONS: Enter from the north, past the narrows at Beach Point through which there is often a heavy current. Be careful of the cable ferry that operates between Beach Point and Old Fort Point. Most boats continue down the five miles to South Gut, but it is possible to lie at the government wharf at Englishtown or anchor at Price Point for the night if you are in a hurry to go elsewhere.

ANCHORAGE AND BERTHS: The best anchorage is in South Gut, in 12-14 feet of water just north of the government wharf. (Good mud holding ground here.) There is reported to be ten feet of water at the end of the government wharf here should you wish to tie up.

As previously mentioned, it is possible to tie to the government wharf at Englishtown where the depth on the end is 11 feet. Be prepared, however, to tie to the windward (south) side of this wharf, as the space inside the L is usually filled with local fishing boats. It is generally considered too deep here to drop an anchor.

There is another anchorage at Price Point, behind the breakwater on a line between Price Point and the lighthouse, though this seems open to the south.

A number of other anchorages may be possible on the west side of the bay from a perusal of Chart #4277, but none of these have been reported on.

REMARKS: This is a very beautiful bay surrounded by hills and mountains.

If you take the highway west from the wharf at South Gut, you will come to St. Ann's Gaelic College, where the Gaelic language, native arts, highland dancing and music (bagpipes and drums) are taught and practiced in a six-week summer session to teenagers. If you plan your cruise to arrive here during the first full week in August, you will be able to see the "Gaelic Mod," a seven-day festival of Celtic culture, complete with an outdoor church service on Sunday in Gaelic. At the college, Gaelic crafts may be purchased, including tartan clothes, blankets and even a Gaelic dictionary. If you have any Scots blood in you, this should not be missed.

FACILITIES: Aside from the items mentioned above, basic campers' supplies may be bought locally. No fuel or water is available.

*This harbor should be entered with caution, as it has not been reported on in the last ten years.

172

INGONISH HARBOUR

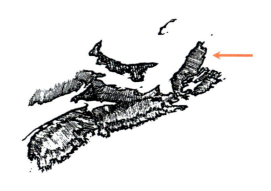

46°38'N, 60°24'W

Chart #4365

Rewritten and condensed from earlier material by O. Gates, P. Richmond, L. Brunton, A. Weld, W. Tobin and update G.Schneider. *2003*

DIRECTIONS: According to the note on Chart #4365, the channel buoys in from the offshore Mo A buoy (KM) may be moved from their charted positions because of shifts in the channel. This channel looks very narrow, but it is considered quite safe except in a heavy onshore wind. Least depth in 2003 was 18 feet.

ANCHORAGE AND BERTHS: Once inside, anchor at the entrance to the cove on the northeast side of the harbor in 14 feet of water with good holding ground. There is also rumored to be a safe anchorage in the extreme north end of this cove, but you must acquire local knowledge to do this. One can safely anchor in 20 feet near the southern point with a good view of the ski area.

The government wharf on the south side of the harbor is reported to have ten feet on its end. However the Schooner William Moir, which conducts whale-watching tours uses it as well

REMARKS: This is a very pretty harbor, and the scenery is like sailing into a Scottish loch. From the anchorage at the mouth of the northeast cove, you get a delightful view of the ski run coming down from Cape Smoky.

FACILITIES: The Keltic Lodge, located 1.5 miles northeast of the harbor on Middle Head (shown on the chart) is owned and operated by the Province, and here is the same quality food and service that you get at The Pines and Liscomb Lodge (mentioned elsewhere).

The town of Ingonish Beach is at the entrance to Cape Breton National Park. There are excellent swimming beaches and hiking trails here. The town itself has a grocery and liquor store, bank, hardware and variety stores. Block ice is available at the Esso station, and the nearest phone is at a motel across the road from the Esso.

No dockside fuel or water is available.

The hike to the end of Middle Head in the National Park is highly recommended— about five miles round-trip.

NEIL HARBOUR*

46°48.4'N, 60°19.3'W
&
NEW HAVEN*

46°49.3'N, 60°19.3'W

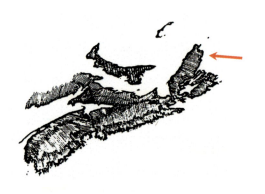

Chart #4363

Rewritten from earlier material by W. Dickson and A. Weld.

These two harbors, located a mile apart from each other midway between Ingonish and Dingwall, complement each other. **Neil Harbour** is for northeast and southeast winds, and **New Haven** is for southwest and northwest winds.

DIRECTIONS: The chart suggests giving the southwest side of Neil Head some room before turning into **Neil Harbour**, otherwise the approach is unobstructed.

New Haven is marked by a green flasher, located approximately 1/2 mile offshore to the east. From this buoy, the entrance should bear 285° (mag.). On entering between the two jetties, keep the small green flasher close to port.

ANCHORAGE AND BERTHS: The best anchorage in **Neil Harbour** is at the head of the bay, and this may be preferable to lying at the government wharf if there is a surge in the harbor. This area, however, is totally exposed to easterly winds. Six feet of draft may be carried into the government wharf (which is small), where you may wish to lie off on a stern anchor rather than tie alongside. Although completely protected, there is considerable surge here during southwest winds.

Inside the jetties at **New Haven** there is plenty of room for anchoring, and nine feet can be carried into the government wharf. This harbor offers perfect protection in a southwest blow.

FACILITIES: None.

*These harbors should be entered with caution, as they have not been reported on in the last ten years.

DINGWALL

46°54.2'N, 60°27.2'W

Charts: #4365, #4363

Rewritten and condensed from material by L. Brunton, A. Weld, A. Chace and J. Hawkins

DIRECTIONS: <u>You</u> <u>must</u> <u>have</u> <u>Chart</u> <u>#4365</u> aboard to get in here.

The chart shows a minimum of seven feet through the entrance channel. In 1987 it was reported that this channel was dredged every two years to a depth of 11 feet. In 1990 it was reliably reported that the channel had a depth of seven feet. Nonetheless, it is impossible to forecast the depth of this channel on any particular date. Remember, however, that Dingwall is a commercial fishing port. Those boats have to get in and out somehow.

The entrance is straightforward. There is an Mo A flasher about a mile offshore, then a pair of buoys before the double-pronged breakwaters, and four channel buoys after the breakwaters, leading into the harbor.

ANCHORAGE AND BERTHS: The preferred anchorage is in the small round bay at the inner end of the harbor. J. Hawkins in 2004 said with excellent holding ground in 20ft of mud it would make an excellent hurricane hole. There is a government wharf just north of the gypsum pile, with a 15-foot depth reported on its outside face.

REMARKS: Dingwall is only eight miles south of Cape North and very handy for anyone wanting to make a daylight crossing to Port aux Basques or Codroy on the Newfoundland side of the Cabot Strait. There is no nearer protected anchorage.

This once was a very active gypsum port, with large ships entering and leaving through a deeply-dredged channel. A large pile of gypsum is now completely overgrown and the harbor is much more attractive than it used to be. If you stop here, it is best to allow enough time to go on to White Point Cove or even Ingonish if you cannot get in due to the shoaling of the channel.

FACILITIES: Basic supplies can be had at a general store 1/2 mile from the harbor.

WHITE POINT COVE*

46°52.5'N, 59°21,2'W

Looking at Chart #4363 you wouldn't realize this *cul de sac* exists. White Point Cove (called Scotch Cove in the **Gulf of St. Lawrence Pilot**) has a breakwater extending from its northeast corner, within which lies a government wharf with a reported ten feet of depth on its end. There have been mixed reports on the suitability of this harbor, from its "providing shelter in almost any kind of wind," to, "I was not happy to get 9 1/2 feet into the cove [in a 30-knot wind and therefore didn't go in]."

*Caution should be used entering this harbor, as it has not been reported on in the last ten years.

ST. PAUL ISLAND

47°12.5'N, 60°09.2'W

Chart: #4450

This is such an intriguing place that there has been no attempt to adapt previous information on the island to a format, and little attempt to edit it. What follows is a dialogue between those who have landed or attempted to land there.

C.W. Bartlett   *1952*

Anyone leaning over a chart which covers the waters between Cape North on Cape Breton Island and Cape Ray on Newfoundland, can't help wondering about that island a part of the way across. Of course, the waters are the Cabot Strait, and the island is St. Paul.

The fact is, that it is about 13 miles NE of Cape North and about 40 miles SW of Cape Ray. It is some three miles long tending in a NE-SW direction. There are lights at either end. The northeasterly one has a diaphone. The R.D.F. beacon is located on Atlantic Cove on the SE side.

That just about tells the story for the person who is going by. For the one who would like to stop, however, more information is in order. Unfortunately, this writer is in no position to supply it in any real detail. His knowledge is based on only one abortive try back in 1951. Perhaps the best way to pass along the information is to tell of it.

The plan was to lay overnight at the island on the way to Newfoundland. Coming up on it around 4:00 P.M., there was an easy southeast wind blowing with apparently little or no ground swell. The two obvious (and only) choices for an anchorage were Atlantic Cove on the SE side and Trinity Cove on the opposite. Trinity, being the lee, was elected. Disappointment number one was the fact that the cove was such a slight indentation that it was very difficult to distinguish, though it hadn't appeared so on the chart. Annoyance number two was the narrowness of the sand

bottom shelf between the beach and a very liberal ten fathoms. The clincher came thereafter, however. With the hook on the bottom and the anchor-down drink being served, the surge took over. For a few minutes all would be relatively calm, and then she would start a roll — not an easy roll but a slam-bang gunwale proposition. After a few cycles of these, it was to-hell-with-it-let's-shove-off-for-Newfoundland. Which we did.

To take a look at Atlantic Cove on the windward side, we doubled back and sailed quite close. There you could see what was going on. Whether you would call it a surge or a confusion of breakers doesn't make much difference. It was no place for anchoring.

One-trip knowledge of a harbor or anchorage is a dangerous thing. It is quite probable that someone who has stopped at St. Paul at some other time or more than once will come forward and be fairer to it. Edward Rowe Snow's book, **Secrets of the North Atlantic Island** (Dodd, Mead, 1950) has a long account of St. Paul and its history. It makes very intriguing reading.

Dr. Wm. Dickson   *1966*

We came in from the NE and circled the island one-and-a-half times. The island is deserted except for the lighthouse keeper on North Point, with whom we chatted. He persuaded us to land at his "dock," a rock in the tickle, but the surge and the current made this too much of a stunt. [The light is no longer manned. ed.] Apparently you missed a spot in the northeast corner of Trinity Cove just north of the 2.2 sounding on the insert of Chart #4450. Here you can proceed into a flume 30-feet wide and 100-feet long, with rock cliffs rising from 50 to 100 feet on either side extending abruptly down to 20 feet of depth. You should take along spikes with rings, i.e. mountaineering pitons, and bridle your vessel bow and stern for an indefinite stay. A northwest blow and surge might give this spot motion, but in general you would be very snug and completely hidden. We landed and could climb out of the flume without any difficulty.

C.W. Bartlett   *1966*

I must admit that Bill Dickson's "spot" in the NE corner of Trinity Cove was missed by me and sounds intriguing. Few will disagree that he has suggested a new high in what the well-outfitted cruising yacht should have aboard, i.e. mountaineering pitons.

Dr. Wm. Dickson   *1972*

In 1966 in a southeaster, we found Trinity Cove tranquil. In 1971, a southwester built up a sloppy surge and made Trinity Cove unenterable. On this occasion we went further north and found good shelter east of the ledge in MacDougall's Cove (insert Chart #4450). The holding ground was good, there was an irregular surge, and there were vertical spinner puffs from the surrounding headlands. One should post watch over two well-spaced anchors and be prepared to move out promptly should the wind shift into the north and west.

H.P. Sullivan   *1977*

We came into Atlantic Cove on the east coast of the island under power in a nearly flat calm. Nonetheless, there was a slightly confused and oily sea, together with a noticeable surge. We anchored beneath the cliff at the south end of the cove and went ashore, landing on a small shingle beach.

Nearby there is a ring fixed to the rock face with a rope attached which helps one climb up to the footpath which runs around the cove about 50 to 60 feet above sea level. The path led to several good-sized deserted buildings on the northern side of the cove and also extended a good way to the south, although that is far more difficult going. This is not a place to linger if weather or sea makes up, and we suggest that anyone going ashore leave at least one person and a loud horn aboard.

John Harries   *1991*

We deliberately planned our visit (in late July) immediately after a cold front passage with a large and building high behind it. We anchored [at Atlantic Cove] with a 45 lb. CQR and a Fortress [Danforth-type anchor], at right angles, in six fathoms, just south of the shallow patch south of Big Dick Rock, as shown on the insert on Chart #4450. With the wind in the northwest, there was a small, but not unduly uncomfortable surge.

After landing just east of the derelict building on the edge of the cliff, on the north shore of the cove, we were faced with the problem of getting up to the cliff. The rock is very rotten, and strong-looking outcrops give way with no warning; the consequences of a fall could be serious. At the top of the cliff there is a clear area that looks as if it were once cultivated. We later found out that the undulations in this field" are the graves of some two hundred victims of shipwrecks.

The next morning dawned sunny and flat calm. We steamed around the island via North Point to anchor in eight fathoms in Trinity Cove. This cove is less easily distinguished, since it is only a small indentation and lacks differentiating land marks. Before anchoring, we motored far enough offshore to confirm our position by a visual bearing and a radar range on South Point light.

Our purpose was to find the flume mentioned by Dr. Dickson in his account of his visit in 1966. We were unable to find any such indentation. We did however; find a flume matching his description, between the islets shown on the chart, but four-tenths of a mile north of Peters Point. From the dinghy, the water there appeared deep and rock-free, with almost no surge. The best bet might be to drop an anchor off the bow, back in and secure the stern lines to the many outcrops. This would supply a very snug mooring, and would make an interesting stopover on the way to Newfoundland. We did not try this, and a skipper contemplating it would be well advised to reconnoiter first in the dinghy.

S. Dumaresq   *2004*

In 2004, *Surprise* anchored in Atlantic Cove inside the shallow spot called Anchor Rk. The rocks on the south side of the cove extend quite far into the cove so one should watch the sounder closely, and keep a look-out on the bow. The water was very, very clear, almost tropical. The wind was light from the Northwest and although we had a small surge the whole time we were visiting the island, we were able to spend a comfortable night at anchor. We found a satisfactory place to land the dinghy. It is about 100 yards south of the derelict boat shed mentioned by John Harries. There is a stone outcropping that slowly climbs up to cliff level thus avoiding the dangers caused by the crumbling granite. We had to carry the dinghy part way up the rocks in order to secure it above high tide. The pathways linking the houses are all overgrown so that exploring the island on foot is now quite difficult

Because of the many shipwrecks in the area, and because of the clear water, this island is very popular for diving expeditions. Those yachts with diving gear and experience might like to explore this aspect of St. Paul's.
We would recommend the book "*Memoirs of a Lightkeeper's Son – Life on St. Paul Island*" by Billy Budge (Pottersfield Press, 2003). This is a delightful account of a young boy's life on the Island in the 1950s.

W.Cook   *2003*

In 2003, *Resolution* stopped at St. Paul Island on the return from Greenland. With the wind in the southeast, MacDougall Cove looked to offer the best protection; indeed it was perfectly calm, and we anchored in the middle of the cove. We also explored the small cove in the northeast corner (2 fathom, 4 foot depth on chart #4450) by dinghy, and it appeared big enough to moor bow and stern (perhaps with pitons?) During the night the wind veered to south-southwest, however, and MacDougall Cove quickly became a dangerous lee shore, with the swells rolling around the point and breaking on the low cliffs. We left in a hurry, lucky to be able to escape undamaged.

MACDOUGALL POND

(Bay St. Lawrence)
47°00'N, 60°28'W

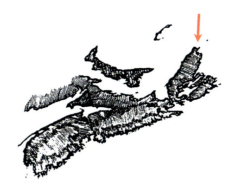

Chart #4363

Dr. Wm. Dixon, Brian Dalton, T.Kenney and S.Dumaresq   *2004*

DIRECTIONS: Find the Mo A Bay St. Lawrence buoy, and steer a southerly course into the jetty. Eight feet of water is reported in the channel to the pond. Entry here in a hard northerly is inadvisable.

ANCHORAGE AND BERTHS: A large portion of the pond is shoal. If you wish to anchor, it would be best to tie to the new T-shaped wharf located on the port hand (east side) of the harbor and inquire about the anchorage. One should stay close to the T shaped wharf as it shoals off quickly. You can tie to the jetty with lots of water, but fishing boats with large wakes have no mercy. Current, wakes and surge make the inner wharf preferable.

REMARKS: This is a very convenient spot on the way to or from Port aux Basques or the Magdalens if you have shoal draft. However in 2003 T.Kenney carried 8.5ft into the harbor on a ¼ rising tide.

The little village with Cape North (1,400 ft.) towering above it to the west is very pretty. This can be a busy place during the lobster and crab season but as the people are very friendly and this is an incredibly beautiful harbor it is recommended.

FACILITIES: The active fishing wharf (pay telephone in the office) at the entrance has water and ice; electrical outlets exist at each hoist here, and at the new pier up harbor there are also differentiated receptacles for oil cans, plastic, and glass. There is a supermarket near the church (one mile away). The 24-hour wharfage charge is $10.00 (Canadian)

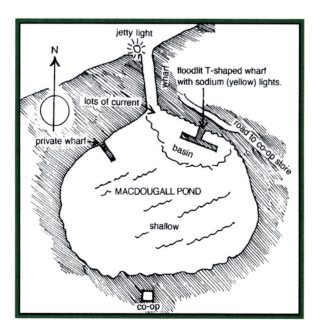

179

CHETICAMP HARBOUR

46°38'N, 61°01'W

Charts: #4449, #4464

Rewritten and condensed from earlier material by H. Barlow, P. Richmond and V. Spooner, with new information by P. and H. Travis.   *1997*

DIRECTIONS: Chart #4449 is far preferable here, as it is a large-scale chart for the harbor, although it is possible to get in using Chart #4464 and following the buoys and ranges precisely.

At the north end of Cheticamp Island, there is a range bearing 109° (true) which will bring you to a point where the harbor opens up to starboard. You will see a RWG sector light bearing 190° (true), with white marking the center of the channel. Alter course to the second bearing. The water is very shallow around the last pair of buoys.

ANCHORAGE AND BERTHS:
Approximately 0.1 mile south of the channel buoys VD 13-14 you are in the main harbor and can anchor anywhere. The holding ground is good mud. There is a depth of 11 feet at the last pair of buoys The T-shaped government wharf is very much available for visiting yachts. However, there may be a lot of activity in the wee hours of the morning when the crab fleet heads out to sea. After entering the harbor, there is a fishplant on the port side. If you are following the buoyed channel, it ends at a small wharf that is also a good place for yachts to tie up. The "lighthouse" painted like an Acadian flag – red, white and blue stripes with a gold star, identifies this wharf. The dock is part of the waterfront boardwalk in the middle of town; it is very handy to the grocery and hardware store as well as other shops and restaurants. In 2004, there was a very good there was seafood restaurant just above this wharf.

REMARKS: Cheticamp (pop. 3,000) is a French-speaking community, though cultural imperialism has forced it to be bilingual. The road through the town is part of the Cabot Trail, and aside from the fish factory, the main industry seems to be tourism. The town consists of houses strung out along the waterfront for a considerable distance, but not extended back. The land is fairly high.

There is a flourishing craft industry here, the main product being hooked rugs, which are acclaimed to be very good.

FACILITIES: This is a good place to provision, as most needs can be found within walking distance— a large grocery store, bank, post office, liquor store, laundromat and some restaurants. People are friendly and helpful. Water is available at the small-craft basin as you enter the harbor on the south, facing the pier. There is no dockside fuel.

MARGAREE HARBOUR

46 21.9'N 61 11.4'W

Charts 4449, 4464

S. Dumaresq   *2004*

Surprise followed the range lights into the harbor just after high tide. Between the red (QR) buoy and green (QG) buoy, our sounder went down to 7 feet. This happened again at the end of the breakwater. Although not shown on the chart, there is a red buoy at the end of the breakwater

There is lots of water at the Fisherman's Co-op Wharf, although we were advised not to go all the way to the northerly end of the wharf. We were able to get fresh water at the wharf. As this was a short lunch stop, we did not explore any further.

Mabou Harbour -see next page

MABOU HARBOUR

46°04.6'N, 61°25.5'W

Charts: #4448, #4462, #4463

Rewritten and condensed from earlier material by P. Pereira, C. Bartlett, L. Brunton H. Sullivan and S.Dumaresq   2004

DIRECTIONS: This harbor can be entered using Chart #4463, but Chart #4448 is preferable.

This entrance can be seen clearly from quite a distance offshore. Mabou Highlands to the north noticeably slope down to Green Point and then suddenly drop off. In comparison, the low land to the south of the entrance is quite conspicuous. When one comes a little closer, one can see Green Point is well named. Its large expanse of open pasture is invaluable for identifying the harbor entrance during the summer.

Pick up the range of 107.5° (true) and follow it in. Mabou has finally been dredged and S. Dumaresq reported a minimum of 7ft two hours after low tide

ANCHORAGE AND BERTHS: This harbor is well protected from every wind, and it is safe to anchor anywhere. If you must come ashore for supplies, it is best to anchor 1/2-mile west of the Mabou River, so that you may take a dinghy under the highway bridge and beach it on the north side of the river and walk to the village.

There is a government wharf at the base of the inside range lighthouse with a minimum of 6ft feet on its face. Upriver at the village of Mabou, there is a floating dock just below the highway bridge. There is lots of water at the dock. Passage to the dock is well marked by stakes driven into the mud banks. *Surprise* made this run to the dock within two hours of low tide and the shallowest point they found was 6ft under their sounder.

REMARKS: This is one of the most beautiful harbors on Cape Breton and a very pleasant place to spend a few days. To the south of the entrance is one of the few sand beaches on Cape Breton. It is peaceful and you may very well be the only boat in the harbor. St Mary's Church is a stunning piece of architecture that dominates the beautiful Mabou countryside.

FACILITIES: Basic supplies may be had in the village. There is no fuel or water available.

PORT HOOD

46°00'N, 61°33'W

Chart #4448

Wallace Feldman, Brian Dalton, and S.Dumaresq 2004

DIRECTIONS: The harbor is south of the breakwater here. (Never be tempted to anchor north of the breakwater.) When entering from the north, round the green flasher at the southeast corner of Port Hood Island and proceed northeast to the second green flasher, leaving it to port. Then head north to the red buoy VM6 (not the red buoy to the northeast (VK14).

The snug harbor on Port Hood Island is to the west and south of the breakwater toward Cape Breton. The three timber wharves encompass a square basin of about 40 square yards (see chartlet). Entrance requires great skill on the depth sounder for the outer and inner approach where it shoals east of the old wharf and off the ramp. [Don't do this if you are faint of heart. -ed.] The "breakwater' on the chartlet is really the remains of an old causeway. The gap in the causeway is a government dredged channel and is marked by one pair of tiny white buoys.

ANCHORAGE AND BERTHS: There is a fine anchorage off the wharf near the light, well-sheltered from west and southwest winds. There is also room for one or two

boats to tie up at the wharf which offers good shelter from winds in any direction.

REMARKS: This former fishing village has become a small summer colony, occupied by U.S. and Canadian residents in equal numbers. The former government wharf noted above is now well-maintained privately. If one wants to learn about the fascinating history of Port Hood Island, it is worthwhile to seek out Earl Smith, a direct descendant of the Bostonian who settled there in 1786.

FACILITIES: There are no facilities here, and as far as we could tell, none on the mainland side either.

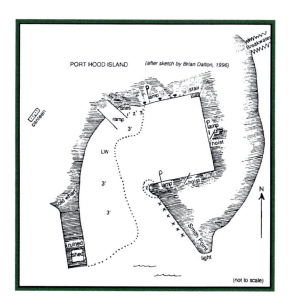

ST. GEORGE'S BAY TO PUGWASH

(Northumberland Strait)
Rewritten and condensed from earlier material by C. Bok and R.M. Black.

Generally, the Strait is blessed with good July and August sunshine, a predictable force four west or southwesterly wind, and almost complete freedom from fog. It is plagued by a short chop in breezy weather, few happy harbors and, in many places, thin water covering sand flats, with occasional rock patches extending to a mile offshore. The water is the warmest for bathing in all the Maritimes. Most shorelines are regular and uninteresting, although the river inlets which form the harbors are usually bordered by wooded hills and have lovely scenery. Sunsets are unsurpassed in variety and extent of color.

The *St. Lawrence Pilot* should be referred to for currents and tidal effects, but predictions will be inaccurate following a period of consistent wind. The ebb, flowing to the east, will be stronger than expected near the Nova Scotia coast after a day or more of steady westerlies.

Charts show the rocky patches quite faithfully, and practically everywhere the bottom is mud or coarse-packing sand and good holding. Summer weather is far more stable than on the Atlantic coast, and visibility is usually perfect.

There is a customary late August storm of two to four days of heavy rain and strong winds from the north and east, preceded by a long period of stable weather. Local short-duration squalls are more common than on the Atlantic, as are waterspouts. Pleasant sailing is the rule, however.

Proceeding west along the Nova Scotia shore, the best harbors after the Strait of Canso are Havre Boucher, Pictou, Caribou, Tatamagouche Bay, Wallace and Pugwash. The passage across St. George's Bay is without obstructions and there is emergency shelter at Ballantynes Cove on the east tip of Cape George. (Chart #4404 has inserts on Ballantynes.) The only aids down the coast to Pictou are the range lights at Arasaig and Lismore, but they are too obscure to be of much help in daylight. However, church steeples at these points and Georgeville are useful for pinpointing, and can be seen from a distance. A yacht can stand in within a mile of the shore with confidence to Lismore, and for most of the remaining distance.

Do not be misled by the apparent harbor shown on Chart #4462 at Antigonish. It does not exist in fact. Antigonish has a lively radio station that gives weather reports and creates the impression that there must be a harbor for such a town. There are no buoys, and the entrance is merely a break in the sandy beach with yellow water in it. Just outside this break a bar makes eastward for one thousand yards; it is not visible but the bottom is decidedly too near the top. The harbor has obviously been abandoned. In any but calm weather, be prepared to keep moving to Merigomish or Pictou from any point south of the strait (except Ballantynes).

Pictou Island is a good landmark, and passage-making can be either to the north or south of it. It has good lights and a buoy off its western tip which can easily be picked up. Give the island a half mile and more at Seal Point at its eastern end.

The foul ground from Pictou to Caribou is well marked, and the two large-scale harbor charts (#4437 and #4483) are good.

The coast cannot be approached as safely west of Caribou. Amet Sound and the entrance to John Bays Brule Harbour, and Tatamagouche (Chart #4497) can be made either to the east or west of Amet Spit. This must be given a wide berth, particularly to the southeast. The spit is square in shape and easily recognized. You will usually be beating when going west and could go to the north of the spit. If heading for Wallace, it may be quicker to use the Eastern Passage. In this case, keep well south of the red cone, and plan to pick up the red spar off Washball Reef to port. There is an unwatched light on the spit and another red cone to the northwest, marking the eastern side of Waugh Shoal. This last has 11 feet and need not be of concern under normal conditions. The other two passages to Amet Sound are evident from the chart. Malagash Point is the tip of the eastern arm of the Sound and has another marker buoy to the south of the buoy at Washball.

On leaving Wallace Harbour (Chart #4402), keep on the second range as far east as the outer buoy, and, on turning north from it, 010° (mag.) will leave Oak Island safely about a half-mile to port. It is well to keep offshore when heading for Pugwash and pick up the buoy east of Ballast Ground.

Pugwash (Chart #4498) is the last good harbor in Nova Scotia. Baie Verte to the west is sizeable but shallow, and the three possible refuges, Northport, Tidnish River and Port Elgin, although regularly used by power cruisers, must be considered only in an emergency for anything drawing over three feet. Even then, high tide is necessary and local knowledge is a must. In Baie Verte there is good holding ground, and in most weather one can anchor 3/4-mile offshore almost anywhere in the Bay. The lights of Coldspring Head and Port Elgin are the only aids except for the red and green buoys off Tidnish River and the pair of reds off Fort Moncton Point.

HAVRE BOUCHER*

45°42'N, 61°31'W

Charts: #4448, #4462

Rewritten from material by P. Richmond and L. George.

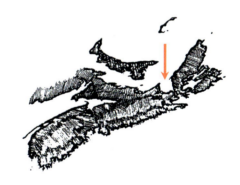

DIRECTIONS: Chart #4448 gives a large-scale view of the harbor, but Chart #4462 is perfectly adequate for getting in. Follow the range in, marked by two fixed red lights on white towers bearing 194.5° (true). Once inside, red and green buoys mark the shallow areas. Except for the area leading to the government wharf, the harbor tends to shoal more on the west than the east side.

ANCHORAGES AND BERTHS: Anchor anywhere you can find room. The holding ground is reported to be uniformly good. The harbor is partially exposed to the northeast, but it is reasonably safe in anything short of a northeast gale. Ten feet can be carried to the government wharf just west of the entrance.

REMARKS: Havre Boucher, about 1.5 miles from North Canso Light, is handy for anyone who has passed through the lock going north and is looking for a place to hole in for the night. It is pretty, was virtually deserted in August, 1988, and is easy to get in and out of.

FACILITIES: Basic supplies can be had at the village (pop. 400). No water or fuel is available.

*Caution should be used entering this harbor, as it has not been reported on in the last ten years.

BAYFIELD WHARF

(Pomquet Road)

45°38.7'N, 61°45.3'W

Charts: #4462, #4447

Robert D. Thompson   *1992*

DIRECTIONS: This artificial harbor is located on the southwest side of St. Georges Bay, just southwest of Pomquet Island. The harbor consists of a 400-foot wharf with a 50-foot "L" on the end. The wharf is protected by a large rock jetty, 600 feet long, approximately 150 feet northeast of the wharf. Chart #4447 gives a large-scale view, but #4462 is perfectly adequate for getting in. Red lighted buoys mark the shoal extending south of Pomquet Island, and the end of the rock jetty.

ANCHORAGE AND BERTHS: Nine feet can be carried on the outer face and both sides of the wharf for about 100 feet. Maneuvering boats on the north side of the wharf is not recommended because of remnants of an older wharf. The outer face probably would not be comfortable in strong east or southeasterly conditions.

REMARKS: This harbor is off the track from Canso Locks to PEI and Northumberland Strait, but it is only 12 miles by road from the large town of Antigonish. The "Love-Me Fish and Lobster Company" is at the head of the wharf, where fresh fish and lobster are available in season.

FACILITIES: Diesel fuel is available here. Water is hard to get and you must carry it yourself.

BALLANTYNES COVE

45°51.5'N, 61°55'W

Charts #4404, #4462

Rewritten and condensed from earlier material by C. Bartlett, A. and J. Doul. Updates by P. & J. Wick, R. Barton, and E. Haley.   *2001*

DIRECTIONS: This artificial harbor is located 1.2 miles southwest of Cape George lighthouse which can be seen for many miles in clear weather. The harbor consists of a 400-foot L-shaped breakwater and dock. Round the end of this breakwater and turn to starboard, and you will find yourself in smooth protected water.

ANCHORAGE AND BERTHS: A new (2001) north-south breakwater west of the original "L" makes a very protected harbor. The basin has been dredged to 10 feet MLW, and a 300 (+/-) floating dock has been added along the new breakwater, with 8 feet of water alongside. This dock is dedicated to pleasure boats only and the fee is minimal ($9 Canadian in 2001 for boats less than 45 feet).

REMARKS: The tuna season starts in September, and fishing boats tie some ten deep along the fishing side of the harbor. Nevertheless, the yacht float will be restricted to pleasure boats during the tuna season.

FACILITIES: Fuel, water, and ice are available at the North Bay Fisherman's Co-op on the Government Dock. Laundry and showers are at the Harbormaster's Building. An excellent fish and chips take-out is nearby.

MERIGOMISH HARBOUR

45°38.5'N, 62°28'W

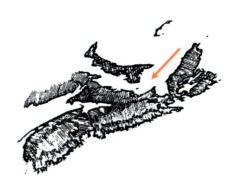

Chart: #4445

Rewritten from material by J. Doull with new information by S. Livingston. *1995*

DIRECTIONS: The entrance is straight-forward. Just follow the channel buoys in.

ANCHORAGE AND BERTHS: Various anchorages are possible and the choice will depend on wind direction. The nearest is a few hundred yards east of Savage Point in four or five fathoms. The holding ground is excellent, but a Bahamian moor is advisable because of the considerable tidal current.

Stanley Livingston informs us there is a tight, narrow, shallow channel into the government wharf and not much room to turn around. He carried six feet in without touching (1995).

REMARKS: This beautiful and unspoiled harbor is not often visited by cruising yachts, although it is one of the few good sheltered anchorages on the north shore of Nova Scotia. In former years, ships of several thousand tons visited it regularly to load pulpwood.

FACILITIES: No supplies are available on Merigomish Island, but an excellent general store at Merigomish Village (pop. 200) can be visited by dinghy by way of the well-buoyed French River.

There is no fuel or water available.

PICTOU HARBOUR

45°41.5'N, 62°40'W

Chart #4437

Rewritten from material by C. Bok, C. Bartlett, A. Phillips, J. Doull and M. Grant, with additional information by H. Jones, W. Saltonstall, S. Livingston and T. Kenney.   2003

DIRECTIONS: The entrance here is straightforward with two ranges and several channel buoys to help you in.

ANCHORAGES AND BERTHS: Although several anchorage areas have appeal, the most convenient is just southwest of the town and somewhere out of the channel, but with enough depth to accommodate your draft.

The only suitable place to tie up is at the Hector Heritage Marina, established in 1993. It is approached to the west of Pier "A", and an entire channel starts just to the west of buoy SJ16 (Chart #4437). The channel is marked with private buoys — cylindrical cans with a white stripe on top, three red and three green. There are eight feet at low water despite the chart readings and excellent protection with modern floats. It is the second marina you come to, on the starboard side as you enter, past the replica of the ship *Hector*, which brought the first colonists to the town in 1773.

REMARKS: Pictou (pop. 6,000) is a fascinating old town, reminiscent of Lunenburg. There are some interesting museums here as well. The town was originally populated by Scots who were swept from their native land by "the Clearances" and brought with them their devotion to education, thrift and hard work. Many great men in Canada had roots in Pictou and were educated at Pictou Academy, one of the great North American schools for its time.

Pictou is close to Halifax, 1 hour 30 mins by road and about the same to Sydney. Dr. Kenney recommends it as a good place to leave a yacht. – better than Baddeck as it is less crowded.

FACILITIES: Pictou offers all the amenities such as restaurants and food stores. At the marina there is electricity, water and pumpout. There are no fuel facilities at dockside. There are washers and dryers at the pierhead and all is very convenient to the town.

WALLACE HARBOUR

45°49'N, 63°24'W

Chart #4402

From material by R. M. Black, with new information by H.B. Jones, Jr.   1993

DIRECTIONS: Entering Wallace Harbour is easy if you follow the two excellent ranges, one from Mullins Point, and the other, an inner range which is unique in that there are five sectors, going from solid red, through flashing red and white, to all white, only <u>one degree</u> wide, and then flashing green and finally solid green. Follow the range and buoys carefully, because the depth goes from about 15 feet to zero in less than a boat length.

ANCHORAGE AND BERTHS: All marks lead to the town dock. Because of the eight-foot tide, a considerable current runs across the front of the dock, so tie up near the end of it on the west side, with eight feet at low water. Anchoring off the dock is not recommended because of the current and narrowness of the channel.

REMARKS: This is a fishing town — small, with few supplies. It is the most westerly harbor on the north shore of Nova Scotia except Pugwash. We were greeted here by Dr. Willard Boyle, who offered to take us by car to the winery just to the east of the town. He is a most interesting man, born in Wallace Harbour, who worked for many years at Bell Labs and has a number of patents on such arcane items as the ruby laser.

FACILITIES: Only basic supplies are available in the town. There is no fuel or water.

PUGWASH HARBOUR*

45°51'N, 63°40'W

Chart: #4498

From material by R.M. Black.

DIRECTIONS: The outer red flashing buoy marks the east side of Ballast Shoal-most yachts need not be concerned about. At the next mark, a red spar a mile south of Ballast Shoal, the ranges should be followed carefully. The channel in from Pugwash Bar is very narrow. Although well buoyed, try to keep strictly to the last two ranges.

The last range ends between a pair of buoys almost on a line between Fox and Pineo Points. From these, keep generally in the center of the channel until you turn southward around the red flasher at Page Point (NK32).

ANCHORAGE AND BERTHS: Anchor in the pool south of the wharf. This area can sometimes be crowded and your swing room restricted, but there is good holding ground. You may also tie up at the south side of the government wharf where there is 20 feet of water at low tide.

REMARKS: Pugwash (pop. 600) is the last harbor on the Nova Scotia shore of the Northumberland Strait going west. It is an attractive town where the street signs are in English and Gaelic, and there is a gathering of the clans at some date every July.

FACILITIES: Basic necessities, food stores and restaurants are available (but alas, no liquor store). There is no fuel or water here.

*Caution should be used entering this harbor. It has not been reported on within ten years.

CANSO LOCK TO PRINCE EDWARD ISLAND
AND THE MAGDALENS

Rewritten and condensed from earlier material by G.P. Gardner, R.&M. Morse, A. Weld, S. Surrey, V. Spooner, W. Feldman, S. Dumaresq, G. Tidmarsh, F. Bissell, and J. McKelvy.

The attractions of cruising the Gulf of St. Lawrence are steady southwest winds, lack of fog, and water warm enough to swim in. The least attractive (though hardly daunting) feature of the area is the paucity of harbors compared to the southeast coast of Nova Scotia.

For planning purposes, look at Canadian H.O. Chart #4023 (Northumberland Strait). You can see that there aren't that many good harbors, lots of inshore shoals and not many navigational aids. This is not an area for making landfalls or departures at night. Plan your passages in daylight with good visibility.

Going north from Canso Lock, you may wish to use the following harbors: Ballantynes Cove, 25 miles northwest of the lock (safe to tie up in, but crowded), or Mabou, 35 miles northwest of the lock around the corner from Port Hood Island. Havre Boucher, seven miles northwest of the lock is adequate but shallow (eight feet in spots), cramped and open to the northeast. Port Hood itself is adequate in settled summer weather. From Ballantynes Cove, it is 35 miles to the Cardigan Bay area of P.E.I., and 40 miles from Mabou. From Cardigan Bay, it is 70 miles to the nearest harbor (Havre Aubert) in the Magdalens, or alternatively, it is 77 miles from Mabou to Havre Aubert.

PRINCE EDWARD ISLAND

Prince Edward Island is Canada's smallest province in area as well as people (110,000 pop.). The island has always had a fishing (mostly lobsters and oysters) and agricultural (mostly potatoes) economy.

Geographically the island is similar to Cape Cod, consisting mostly of reddish sand and bound by shallow bays and harbors which need occasional dredging. The best harbors, particularly when headed for the Magdalens, are on the east side. Souris, located 12 miles west-southwest of East Point, is not recommended as a cruising port because it is dirty and noisy (though it offers adequate shelter). Particularly recommended are the harbors off Cardigan Bay, especially in the Montague and Brudenell Rivers.

Charlottetown, 20-30 miles west of the rhumb line to the Magdalens, is the capital of the province. It is a good harbor and here are the "bright lights" if you want them; however, unless you're cruising into Northumberland Strait, it is easier to see Charlottetown by cab from a harbor on the island's east coast, rather than sail half the length of the island just to see it. This city is not famous for its sights, watering holes or eateries, and the real charm of the island lies in its small towns in places like Montague or Summerside.

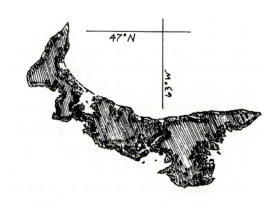

THE MAGDALENS

There are twelve islands in the Magdalen Archipelago, most of them uninhabited. The five main islands are linked by sand spits which form shallow lagoons. A road runs over the sand spits, connecting the islands for vehicular traffic, and the three sheltered harbors in this area (S to N) are: Havre Aubert, Cap aux Meules, and Ile de la Grande Entree. Six miles north of this group lies Brion Island (now deserted), and 15 miles northeast lies Bird Rock, famous to ornithologists as a nesting ground for Gannets, Murres, Kittiwakes, Razorbills, and Puffins. These islands have no harbors and there is an unpredictable current in the area, so landing on them without local knowledge is dangerous. The islands are part of the Province of Quebec, and French is the principal language spoken (though English prevails in the more northerly ones). In spiteof the fact that the provincial government spends considerable money to promote tourism here, the economy depends mainly on fishing.

These islands are wild and desolate with a subtle beauty that grows on you. They are treeless — their timber having been cut down long ago. Entry Island, the first landmark one sees coming from the south, rises like a green velvet mountain out of the sea. Miles of deserted beaches offer excellent swimming, and if you prefer very warm water to bathe in, try one of the lagoons. It is worth hiring a car to see the main islands, and as you ride over the treeless terrain, imagine what it must be like in winter when the Gulf is frozen, the wind howls out of the north and the little houses stand gaunt and unprotected from the cold.

SOURIS

46°21.1'N, 62°15.1'W

Charts: #4419, #4403

S. Dumaresq W. Saltonstall and S. Livingston.
Update by E. Haley. 2001

DIRECTIONS: The approach to Souris is unobstructed. Just round the breakwater and you're there.

ANCHORAGES AND BERTHS: In 2001 one correspondent was warmly welcomed by the local fishermen who directed them to the inner pier by the Coast Guard wharf as a safe and secure berth. There is no anchorage.

REMARKS: This harbor is the closest from P.E.I. to the Magdalens.

FACILITIES: Although it is a ½-mile walk to town, there are new restaurants, grocery stores, pharmacy, propane and jerry jug fuel.

GEORGETOWN

46°11'N, 62°32'W

Charts: #4403, #4422

Robert D. Thompson.   *1992*

DIRECTIONS: Chart #4403 is satisfactory to get you to Georgetown, but it doesn't show the flashing red buoys on Knoll Shoal and Thrumbcap Spit. After rounding NH12 off Thrumcap Spit, head straight into the center of the harbor.

ANCHORAGE AND BERTHS: There are two floating docks for yachts, each able to handle two boats up to about 45 feet, located just to the west of Queen's Wharf (government wharf). The depth is reported to be six feet at low water. You can also tie up at Queen's

Wharf and the Railroad Wharf, although the latter is still used by commercial traffic. There is also plenty of space to anchor.

REMARKS: Georgetown is a delightful old town with a post office and supermarket within an easy walk of Queen's Wharf.

FACILITIES: Water is available at Queen's Wharf (on its east side about halfway out) and the Railroad Wharf. Groceries are available as mentioned above. The lobster pound at the head of Queen's Wharf has live and cooked lobsters. There is no fuel available.

MONTAGUE

46°10'N, 62°40'W

Charts #4422, #4403

P. Wick, R. Barton, S. & M.E. Taylor.   2001

DIRECTIONS: Passage up the Montague River from Cardigan Bay is straightforward between well-marked mussel farms on each side. Marked with red and green floating buoys along the mussel farms, this river is like a "runway"—a little shallow at a couple of turns but no problem with 6-7 feet at low tide.

ANCHORAGE AND BERTHS: Montague Marina at the head of the river on the north side has all services and uses the old railway station as its base of operations, with showers and tourist information.

REMARKS: Care must be taken to avoid the concrete small boat launching ramp extending into the river near the fuel dock. (It stands

above the mud bottom and has only 4-5 feet over it at low water; more at high tide). The river current runs swiftly at mid-tide at an angle under the docks, so observe it carefully while planning your tie-up or departure before getting close to the steel I-beam pilings that secure what are otherwise very nice docks and floats.

Occasionally, in certain conditions similar to "red tide," large broadleaf algae blooms are found in this river and can be a nuisance clogging seawater intakes.

FACILITIES: At the Marina, water and 20-amp electricity are available on the floating docks; gas and diesel on the fuel float. The town has multiple supermarkets, a large hardware store, rental car agencies, laundry, restaurants, banks, car dealers, realtors, etc.

BRUDENELL RIVER

(Provincial Campground Anchorage)

46°11.9'N, 62°35'W

Chart #4422

R. Barton, Steve and M.E. Taylor.   2001

DIRECTIONS: The channel into the Brudenell River is buoyed, but beware of the mussel rafts moored between the shore and channel. In dull weather the buoys marking the anchor lines to these rafts can be confused with the navigation marks. The Rodd Resort and Conference Center (902-652-2332) is located between Brudenell Islet and Gordon Point, about one-and-a-half miles up river from Georgetown.

ANCHORAGE AND BERTHS: There are moorings and plenty of room to anchor in good mud off the campground which has small boat floats and places to secure dinghies.

REMARKS: This is a beautiful resort, and a good place to put into if you are cruising with children.

FACILITIES: There are two beautiful 18-hole golf courses, the older one called "Brudenell" and the newer one, "Dunderave" (902-652-8965 or 800-377-8336—same numbers, both places). In addition to the campground, there are meeting facilities, rooms or cabins to rent, a swimming pool, exercise room, and showers.

The two excellent restaurants accept cruising attire.

MURRAY HARBOR*

(Greek & Mink Rivers)

46°02.6'N, 62°31.7'W

Charts: #4420, #4403

Rewritten from earlier material by S. Dumaresq.

DIRECTIONS: Buoys mark the channel past the range lights at Sable Point to the mouths of the Greek and Mink Rivers. The controlling depth of the channel is six feet [but you had better enter this area on a rising tide if you draw six feet. -ed.]

ANCHORAGE AND BERTHS: There are no wharves. Anchor anywhere in deep water.

REMARKS: This is a very well-protected harbor. It is secluded and there are seals at the entrance.

FACILITIES: None.

*Caution should be used entering this harbor as it has not been reported on in the last ten years.

CHARLOTTETOWN

46°12'N, 63°15'W

Charts: #4466, #4460

From material by W. Feldman and F. Bissell. Updates by Ed and Nancy Haley and T.Kenney   2001

DIRECTIONS: The entrance to this harbor is straightforward through a buoyed channel.

ANCHORAGE AND BERTHS: Slips are available at the Charlottetown Yacht Club. Quartermaster Marine, just north of the yacht club, also has slips. Anchoring in the bay to the southwest of the town is inadvisable, as the area is at the confluence of three rivers and is swept by the tide, which may cause your anchor to break out unexpectedly.

REMARKS: From the marina or Yacht Club, it is a short walk to the center of town which has a fine hotel (the Prince Edward), the Confederation Center (which runs a summer theater), and shops to supply most of your needs. This town gets a bad rap. It has a new waterfront development with many trendy and good restaurants.

FACILITIES: The Yacht Club has water and electricity. Quartermaster Marine has fuel, water, electricity, showers, a laundromat, and a new waterfront complex of restaurants and shops. The dockmaster guards VHF Channel #16 from 08:00 to 21:00, and there is also night security.

SUMMERSIDE

46°23'N, 63°55'W

Chart: #4459

From material by W. Feldman and T.Kenney. 2004

DIRECTIONS: The entrance is straightforward with a buoyed channel with two lit ranges from the outer breakwater to the government wharf.

ANCHORAGE AND BERTHS: Slips are available at the Silver Fox Yacht and Curling Club, located inside the inner breakwater (labeled "Summerside Yacht Club" on Chart #4459). Anchoring is possible off the government wharf or further to the southeast in the mouth of the Dunk River.

REMARKS: This is considered the better cruising stop than Charlottetown, which is now much improved, in terms of facilities. Tom Kenney described it as a wonderful stop.

FACILITIES: Showers, water, fuel, a restaurant and electricity are all available. The electric lines have only 20 amp circuits, and you should test the polarity before using one.

CAP AUX MEULES*

(Grindstone Harbour)

47°22.6'N, 61°51.4'W

Charts: #4956, #4951

Rewritten from earlier material by A. Weld, S. Dumaresq, and W. Feldman.

Cap aux Meules Harbour in 2004

DIRECTIONS: Cap aux Meules is a man-made harbor behind a breakwater which presents no difficulty entering. There is a marina behind the new breakwater south of the old breakwater. Don't immediately enter the main harbour, but proceed south from the main breakwater and look for a red light on a tower at the marina, and enter here. Do not attempt to leave this marina in a strong southerly because of the risk of being driven onto a lee shore.

ANCHORAGE AND BERTHS: Berths are available at the marina for a reasonable sum. Presumably one can berth in the commercial harbor as well, but this is where the ferry lands and many trawlers tie up, so berthing here probably isn't worth it. There is no anchoring in either harbor.

REMARKS: This is not an attractive town, but makes up in services what it lacks in scenery. One correspondent writes, "The sight of five American sailboats [at Cap aux Meules] attracted a steady stream of visitors. Almost everyone spoke English, and nobody seemed to resent our monolingual group." [Anyone who has experienced Gallic resentment will appreciate this. -ed.]

FACILITIES: Fuel is available at the gas station in town if you wish to carry it to your boat. Otherwise, there is ice, showers, (anemic) electricity, and a marine electronics store at the marina. A liquor store and some grocery stores are located in town.

*Caution should be used entering this harbor, as it has not been reported on in the last ten years.

HAVRE AUBERT

47°14'N, 61°50'W

Charts: #4957, #4951

*From material by A. Weld, S. Dumaresq and
update J.Hawkins*   *2004*

DIRECTIONS: From the south, it is necessary to use the channel between Entry Island and Sandy Hook. This is well marked; use caution to avoid the bar as you steady up to a southwest course for the harbor after passing the northernmost mark (green flasher YM11). A new flashing buoy, YK1, is located between YM11 and the channel entrance due to the advance of the sand shoal into the bay. Leave it to port going in. A lit range (213.5° T) leads into the buoyed channel, past the large small-craft wharf. From Y22, turn to starboard northwest, and proceed up the buoyed channel, staying in the middle. At half tide, you can carry six feet through here.

ANCHORAGE AND BERTHS: Berths may be had at the first pier on the way in. This is a big commercial wharf, and depending on the season, there may be much commotion and not much privacy. The small-craft wharf mentioned above has berths, but the water shoals as you move up toward the land. A third (and possibly quieter) berth is at the fish pier opposite Point Fox in the channel leading into Le Petit Basin. South of the last channel buoys (YK22 and YK23) is a small anchorage (called "Havre Amherst" on Chart #4957) with good holding ground in sand and mud.

REMARKS: Most correspondents find this a delightful harbor. An interesting marine museum is ashore where you will find friendly folk with suggestions about what to see and where to go in the islands. There is an excellent walk up to the cross on the hill above the harbor where there is a panoramic view of the island. The flats west of Sandy Hook have clams, and the nearly deserted beach across the dunes is reported to occasionally have nude bathers. The atmosphere is decidedly French.

The small-craft wharf is operated by a local marina club, "Les Plaisanciers du Havre." Water and electric service are on the wharf. The club provides showers, ice, telephone, a lounge and other helpful conveniences. Dockage is 75 cents (Canadian) per foot (1994). The staff is friendly and bilingual. The marina is open from the middle of June through the first week in September. They monitor VHF Channel #68, and the telephone number is (418) 937-5283.

On the beach at Havre Aubert, an international sand castle contest is held annually at the end of the first week in August (or the second weekend if rained out on the first). The event attracts large crowds to the community. A very nice guide to the islands may be obtained locally, or from the **Association Touristique de Iles de La Madeleine**, C.P. 108, Cap aux Meules, CANADA G0B 1BO.

FACILITIES: There is no fuel here. Water is available at the small-craft wharf (mentioned above), but check the depth of the water at the small-craft wharf before going in.

The town has a good seafood bar-restaurant, and there is a grocery store where beer and wine may be purchased. There is also a bakery, and fresh seafood (especially crabmeat) is available in season.

HAVRE DE LA GRANDE ENTRÉE*

(Not to be confused with Entry Island)

47°36.5'N, 61°33'W

Charts: #4954, #4952

Condensed from material by A. Weld,G. Tidmarsh and S. Dumaresq.

DIRECTIONS: Use Chart #4954 for this occasion.

The salt mine has caused a channel to be dredged all the way into this shallow lagoon. The fishing boats all use the basin immediately east of Pointe de la Grande Entrée.

In an ebb tide and a southwest wind, a short, steep chop kicks up from the outer entrance buoy (YC1) to YC14 (enough to flip an 11 foot Whaler dinghy on one occasion).

To enter the basin at Grande Entrée, turn tightly around red buoy YC14 by the lighthouse, then stay parallel to the wharf, and south of a line extending from the northern (outer) pier that forms the small boat basin. Be aware that the ebb current flows past the basin unexpectedly fast, creating a back eddy which makes turning around difficult.

The ship channel to Dune de l'Ouest leads to the loading pier for the salt mine. There is an anchorage here that is perfectly safe from ships docking and maneuvering (see below).

ANCHORAGE AND BERTHS: The basin at Grande Entrée is extremely busy during the lobstering season (May, June and early July), and is moderately busy during the rest of the summer. Moor along the ends of the piers to avoid having to move at four a.m. when the fishing fleet leaves. There is no anchoring here.

At Dune de l'Ouest there is a good anchorage with a sand bottom in 15 feet, halfway along the south side of the pier. Here you are out of the way of the ships. Do not plan to spend the night here, as there is no protection from southerly or easterly winds. Tying to the wharf is also not recommended.

REMARKS: The wharves at the Grande Entrée basin are crowded, and fishing boats leave constantly between 3 and 4:30 a.m., disturbing your sleep. Also the town at Grande Entrée is quite a distance away. There is, however, a nice beach on Iliot C.

At Dune de l'Ouest there is excellent clamming on the flats south of the pier, as well as a beautiful, deserted beach available after a short row and walk (1/3 mile) across the dunes.

This is not a useful stop unless you are progressing northward to Brion Island or Bird Rock. Nonetheless, it has an intrigue and charm worth seeing if time permits.

FACILITIES: At the basin there is no fuel or electricity, but fresh fish and chipped ice are available at the Madelipeche Fish Plant located on the wharf. There are no facilities at Dune de l'Ouest.

*Caution should be used entering this harbor, as it has not been reported on in the last ten years.

HAVRE L'ETANG DU NORD

47 22'N 61.57'

Chart: #4591

J. Hawkins   *2004*

Located on the west side of the Island (with Cap aux Meules on the east side) it is the harbor nearest the Gaspesie, about 116 miles from Anse de Beaufils. Entry is straightforward. Outside of fishing season, it provides a convenient port with room for several pleasure craft. Pleasure boats usually, but not always, tie on the north side of the main wharf. Wharfage in 2004 was about $1.00cnlfoot. This is a French-speaking fishing port that has adapted only minimally to a marine tourist trade. There are no official services, but if you have enough electric cabling, you may be able to reach an outlet on the dock. Water is available if your hose is long enough. But you are on your own to figure it all out. Bathrooms, (locked at night, you get a key) and shower are a hundred yards from the wharf attached to a good restaurant open from breakfast through dinner. A classy tea room serving lunch, as well as tea and pastry the remainder of the day also has creative artwork, dolls, etc. A lovely walk on the bluffs by the sea, several kilometers long, starts near the wharf. Ice is a little more than two kilometers away. The coop grocery was not open in 2004, the nearest alternative being about five kilometers away in Cap aux Meules. There is continual dock traffic, both foot and vehicular.

ENTRY ISLAND

47 16'N 61 41'W

Chart : #4591

J. Hawkins   2004

Lying on the east side of the channel from the land spit guarding Havre Aubert, Entry Island is noted for its high hills and the trails up to the top from where you get a lovely view of the Islands and Cape Breton on a clear day. The harbor is small, but has enough turning room for small craft. There is 10' of water along the docks. Tour boats come and go all day bringing hikers from Cap aux Meules. The dock nearest to the breakwater is reserved for these boats, but can be used by pleasure boats for brief landings or after the last hikers leave for the day. A dock attendant takes name and address and the town sends wharf bills by mail. There is no accessible electricity or water. A poorly maintained public bathroom is at the head of the wharf. A number of English speaking families live here. Island teenagers whoop it up until about 11:OOpm on the breakwater. The Island makes for a good departure point to Cape North or Cheticamp on Cape Breton. To enter, find red buoy YM 12. Leave it well to port. Track toward the bluff which faces the water south of the harbor until the entrance opens up, then go straight in.

ANSE DE CABANE

47 13'N 61 58'W

Chart: #4951

J. Hawkins   *2004*

This small fishing harbor lying on the SW corner of Isle de Aubert is the closest point to Cheticamp on Cape Breton. The harbor makes a good interim stop enroute to or from other Island harbors. Outside of fishing season, you can find one or two spots at the dock. Wharfage in 2004 was free, but there were no services. A small but good restaurant is a five-minute walk away and basic groceries are about 15 minutes away on foot.

INDEX

Liscomb Harbour